Our Journey

(Temple Of Pentecost)

and Beyond

(Heaven)

The Story of Wayne and Patsy Huntley

By Patsy Landtroop Huntley

Just married! (50 years ago!)

The most important people in our lives–family

Copyright © 2025 Patsy Huntley

All rights reserved. No part of this publication, including pictures, may be reproduced, stored in a retrieval system, or transmitted in any form or by any other means, electronic, mechanical, photocopying, recording, or otherwise, without the prior written permission of the author.

Biblical references cited: The Holy Bible: King James Version (KJV)

Dedication

This book is dedicated to our remarkable family: Christy Huntley Ballestero, our daughter, who is a very dedicated and real Christian, a fabulous mother, an anointed singer and songwriter who wears the title "Pastor's Wife" with dignity, grace, and compassion. I have confidence in your walk with God and your love for your dad and me. I do love you with all my heart.

To our grands: Huntley, Christyana, Christian, Caison, and Gentson, who always make our world a more fun-filled and exciting place and are "the crown of old age!"

To Reverend Bryan Starr Ballestero, our son-in-love, our pastor, and the person who takes good care of us and continually makes our lives comfortable and fulfilled. Thank you for always being the best dad to our grands; they are truly blessed.

To Frances Huntley and Josie Landtroop, our precious mothers, who were the wind beneath our wings. They gave us life and were the foundation on which our lives were built. We love you and thank God that you were always there for us.

Josie Landtroop *Frances Huntley*

Thanks to our sister, brothers, sisters-in-law, nieces, and nephews–the earthly family Wayne and I were born into. You have helped mold us and have loved us unconditionally through the years.

Thank you, Temple of Pentecost family, for your part in our story. Without you, we wouldn't have much of a story at all.

To our friends, you are the main reason I decided to write this book in the first place.

Wayne Huntley, the one I love above everyone on this earth, I trust that as I have told *our stories,* I have given insight into the man you really are. It is my desire that all those who love you, after reading this book, will know you in a way that was impossible before now.

These are the things that make up the man that I love, respect, and admire. Wayne is a man above men and one that God truly loves, and He has shown that repeatedly. He is absolutely worthy of all these accolades. I should know, for I have walked by his side for over fifty years, and if anyone truly *knows him,* it is me, Mrs. Wayne Huntley.

Table of Contents

Foreword..i

Preface..iii

Introduction...iv

Chapter One—Patsy Sue Landtroop..1

Chapter Two—Ronald Wayne Huntley....................................31
    —Texas Bible College, 1968

Chapter Three—Wayne and Patsy...55
    —We Said, "I Do."

Chapter Four—Mr. and Mrs. Wayne Huntley..........................69
    —Texas Bible College, 1969-1971

Chapter Five—Rev. and Mrs. Wayne Huntley.........................81

Chapter Six—Evangelist and Mrs. Wayne Huntley.................90
    —Daddy and Mother
    —Christy Renee Huntley
    —Emotions of a Mother
    —Evangelist and Mrs. Wayne Huntley, and Christy

Chapter Seven—Pastor and Mrs. Wayne Huntley..................125
    —Christy Renee Huntley Becomes
    — Mrs. Bryan Starr Ballestero
    —Grandbuddy and Grammommy

Chapter Eight—Senior Pastor and Mrs. Wayne Huntley..215

Chapter Nine—Bishop Wayne Huntley and Your Bishopness, Patsy Huntley.....................................231

Chapter Ten—The Golden Years...259
    —To Sum It All Up

Chapter Eleven—Conclusion...283

Epilogue—Words from Family, Friends, and the Field..........................287

Family Photos ………..……………………………………….........................323
    —Wayne and Patsy Huntley Through the Years
    —Wayne Huntley Ministering
    —The Huntley Family
    —Huntley Starr Ballestero
    —Huntley and Abigail Ballestero
    —Christyana Content Ballestero Blake
    —Christyana and Jordan Blake
    —Clara Content Blake
    —Christian Bryan Ballestero
    —Caison Judah Ballestero
    —Gentson Hebron Carl Ballestero

Foreword

Throughout the centuries, God has called dedicated men and women to work in His Kingdom. Few, however, have made as indelible a mark on Pentecost as Brother Wayne and Sister Patsy Huntley. Their lives are above reproach, having answered the high calling of Jesus Christ. Since the beginning of their ministry, they have been fully sold out to God, His work, and His people. Brother Huntley has preached messages at various conferences, camp meetings, and special services, impacting the lives of many over the years.

I first met Brother and Sister Huntley during Christmas in Shipshewana, Indiana, with my family, my brother, Martyn Ballestero, and his family. They were down-to-earth and personable. No matter who you were, they treated you as if you were special. I was thrilled when their daughter, Christy, became my niece by marrying my nephew, Bryan Ballestero. The Huntleys' love for Christy, Bryan, and their grandchildren reflects their roles as devoted parents and grandparents, imparting wisdom and guidance in the fear of the Lord. Their path, marked by hard work and sacrifice, reflects their unwavering dedication and passion for serving God, positively impacting countless lives.

Now, through these pages, Sister Patsy Huntley invites us into her story — to experience their journey. You will discover their hunger for winning the lost and gain insight into their character when tragedy strikes or they face trials; through it all, their faith never wavers. Sis. Huntley is transparent in her narrative. She is authentic, never hiding behind a façade, but inviting you to witness her laughter and tears. You will discover her words of wisdom, lessons learned, challenges overcome, and moments of profound faith and answered prayer. As you turn these pages, may their journey challenge and inspire you.

It is with great joy that I introduce the remarkable lives of Brother Wayne and Sister Patsy Huntley. May their story be a blessing to you, as their lives have been a blessing to many others.

Sincerely and with much affection,

Nila Ballestero Marxer

Preface

It's a wonderful life, living for the Lord. ***Our Journey to the TOP*** *(Temple of Pentecost)* has truly been "a wonderful life" living for the Lord. Our short journey before we arrived at the Temple of Pentecost was most surely in preparation for coming to this place, this city, God's will for our lives.

…and Beyond *(ultimately, Heaven!)* God has more plans for us than just coming to the TOP, to this city, Raleigh. He has "a heavenly City" prepared for us and for those who love Him.

"But now they desire a better country, that is, an heavenly:
wherefore God is not ashamed to be called their God:
for he hath prepared for them a city."
(Hebrews 11:16)

> *I can hardly wait to see my blessed Savior's face,*
> *And to view that beautiful place.*
> *My family and friends, saved by divine grace,*
> *Will be privileged, once more, to finally embrace.*

Introduction

This book is written about our lives. It's about our thoughts as we have traveled our paths from birth to the end. During our journey to the TOP (Temple of Pentecost) and beyond (our ultimate goal: Heaven), we have met many people along the way. We certainly could not mention everyone who has been a part of our lives. If you are mentioned on these pages, and it's not exactly as "you" remembered, don't forget one small detail: this is "our" book as "we" remembered it happening. (smile)

I wish there were enough pages to tell every detail, but alas, that would be too long and boring. Wayne and I want to thank everyone who brought happenings and happiness into our lives. Even if your name is not written down here, know that we do remember and thank God for all the friends He blessed us with.

One small thing to consider as you read this book: Please note that it is written by Patsy, and many things are written here not by Wayne Huntley's *recommendation* but rather with his *permission*.

If you know my husband or me by a specific title, for example, Brother Huntley, Sister Huntley, Pastor, Bishop, Your Bishopness, Dad, Mother, Grandbuddy, Gramommy, Uncle Wayne, Aunt Patsy—please note again, Patsy wrote this book, and I call us Wayne and Patsy. I have always had the privilege of calling my husband Wayne. I have never called him Brother Huntley unless I was talking to someone who respectfully calls him Brother Huntley. I have never called him "Daddy, or Dad" unless I was talking to Christy or Bryan. And then only for reference. So, when *"I"* am speaking, I use the name that I call that person, not the name "you" call them.

First of all, I cannot express my gratitude enough to the many, many friends and church family, both here at home and around the country, who have encouraged me not only to start writing this book but also to finish it. This turned out to be much more time-consuming and a far greater task than I had originally anticipated.

- Cassidy Sanders Gilbert, your input and help were invaluable in getting me started on the road to correcting this manuscript.

- Jay Douglas, thank you for your expertise in the audio production of this book.

- Nila Ballestero Marxer, how can I ever thank you enough for your profound wisdom in editing, your encouragement to make me feel that my writings are worthwhile, and your enduring patience to see this project completed?

I hope all who read these words from my heart will find encouragement, strength, and hope. If our good Lord can do it for the Huntleys, He can and will do it for *you*.

The chapters in this book run chronologically, although not all the stories do. There are times when a story is inserted that fits the location, even though it may not fit in the time frame.

Chapter One

Patsy Sue Landtroop
Waco, Texas, 1948

It was just after Christmas in The Lone Star State, in the year of our Lord, 1948–December 29th, to be exact. My sweet mother, Josie Lue Kissinger Landtroop, was in labor at Hillcrest Hospital, Waco, McLennan County, Texas.

A week earlier, she had ridden a bus, alone, from her home in Hillsboro, Texas, to Waco, Texas, thirty-two miles away. She would stay with her stepsister, my Aunt Marie Chapman, to await my arrival. It seemed her lot in life was to always care for herself. She never had a network of family to fall back on or to lean on in times of need.

I was the only one of my siblings born in a hospital. Well, if the truth be told, I was born in Hillcrest Hospital Annex, a clinic where poor people could get medical help, not the actual hospital itself. Nevertheless, it is as close as you could get to the hospital without being there.

Patsy at 6 months

I was number six in a family of six children, always my mother's baby. My oldest brothers were Garth Wayne (G.W.), Kenneth Earl (Red when he was younger, and Ken as he grew older), and Malcolm Cecil (Lanky when he was younger, and M.C. when he was older). My sister, Lenda Jo, was five years older, and Garth was fifteen years older than I was. Baby number four was a brother, Travis Weldon, who died as an infant when he was almost a year old.

My father, Cecil Lawrence Landtroop, picked Mother up from the hospital and brought us home. However, he was not in attendance at my birth, and he was not at most of my day-to-day living or life events as I grew older, such as my baptism, graduation from Waco High School, or my wedding. None of these events found him in the audience.

When my mother brought me home from the hospital, our family lived in Hillsboro. My sister, Lenda, had just turned five in October, and I was born in December. The following fall, during cotton picking time, I was not quite a year old. Lenda had to take care of me while Mother worked the fields just down the street. She had to change my diapers and feed me. I would crawl up on the kitchen table and eat butter with

Patsy - age 3

my hands. My mother always left it out in a bowl so it would be soft and spreadable. I still love butter (especially the Amish Country Roll Butter) and leave mine on the counter in a covered dish at room temperature—like mother, like daughter.

I say, "My sister cared for me when I was a baby so that I could care for her when we grew older." I love having my sister live near me. She lives in my backyard, in what had been my mother's little house. When Mother lived there, she had watched Wayne and me go in

Lenda and Patsy

and out every day, and she said it made her tired just watching us! We remodeled the little house for my sister. She had been saying that she wanted a tiny house. Well, she got one. It's truly a tiny house, but it's hers!

My mother always said to us about our father, "It doesn't matter what he has done or what he is; he is still your father." She never talked badly about him or ran his image down, so my siblings and I always tried to have a reasonably civil relationship with him.

After I had been married for many years and had moved to North Carolina, my daddy and I had a decent relationship. However, he always seemed more of a distant relative than my father. That was his loss. I never really got over longing for my father's love. But despite this, I am very thankful for him and my paternal grandparents, Lawrence Pearl and Rena Marinda (Rendi) Hamilton Landtroop. They had two children: Cecil Lawrence (my father) and one daughter, Irene Landtroop Cathey. (I am also thankful that many of my Cathey cousins continue in the Apostolic faith as pastors, ministers, and saints.) Because of my grandparents, my family and I came to know the Truth.

Lawrence and Rendi Landtroop

They were backsliders when a revival, held by Rev. Pal Sojourner, came to Gorman, Texas, in 1934. He was quite a preacher. My grandparents had gone to the tent revival, praying and renewing their walk with God. They wanted my parents to go with them to the revival meeting. My oldest brother, Garth, was only a babe in arms, less than a year old.

Now, my mother knew nothing about Pentecost except that when she was a young girl, she and her family had gone to a tent revival, and God touched her soul. Her father, Jesse Monroe Kissinger (pronounced Kiss'-sanger by my mother), thought those people were crazy and didn't want anything to do with them, but my mother was different. She felt something calling her and wanted more. From then on, she sensed the Lord leading her. She had a real hunger for God, so when she went to the tent revival that night with her husband and his parents, she began her lifelong journey with God that lasted seventy years.

Mother and Daddy, with Garth and Kenneth

My daddy received the Holy Ghost that first night, and three days later, my mother was filled with the Holy Ghost in a morning cottage prayer meeting.

For a while, my father did well. He felt his call to preach and began preaching, but his roots needed to be deeper. He didn't have enough teaching and preparation before working for God, and as a result, his flesh got the best of him, causing him to fall away from God. Although he strayed far from Him, in his later years, he did recommit and serve God for the last several years of his life—a true testimony of God's great grace.

So, my daddy would stay with my mother, and then he would leave, be gone for a while, and then decide to be elsewhere. Maybe he would just come and take the money that she may have saved. This way of life went on for years.

Mother always had money. She taught me how to handle money, and here it is in a nutshell:

When you get your paycheck,
You pay your tithes and offerings first,
You pay your bills next,
And put a little back for a rainy day.
IF you have any left,
You may spend some,
But ONLY after you have done those three things,
In that order.

My daddy had no trouble taking money from the ever-growing family. My mother loved him with all her heart and would forgive and take him back whenever he decided to come home.

Some of the time, Ms. Josie worked at a café. She had growing boys at home but not much money, so when customers would leave meat on their plates, my sweet mother would take that meat home to her boys. You might say, "I would NEVER do that!" Maybe not. Maybe you just haven't been as hungry or needy as she was. Sometimes, you just do what you have to do.

Finally, about the time I started school, Daddy left for good. My mother mourned. I never knew at the time how much she was hurting. I didn't understand her loneliness and broken heart. I never realized until I was grown how much she had sacrificed for her children. She told me she made a concerted commitment to see that her children loved and served God. She did that, and all her children, most of her grandchildren, and great-grandchildren live for God today. Many of them are preachers and preachers' wives. There are seventeen in her lineage at this writing, and more coming on in the future.

It started with her. She had no Pentecostal heritage, but she began her own. What a great legacy she left behind when she left this "church militant, for the church triumphant" on September 30, 2004, at the ripe old age of ninety-one.

She never, not even once, talked about her family. Now, I wish I had asked her about it, but I only saw my maternal grandfather a couple of times. (Her mother, Minnie Lee Bramblett Kissinger, died when my mother was only eleven years old, which was another reason Mother had no one but herself to depend on.) I don't know if they didn't want her to marry my daddy, if they didn't care for Pentecostals, if they weren't a close family, or what the situation was. We had no relationship with them at all. I know that none of her blood relatives—no brother, sister, father, aunt, uncle, or cousin—ever received the Holy Ghost, or was water baptized in Jesus' name, or, to my knowledge, ever attended a Pentecostal church service.

Because my daddy left us when I was so young, I hardly remember him living in the home.

I didn't know I was poor. I always had plenty to eat, even if it was only cat-head biscuits (giant, fist-size biscuits), water gravy, or rice with sugar and cream for breakfast. Our Sunday dinners consisted of hamburger meat, wieners, or chicken; we usually had macaroni and tomatoes and sugar pies for dessert during the week.

The morning of May 11, 1953, was a day like most others in Waco, but by the time the sun set that night, there were 144 dead and 895 injuries. The deadly F-5 tornado that swept through my hometown left much devastation. I was four years old, and I still remember it pretty vividly.

My first memory of that devastating tornado was of my mother, my sister Lenda, and me praying in the kitchen next to the refrigerator in our little rented duplex on McKeen Street. It was almost dark as night, and the sound we heard was like a train running over us. It was so loud you could hardly talk. The wind was whirling things by the window, like horses, and whipping large pieces of metal around as it flew by. Everything was so loud. There was crashing and banging all around us. My sister and I ran to the window, and Mother quickly called us back. We were praying with all our might. Let me tell you that prayer works!

There was an eerie, deadly silence when the tornado passed over and the wind stopped. We went outside and looked around, and that's when we knew God had heard and answered our prayers. Telephone poles lay across roads, electrical wires ran over sidewalks, and debris lay everywhere.

Our house was on a corner with only the road on one side. The house on the other side of us, a long shotgun-style house, was split right down the middle. Half was falling forward, and half was falling backward. The house across the street from us looked like it had been picked up from its foundation and dropped back down. It was just a big pile of rubble. Our little house stood tall with just a few loose shingles. Yes, prayer works. The owner of that McKeen Street dwelling should have thanked us for saving his little rental apartment house that horrific day.

For days after the tornado, Mother would come outside and find me sitting next to the house praying, "Lord, please don't let another tornado come." I was so

Patsy and Lenda

serious about that and terrified, but I knew He answered prayer.

Shortly after that, we moved from McKeen Street to Plum Street, which was still in East Waco. There, I met a lifelong friend, Hazel Pearl Laura Harley Faltesek.

Patsy and Hazel

She has been in my life, off and on, all my life. We went to school together, from kindergarten through part of fourth grade, when my family moved from East Waco to South Waco to the address on South Fifth Street. Later, when we were in eighth grade at West Junior High School, we went to school together again after a few more moves by our family.

I began witnessing to her, and she started to come to church, riding with some of the church members who lived near her, Brother and Sister Willy Saulter. She received the Holy Ghost and was baptized.

Not long after, her father passed away, and she and her mother moved to Houston, Texas, to be with her brother. I lost contact with her for a few years until I went to Texas Bible College (TBC) in 1969. She was attending TBC and was also going to Brother James Kilgore's church, Life Tabernacle. After Bible college, we again lost touch for a while, but I have always prayed for her and felt a special spiritual connection to her. She came to our fortieth wedding anniversary celebration in Raleigh. We have talked on the phone and kept in touch from time to time.

At five years old, we lived in a two-room house on 1825 East Walnut Street without indoor running water or restroom facilities. We had a water pump in the front yard and kept a jar beside it to prime each time we wanted water. You would pour the water from the jar into the pump and start pumping the handle up and down. It made a suction to bring the water up and out of the spout. We had an outhouse in the backyard down a short path.

This yard also had a big black walnut tree full of asps. Those little furry crawly worms stung like crazy if you touched them or accidentally stepped on them barefoot. There were thorny stickers in a section of our yard. Many of them pierced my feet since I was always barefoot, and I still am most of the time.

In this humble abode, I received the precious gift of the Holy Ghost, evidenced by speaking in tongues as the Spirit of God gave me utterance. My mother, Lenda, and I had our usual prayer meeting before bed. As was her custom, Mother made sure she could *hear* us praying and not just *her* bombarding heaven. We prayed every night before bed. I may have been bad during the day and done things wrong, but when my mother started praying and made me pray, the Holy Ghost would

Patsy age 5, Lenda age 10

begin to move on my soul, and I would start crying, repenting, and praying. This is one of the most significant things in my life that helped me stay saved and close to God. I have not always made one hundred percent on every test serving God, and have done many things I should not have done through the years, but those nightly prayer meetings kept me on the straight and narrow. They were my "plumb line" that held me on course. This particular night, when I was five, I started crying, and Mother said, "Do you want the Holy Ghost, Patsy?"

Pastor and Mrs. J. J. Hennigan

I said, "Yes!" I raised my hands and began speaking in tongues like they did in the second chapter of the book of Acts. Later, my pastor, Brother James Hennigan, baptized me in the most precious name known to man: Jesus Christ!

Lenda and I played church, as do most Pentecostal children. I don't remember what *she* did; I just recall what *I* did! We had a box purse made out of metal with a hard plastic lid and handle. It was approximately 8" x 4" and 4" high. I would slip my left hand inside the handle (as you do with the leather strap on a real accordion), holding on to the purse with my fingers. I would move my arm back and forth like I was playing an actual "squeeze box" and sing to the top of my voice. I remember *how* I felt. It felt so real, and I loved it! In later years, I would feel that same feeling as I played my "real" accordion and sang in revival services while on the evangelistic field.

In elementary school, someone brought us a basket of food for Christmas. In it was a brand-new little blue sweater for ME. I was so proud–my very first new sweater. I usually got my clothes from Goodwill and was glad to get them. I still like a good deal from the Goodwill, thrift store, or yard sale. My first new school dresses came from a Levines store, where my Aunt Marie worked on Elm Street (pronounced THEN as El-Mm) in East Waco. I got three new dresses. I felt like I was clothed in Paris or Vogue!

At Christmas time, the principal of Nalley Elementary School, Mrs. Dixon, would stand out in the hall and mentally note kids who needed new shoes. She gave this list to the Salvation Army. They, in turn, had a big day when the children who were deemed needy, along with what seemed like hundreds more from around the city, would go to this big warehouse. The boxes of shoes were stacked (it appeared to me as a kid) almost to the ceiling. We each got a NEW PAIR of shoes (not second-hand) and a bag of fruit and nuts with candy. It was indeed heaven. Nowadays, I feel it's important to make a donation to the bell ringers at Christmas to try to pay it forward. I have a lot of forward-paying to do in my life. God has been so very good to me. My friend, Debbie Barnhill, will, without fail, text me each December and say, "I just made a donation to the Salvation Army bell ringer in honor of my friend!" Maybe some other little girl will have a better Christmas because of us.

Patsy – fourth grade

We were always on the list to receive free lunch at school. Wow, did I ever love those hot lunches! Especially those big, fluffy yeast rolls with butter. Some things never change. As a preacher friend, Brother Tim Mahoney, once said to Wayne, "I never met a biscuit I didn't like." That's me and yeast rolls!

We had some special friends that Mother had known since I was a baby, when we lived in an apartment called "First and Last Chance." They also lived in one of the apartments. It was a mother, Annie Singleton (whom we called Saintie), and her grown unmarried daughter, Sue Hastings, for whom I am named, Patsy "Sue." Through the years, they were so good to us. We would visit their house, and they would cook delicious meals. We would ride a taxi cab to downtown Waco to shop at S. H. Kress & Company, a general store on Austin

Avenue. We would get to eat at the Woolworth's five-and-dime lunch counter on special occasions.

If not for Saintie and Sue, I would not have had the special dolls that I did. They bought me new dolls, and I loved them. They were my babies. There was Baby Vicky, a small, wetting doll. She had a bottle, diapers, a tiny roll of toilet paper, and a small bottle of baby powder. I felt like she was alive and real. Then, they gave me a baby doll dressed in a christening-type dress and also a walking doll. She was a beauty with long blond hair. One day, I sort of backslid and cut her bangs. Unfortunately, they didn't grow back, so with a chuckle, I say that that is a sin I have had to live with. These dolls have been so important to me all my life. Mostly, I kept their original clothes and have always felt they were almost real because of the extreme happiness they brought me as a little girl.

After our house fire in 2016, which I will tell more about in Chapter Nine: "Bishop and Your Bishopness," I will also reveal a most unusual story about these remarkable, almost real dolls!

Since Mother never had a driver's license, we had to find rides to church in any way we could. One such era of time, when I was in elementary school, we rode with some folks who went to church with us and lived within walking

distance of our house. She was a sweet, saintly woman, but her husband was never in the church. He drove us because she didn't drive either at this time. Later, she did get her license. We would walk up to their house before church to ride with them. After church, sometimes, my sister and I would sleep on the way home. The layout of the land was that their house came first on our drive home. Their house was on the left side, at the end of a long "S" curve sweeping first to the left and then to the right. As we were driving, the car would sweep to the left, then sweep back to the right, and stay straight to take us home. Sometimes, he would drive us home; sometimes, he would not. As we started making that sweeping curve to the left, I remember praying, "Lord, please help him stay straight at the end of the curve, take us home, and not sweep back to the left into their driveway!"

When he made that sweeping left into their driveway, our Mother would grab one of my hands and one of Lenda's and take off down that dark road with the scary bridge over the creek we had to cross. I'm sorry, but what kind of person, what kind of "man" makes a mother and her two small daughters walk home after church in the dark, with them stumbling and crying because they were sleepy and cold? He's dead and gone now, so I will say it—not much of a man! He was unfeeling, mean-spirited, and selfish; I shall leave it at that!

Suspension Bridge

We had no choice if we were to get to church. We never missed a service if we could hitch a ride, or on numerous occasions, we would walk.

It was just under three miles from East Waco to 1601 Clay Avenue. We would head down Spring Street to Elm Street and take a left. Then, we would cross the historic suspension bridge at First and Main Street, which we called "The Swinging Bridge" (completed in 1870). Then, we would continue a few blocks east and sixteen blocks south to 1601 Clay Avenue.

After church, if Mother stayed a little longer praying and our ride left, we would walk in the dark, retracing our steps back to our home in East Waco.

Because we always had to "hitch" a ride, after pastoring the Temple of Pentecost for several years, I decided I had a debt I hadn't paid. We had several elderly saints, along with a few others who didn't have cars or a ride to church. For a couple of years, on Wednesday nights, I drove our shuttle bus and ran the route to pick them up for church. I remember always needing a ride myself until I got old enough to drive and bought a car, and I wanted them to have a ride with someone who didn't resent the fact that they *needed* a ride. I wanted to pay my dues and pay it forward!

We also had to walk to get groceries and anywhere else we needed to go. My mother walked so fast. She dragged me all over town, and I had to run as a child to keep up with her

As she grew older, she and I would walk together in places like the grocery store, second-hand shops, or Walmart. I walked fast, just as she did as a young woman. I told her it was payback for all those times I had to run to keep up with her. You know, they say, "What goes around comes around" (smile).

I remember people asking me to sing for them when I was young. They would stand me in front of them, and I would sing. They would comment and say, "She can really sing." I would feel embarrassed but proud.

In the old days at church, people would send requests to the platform for someone to sing a "special." The first time I got a request, my mother somehow got ahold of the request paper. It simply said, "Please have Patsy Landtroop sing, *Then I Met the Master*." Mother was so proud. She kept this memento for years.

This song turned out to be one of my mother's favorites. I sang it at her funeral many years later, in 2004.

We moved from East Waco to South Waco in the middle of my fourth-grade year to South Fifth Street. I could see the Brazos Valley Cotton Oil Company silos (the now-famous Magnolia Silos) from my front steps and yard. At that time, they were still processing cottonseed oil, which was commonly used then for industrial and culinary purposes. It didn't close for that purpose until the mid-1960s. It had little use and sat empty for many years until it was purchased by Chip and Joanna Gaines in 2014. When I was living two blocks from these mammoth structures, I had no idea they would one day become so famous.

Patsy – 11 years

I was twelve when my sister married and left town to live in nearby Hillsboro, Texas. From then on, I was alone after school, which was a challenging time for me. We did not have a telephone in our home, and my mother did not drive, so her employer would have to come and pick her up for work and bring her home in the evenings.

Patsy at 12 years with her mother

Mother was a hard worker. She cleaned houses and worked as a babysitter. This was before the era of housekeepers and nannies, when such jobs were not trendy or profitable like they are today. It was a poor person's job, which was all she could ever do.

By this time, she worked for Mr. Sam Pass, caring for his two children, Samuel Lindsey and Carol Lynn, and cooking and cleaning. She would have to wait for Mr. Pass to finish working before he could bring her home. He owned his own insurance company. Many times, in the winter, it would be late and dark by the time she arrived. Train tracks ran close to our house. I often stood on the front porch in the dark, crying because I was afraid—afraid of the darkness and fearful that the rapture had occurred, Mother was gone, and I was left behind. Only Pentecostal children have this great fear, but many do.

This was the time of day when trains came through town. Standing there was terrifying; hearing that eerie train whistle was almost more than I could bear. Years later, trains still make me sad. Sounds can transport you back to the past and evoke a range of emotions, from good to bad, happy to sad, or fearful. Wayne is mostly with me now, taking my hand when I hear that lonesome whistle, and this gives me a warm, good feeling instead of fear, emptiness, and loneliness.

I have felt the hand of God on my life all my life! I always just had the awareness that I would marry a preacher. It was my calling. I didn't know that

He would save the very best one in the world for me! How did I ever get so blessed as to become Mrs. Wayne Huntley?

Anyone looking at me when I was growing up would never have placed me in the position that I would eventually be in. I came from a broken home, raised by a hardworking woman who took in ironing, cleaned other people's homes, and babysat for their children to make ends meet. Church people and our pastor often paid my way to the Texas District Youth Camps in Lufkin, Texas, where I made consecrations and dedications that have lasted my whole life.

One "fireside consecration service" occurred in the field behind the tabernacle. We, young people, took pine cones and threw them in a bonfire, representing our commitments to God. I had no idea a new tabernacle would be built in that field years later. I did not know that as a pastor's wife from Raleigh, North Carolina, I would speak at a Texas Women's Conference here on the campgrounds and that the pulpit I would stand behind would be almost in the exact location where I had made those consecrations. I did not know that my five-year-old daughter, Christy, would receive the Holy Ghost right near that same spot when my husband preached at their Junior Youth Camp.

Patsy and Waco friends at Texas Youth Camp

God knows how to elevate you into what He wants you to be and where He wants you. We must place ourselves in His hands, follow Him, be patient, and wait on Him.

When I was around twelve years old, I also started trying to play chords on the piano. Some of my friends would instruct me on the platform piano after church. My pastor, Brother Hennigan, would hear me trying to play. He told my Mother, "I believe if Patsy had a piano, she could learn to play." He purchased an old upright piano for fifteen dollars and delivered it to my house. I banged, played, practiced, and learned to play — not too well, but pretty good for the style of the time. I would pay a lot of money to have that piano again. We moved around a lot when my mother found a better deal on rent. She was always trying to save money and was good at it, but my brothers, who moved us, got tired of moving the piano because it weighed a *ton* and refused to move it again. Alas, my precious piano ... gone!

When I was about thirteen, my very good friend was Irene Seith. She was a married lady who had moved to Waco from Mississippi when she had married Clarence. She possessed an accordion that she had for sale. It was a beauty. My sweet mother purchased it for me for one hundred dollars. That was more than a week's wages for her. She worked very hard manually to earn her money, but bought it for me. I was so excited to have my very own accordion. I still have that accordion and my electric Scandalli accordion, which I purchased when we evangelized. Back then, an accordion and a guitar were almost synonymous with evangelizing. You could hardly be an evangelist without them.

At the age of fourteen, I had a severe sickness that I *think* was the flu, which turned into pneumonia. I had a fever and missed a couple of days of school. On Saturday night, our church's young people were going to Cameron

Patsy age 14

Park to play volleyball, which I loved. My mother would not let me go because she said the night air wouldn't be good for me since I just had a fever. I begged and begged and begged, and she finally relented. Sorry to say that I should have listened. "Mother knows best!" I did have a relapse, and it was much worse the second time.

I experienced a high fever, hallucinated, and had to rush to the restroom. Everyone told my mother I needed to go to the doctor. Initially, I didn't want to go, and Mother was afraid to force me after I had gotten so ill. She was scared that I would die. I'm not sure, but I might have. In those days, more people trusted God without the medical field being involved.

I'm not saying you shouldn't go to doctors; I know I wanted to trust God. During the night, I would wake up and see my pastor, Brother Hennigan, praying in a straight-back chair on the other side of my room. His son, David, was sick at the same time, so Brother Hennigan would go from one of us to the other, praying. I thank God for a praying pastor. We both recovered and grew into adulthood. I don't know; maybe his prayers on those long, weary nights were for me to be used by God. Perhaps he asked God to spare my life and place me into the Gospel work. I am forever grateful for his influence in my life, and I probably wouldn't be alive if he hadn't prayed for me through those hard nights of sickness. After I started to feel better, my mother took my temperature; it was 107°. I know you might think that's impossible! But God!

Because of the high fever, my hair began falling out. It came out in chunks from the roots and looked like I had just cut it with scissors. Mother would have to brush it for what seemed like hours because the clumps coming out got all tangled up with hair still attached. It was a mess. I became so worried that I had my pastor pray for me because I was afraid I would go completely bald. God heard my prayer, and from that day forward, it stopped coming out. Another time, I was having trouble with styes on my eyes. I remember one time I had three styes at once. They were so large that they were as big as the striking end of a kitchen match. They were so very painful. Mother would take a needle, sterilize it with alcohol, and prick it, allowing the infection to drain. This would aid the healing process. That was the home remedy the doctor would refer to as 'lance' today. Again, I had my pastor, Brother Hennigan, pray for me, and I never had another one until years later, in 1972, when Wayne, Christy, and I were evangelizing. We were preaching for David and Myra Hennigan in Haynesville, Louisiana. David and I were raised in Waco when his daddy was our pastor. I was telling them the story about the healing of the styes on my eyes. The following day, when I woke up, I had the largest stye ever on my eye, and it was throbbing! I took authority and rebuked 'lying symptoms,' saying that God had healed me all those years ago, and I would not receive them back. And then, praise the Lord, I have never had another one. We don't have to take everything the devil tries to throw our way!

My sister, Lenda, did not have a good marriage and struggled for years. She decided to go to New Orleans to escape it all, but it turned out to be a poor choice. Mother was so worried and scared for her. I remember my mother waking me up in the middle of the night on several occasions, wailing in the living room. She sounded like a wounded animal, moaning and groaning.

It made me mad, not mad at Mother for what she was doing, but angry at my sister for living in such a way that caused my mother to become so burdened. I wasn't as spiritual as I should have been, or I would have joined her instead of getting angry at being awakened. A Mother has a special love for her children and will go to great lengths for them. Her daughter was in trouble; she was lost and needed God to intervene. I don't doubt that because of her prayers, my sister was saved, returned to God, and is in the church today. God does answer prayers.

Patsy, Mother, and Lenda

M. C., Patsy, and Dorothy

My brother, M.C., his wife Dorothy, and I made several evangelistic trips during my teen years. We went to Gloryland Church in East Texas. (Isn't that a great name?) The pastor was Brother R. V. Cranfield, who was such a Christian gentleman. His wife had left him many years before because of the church. We stayed at his home that weekend. It was in the country, so everything was quiet. There were no city noises during the night, only the chirping of crickets and the buzzing of locusts in the trees. I remember so vividly hearing Brother Cranfield stirring in the next room, and every time, he would exclaim some form of worship or praise or speak in tongues. This made such an impression on me. He was so prayerful, even when he slept. That may be what the Bible means when it says to *"pray without ceasing."*

We went to my brother Garth's church in Gainesville, Texas. I remember one particular time when we had to drive home to Waco after a Sunday night service because we had to go to work and school the next day. It seemed to be about a three-hour drive. We were tired when we started on our journey, and we sang and told funny incidents to try to stay awake. But oh, how great it felt to be a part of the ministry.

Garth, Bobbie, Loretta, and DeWayne

Every summer, I would spend several weeks at Garth and Bobbie's house, having a blast. I would sing and play the piano both in church and at home, spending hours immersed in music, singing and playing the piano. I would also enjoy snow cones and have fun with my nephew and niece, DeWayne and Loretta. A family friend, Ed Porter, had an old "hoopy car/truck" that we called "No Door." It was part car, part truck, and literally had no doors. But it drove, and that's all I cared about.

I rode the bus from Waco to Gainesville on July 18, 1964. When I arrived, my brother informed me that Brother Hennigan, my pastor, had died. He had been sick for a while, but we thought he was improving. I felt complete devastation and sadness. Spiritually, I felt much like I had felt physically when President John F. Kennedy was assassinated in 1963—floundering and scared! No one influenced me more for the Gospel, the Truth, and loving and living for God than Brother J. J. Hennigan. He put the desire for holiness and godliness

deep in my heart, which has lasted my entire life. It's not just something I want to do; it's a conviction for which I would give my life! I love and appreciate him more than I could ever express! God was our help, and we made it through that trial.

Brother and Sister Lonnie Marcus came and pastored our church for approximately two years after Brother Hennigan's death.

Sister Christine Marcus came at a time when I needed her preacher's wife's influence. And influence me she did.

Much later in my life, she came and spoke at a Mother's Day service at our church in Raleigh. Watching her in action then made me realize how much of her I saw in myself—how I carried myself, how I sang, and how I directed our choir. On that day, it was my happy privilege to introduce her, to honor her, and to tell the world, *my world,* just what she meant to me. I love Christine Marcus and am forever indebted to her. She may not feel she has influenced many people, but I am one of them.

Thank you for giving to the Lord.
I am a life that was changed.
Thank you for giving to the Lord.
I am so glad you gave."

Ray Boltz

In October 1964, we made our debut at the United Pentecostal Church International (UPCI) General Conference, held in nearby San Antonio, Texas. Malcolm, Dorothy, and I stayed at the Dun Wandering Motel. I can still feel my excitement from that moment; it was probably my first experience staying in a motel.

The next pastor of our church was Brother and Sister William Harvey (Bill) Davis, along with their two children, Pam and Sam. Oh, what fun we had with them.

From my early teens until I was about eighteen, we would drive to Killeen, Texas, for youth rallies and services. Killeen was home to Fort Hood, a large Army base located roughly sixty miles from Waco. Their church primarily had young men; in ours, we mainly had young women, thus the drawing power. During my youth, one of the pastors at the church was Brother Bill Dean. I had no idea that my life would later intertwine with some of their children, Johnny and Jerry Dean, even though we had grown up, married, and taken very different paths to work for the Lord.

Johnny, his sweet wife Debbie, and their children, Jonathan, Tammy, and Chantry, visited North Carolina, and we enjoyed the Outer Banks of North Carolina together. Later, their family was blessed with another girl, Brooke. We also visited them in Bentonville, Arkansas, drove to Branson, Missouri, and enjoyed great fellowship. Our only regret is that we don't get to spend as much time together as we would like. It seems that life gets in the way. We've gone back and forth to each other's houses and churches several times, and it always feels like we're spending time with family we don't see enough!

I graduated from Waco High School on May 30, 1967. Brother and Sister Davis were in attendance on that exciting day. It was truly special for them to share in my accomplishments. I was the first from my immediate family to graduate, and I was proud of myself.

My one and only sister, Lenda, who was expecting her fourth child at any time, had come down from Hillsboro to celebrate my graduation. But, as fate would have it, she was not to be in attendance.

That morning, she went into labor, and I had to drive her back to Hillsboro. On my graduation day, Charles Edward unexpectedly entered the world. I can never forget his age and birthday. Lenda's children are Denise, Steven, Marietta Kay, and Charles Edward.

At graduation, I was thinking exciting thoughts about my future, believing that God had great things in store for me. I was looking up to the stage, headed toward that special moment when I would reach out my hand and receive my much-anticipated diploma. I was walking down the aisle to "Pomp and Circumstance." No! Wait a minute! It was the "Wedding March." But hold on, I'm getting ahead of myself. There was a lot of exciting living between my graduation and the "Wedding March."

I must tell you how I met and fell in love with my sweetheart. It's a wonderful story and a great miracle how God brought him from Charlotte, North Carolina, and me from Waco, Texas, to Houston. Only God could have orchestrated our lives as beautifully as He did. We were two poor, underprivileged young people from different parts of the USA back in the days before social media and cell phones. We even had to call our parents and family from a pay phone. What an exciting time it was in our lives!

Not long after my high school graduation, my brother, Malcolm, was elected to pastor in Carthage, Texas, a small city of just under six thousand souls in deep East Texas, twenty miles west of the Louisiana state line. I pulled up roots and moved there for a few months to play the piano and sing for that church. He, along with his wife, Dorothy, and their children — Mike, Dennis, Retha, and Kevin — excitedly became residents of that town.

Even though their children were born in Waco, Carthage became home to them. My brother and his wife lived the rest of their lives there. All four of their children and some of their families still reside in Carthage, and, in fact, Dennis has pastored there since 2007. Although he spent time in Raleigh with us and several years evangelizing and pastoring in North Carolina, like a 'homing pigeon,' he felt the pull to return to his Texas roots.

After high school, I began to feel the need to attend TBC, but I had to wait until the second semester of the 1968-1969 school year so I could raise some funds!

A significant event occurred in my life on September 3, 1968, around the time Wayne arrived at TBC in Houston. We were having a 'teaching' revival at our church, the First Pentecostal Church, located at 1601 Clay Avenue in Waco, Texas. The teacher was an elder minister named Reverend Arthur W. Sassman. He was sixty-one years old, much younger than I am right now, but to a nineteen-year-old, I thought he was elderly.

That night after service, Brother Sassman called to a group of us young ladies talking in the foyer and said, "Girls, do you want to know how to get a good husband?"

Husband? Good one? Get one? Sure!

He gathered us around and gave us a list of scriptures to memorize, pray over, and take to our hearts. I took it seriously. I had prayed for my husband all my life, for as long as I could remember. In fact, once, in particular, I had a real burden for my then-unknown future husband. I travailed and interceded for him. I never knew exactly what that prayer was for, but God knew! It was probably when Wayne was struggling with his call to preach and the consecrations he was making.

After Brother Sassman spoke to us that night, I went home, and below is the note I wrote in my journal.

In obedience to the words of Brother Arthur Sassman,
I read, memorize, and believe these passages.
Signed, Patsy Landtroop

9-3-68

"Delight thyself also in the LORD; And he shall give thee the desires of thine heart. Commit thy way unto the LORD; Trust also in him; And he shall bring it to pass."

(Psalms 37:4-5)

"Thou hast given him his heart's desire, And hast not withholden the request of his lips."

(Psalms 21:2)

"Jesus said unto him, If thou canst believe, all things are possible to him that believeth."

(Mark 9:23)

"Therefore I say unto you, What things soever ye desire, when ye pray, believe that ye receive them, and ye shall have them."

(Mark 11:24)

Less than one year later, I was sitting in that same church with that same journal with Wayne Huntley by my side. He picked it up and wrote on a random page, *"I love you."* It had come to pass! God had heard, honored, and answered those prayers and commitments.

On a personal note, I did not have a date until I was eighteen, mainly because I purposed in my heart not to date anyone who did not share my core values or faith. You would find me at the girls' table of 'stags' or those without dates or companions at church events. We mainly had girls in our church, so the male gender was few and far between. I had had opportunities in high school, but it scared me to even think about dating an unbeliever. My actual first date came, as I mentioned, at the age of eighteen. I felt quite old to be having my first date at this ancient age. My goodness, two years have passed since the dating age of sixteen. Was I destined to be an 'old maid'?

On this first date, we went to a church service about thirty miles away in Hillsboro, Texas, at Brother N. J. Jones's church. If I remember correctly, he had a new 1967 Mercury Cougar sports car. He even let me drive? I felt exhilarated to be driving a new vehicle, which was surely not something I could ever afford.

When I arrived at TBC on that chilly January day, God honored that small commitment by arranging a date almost every weekend. It is astounding how God pays back even your smallest consecrations. I have found over the years that He will not be indebted to you.

So it was, in the year of our Lord, 1969, in January, that I rolled onto the Texas Bible College campus, so excited for my future and, oh, what a life God had planned for me.

M.C., Lenda, Mother, Patsy, and Garth

Garth, Ken, Lenda, and Patsy

Chapter Two

Ronald Wayne Huntley
Charlotte, North Carolina, 1949

It was Christmas time in The Old North State, in the year of our Lord, 1949–December 25, to be exact. It was Christmas Day, and Mary Frances Wix Huntley was in labor at Mercy Hospital in Charlotte, Mecklenburg County, North Carolina. Frances had no way of knowing just "who" was about to be delivered or how this baby would affect his world.

Wayne was born into a family that was, by all accounts, very dysfunctional. He had a poor, working-class mother and a mostly absent father. When he was present, he caused havoc because of extreme alcoholism. Like my father, he didn't go to the hospital when this precious, God-sent baby came, but our Heavenly Father was in attendance, as He would be for the rest of this chosen son's life.

Melvin, Frances, and Wayne Huntley

Ronald Wayne Huntley was the firstborn of Frances and Melvin Huntley. Only one other son would be born to them–Melvin Gerald Huntley, born twenty months later on August 7, 1951.

Frances and Melvin Huntley

Frances's background, like Josie's, also had no Pentecostal heritage. She came to the knowledge of this Truth through her husband. Not one of her blood relatives ever did — not her mother or father, sister or brother, aunt or uncle, or cousin — but she started her own Pentecostal legacy.

His mother was also a very dedicated worker; she tried hard and did her best to care for her two boys. Before my husband started school, his father was also a preacher. Although Wayne doesn't remember his father preaching, one of his sweetest memories as a very young child was when he and his brother Gerald were placed, standing on the altar in Tarboro, North Carolina, singing:

Wayne and Gerald

"Sweep over my soul, sweep over my soul,
Sweet Spirit, sweep over my soul.
My rest is complete as I sit at His feet.
Sweet Spirit, sweep over my soul."

Unknown

Those were surely fonder times, better times, and the best of times before almost complete deterioration and ruination! But God was in total control, and sometimes what we would change about our lives the most is what makes us into what God can use for His glory!

How coincidental that Wayne was in Tarboro with his father, who was trying to pastor a fledgling church. His father was unable to make a go of it, but many years later, Wayne would be instrumental in planting not one but two Carolina Crusade churches in this city – an English-speaking church and a Spanish-speaking church. (More about that in Chapter 8: "Senior Pastor and Mrs. Wayne Huntley.")

Wayne's earliest and most constant young memories include disappointments, broken promises, fear, rejection, sadness, his father fighting, cursing to the top of his booming voice, and ranting and raving all day and all night without stopping. Many nights were spent sleepless because of an uncontrollable drunk, slapping his sweet mother around, falling on, and breaking furniture. Some people get passively quiet and prefer to sleep when drunk… but not so was the case with Melvin Huntley! He turned into a raging maniac who wanted to fight any and all people.

God does use our hardships and trials to make us better people. For instance, Wayne would change that his father was a very addicted alcoholic, but he probably would not be the man he is without these trials, hardships, and tears. His childhood was filled with uncertainty and heartache.

The pastor of their little church in Charlotte, North Carolina, gave Wayne's family a key to the church. On nights when it got to be more than was physically bearable, Mama Frances would come to the boys' bedroom and say, "Get up, boys, we have to go." She knew when it became too dangerous to stay at home, so they would go to the church and sleep on the pews. The church has been and continues to be a *safe haven* for many people, including my husband, his mother, and his brother.

Wayne didn't know until 2022, when he participated in his former pastor, Brother Sechrist's, funeral, why his pastor had been so compassionate toward Mama Frances and her young boys by allowing them to sleep in the church. He was also raised in an alcoholic's home, so he understood!

Mama Frances sometimes received a note from the boys' teachers: "I don't know what is happening, but the boys need more rest. They are sleepy and dozing in class." Mama Frances was doing all she could, but things were out of her hands.

To the extent that when Wayne got a little older, he told the Lord, "If you get me out of this, I promise I will not have arguing and turmoil in my home, but it will be a place of peace." When I was a young bride, he made it clear that there would be no arguing in our home: if so, I would have to do it alone.

In elementary school, Wayne remembers living in a little shotgun apartment. His mother would have to go to work early, so she would get the boys up and dressed for school. Then, on the cold, frosty morning, she would walk the sleepy, grumpy little boys a couple of blocks to her parents' home at 204 Jones Street, Charlotte, North Carolina. William J (Bill) Wix and Eva Riggs Wix's house had a gas space heater in the front room where they would lie on the floor, warming themselves and dozing until it was time to catch the bus to school.

Wayne and Gerald

PawPaw Wix was a barber by trade and owned his shop. He would sometimes take the Huntley boys to his shop on Sunday afternoon and give them a free haircut, or as he would call it, "get their ears lowered." Wayne can still hear the scissors clicking and smell the *Royal Crown* shaving lotion. It's funny, the little things we remember.

Frances and her two boys often had to live with relatives to have a roof over their heads. They were so kind to take them in, although sometimes Wayne said he felt unwanted and therefore rejected. It was like, "We must help Frances and the boys again, or they will be on the streets." I'm sure it was also a hardship for those families.

This attitude carried over into Wayne's adulthood, and any time he felt rejected or unwanted, he did not respond positively. That's all I'm going to say on the matter, but as a young wife, I had to make sure I never projected anything that gave him those feelings, or it would not be happy for me in our household. He never argued or said unkind remarks; he just got quiet. Therefore, I knew he felt hurt, and "I" couldn't stand that.

PawPaw and MawMaw Huntley

Many of us must overcome feelings brought about by negative happenings in our youth. God repaid Wayne many times for some of his youthful uncertainties. As an adult, he is very much loved, sought after, and wanted.

PawPaw (Carl Huntley, affectionately pronounced "Carol" by his wife) and MawMaw Huntley (Odessa Leveret Huntley) were very influential in Wayne's life. Without PawPaw and others in the family, Wayne would not have had school clothes or supplies. PawPaw took him carp fishing to Wallace Lake, paid the fee to fish, taught him to fish, and bought fishing rods, "Wilson Wallace" egg sandwiches, and drinks and snacks. Wilson Wallace was the owner of the carp lake, and he made egg sandwiches and sold them there at a little grill. It's like a scrambled egg sandwich, except it is not scrambled *in the pan* but spread thin, cooked, and turned over in one piece. So, at our house, we make "Wilson Wallace" egg sandwiches in honor of Wayne's happy thoughts of fishing. Oh, what fun it was for a boy who would not have been able to go otherwise.

Wayne was much older and a grandfather himself before realizing how much it meant. He wished that he could have the opportunity to hug PawPaw again and tell him how important it was for all the time, money, energy, and love that he had poured into his young life. Thank you, Paw Paw! You are remembered fondly, and one of Wayne's grandsons is named after *you*, Gentson Hebron *Carl* Ballestero.

*My Hero,
Uncle Bill Padgett*

When Wayne was thirteen, his Uncle Bill Padgett, his Aunt Hazel Huntley Padgett's husband, was pastoring the church in Charlotte, North Carolina. He came to Wayne's house and asked his mother if he could take Wayne to a church camp in Batesburg, Georgia. He told her he would pay for everything and take care of him. Uncle Bill surely did not know how important this would be to Wayne, or the many who would one day hear him preach, and the many ministers who would be encouraged, spirits lifted, and lives changed for the better because of the outstanding preacher of the Gospel that Wayne would one day become. To my knowledge, Uncle Bill never preached at any big meetings. He was not known as a "camp meeting preacher," but he did, like Andrew in the Bible, know how to bring someone to Jesus, that Jesus could use mightily. Andrew brought his brother, Simon Peter, to Jesus. Jesus used him to preach the Day of Pentecost message to those in the upper room when the Holy Ghost fell for the first time. Uncle Bill may not have been a well-known preacher, but in later years, Wayne Huntley would be known by name to many ministers in the UPCI. Somehow, I believe Uncle Bill will have a part in anything Wayne has been privileged to accomplish.

So, Wayne went to the youth camp. Brother Doyle Spears was the evangelist, and Brother Benny Cole was the youth president. On the second night, Wayne received the Holy Ghost, with Brother Cole praying for him!

Oh, the far-reaching effects of this one decision! When Mama Frances said, "Yes, Wayne can go to camp," it would affect not only Wayne's life but also those thousands who would one day hear him preach, be taught a home Bible study, or sit under his ministry in Raleigh, North Carolina. It was a pivotal moment, *"The Intersection of Tide and Time."* It's like the stars lined up just perfectly. Look at the end result of this <u>one</u> decision.

After church that night, Wayne went to the boys' dorm. He looked around and saw some boys reading their Bibles and others praying before they got into their beds. Wayne said to himself, "I am one of these Christians now, so if that's what Christians do, that's what I'm gonna do." He got his Bible out and began to read.

After he returned home from camp, his uncle Bill Padgett baptized him, his mother, and his brother in the name of Jesus.

Mary Frances Huntley, like Josie Lue Landtroop, never learned to drive. As a result, Frances and her two boys also had to "hitch a ride" to church, just like Josie and her two girls. Their rides were not always dependable. Sometimes, they would come; sometimes, they would not.

Wayne and Gerald

Mama Frances would have the boys sit on the couch, all dressed up in their Sunday best with their little white shirts, ties, and church shoes, along with a handkerchief and a comb in their pockets, and always with at least a little bit of offering. While waiting for their ride, they would take the hymnal songbook and sing. If their ride didn't show, she would not let the boys change into play clothes until it was time for church to end. They would sing, sing, and sing every song they knew in the book.

Wayne and Gerald were excellent ball players in elementary and junior high school. They played on community and school teams, winning many trophies. On one baseball team, Wayne was the pitcher, and Gerald was the catcher—the Huntley duo.

At that particular time, sports were essential to Wayne and his self-image. Because he was quite the athlete, he had the respect of students, coaches, and parents. This opened many doors for him that otherwise would have been closed. It put men in his life who were positive influences and taught him discipline and traits to become a confident man and a respectable person.

One such man was Sergeant Black. This was his friend, Raymond Black's father, a police officer. Raymond played on the ball teams with Wayne, and they were best friends.

One day, Sergeant Black brought a brand-new bicycle, still in its box, to Wayne's house and asked him to assemble it. Wayne complied, and after it was all done, Mr. Black told him, "It's yours." Wayne certainly couldn't afford a new bicycle, but he had one now!

Gerald and Wayne

Wayne always had so much drive and passion. He tried out for one team, and some players told him that a certain boy *was* the shortstop for the team. Wayne decided right then and there that if that other person got that position, he would have to work, hustle, and battle for it. Wayne came early, stayed late, and gave it all, even though sometimes he didn't even own his baseball glove. He shared with one of his more prosperous friends. Wayne got the position! Sometimes, you don't accomplish things because you don't work hard enough. This would be his modus operandi for the rest of his life's journey. He might not be the best at anything, but no one would be more diligent or outwork him! This would help him build a fast-growing church in Raleigh, North Carolina, many years later. He is consumed by a passion for what he believes in and loves!

Because Wayne played ball and was so good, he was in with the "cool kids" at school. He was accepted because he was one of the star players. They didn't know how poor and dysfunctional his family was. They just thought he was as good as they were. Wayne always had a little girlfriend from school. One of them, he would walk home, carrying her books. He walked right by his poor, little, shabby, shotgun house, headed toward her better and newer place on the more prosperous side of town, and she never knew. When he walked by his house, he didn't acknowledge that he lived there.

Another such school girlfriend, God gave him a dream. He dreamed he was at a funeral home, standing in line with her to walk around and view the body. As he stood in front of the casket, he looked into it, and he was looking into his own face. It scared him so much that he immediately broke off the relationship with her. God knows how to get your attention. On numerous occasions, God unmistakenly called him. God wanted him!

When God began to call Wayne to preach, he was in a spiritual struggle with God. It was not because he didn't want to do the will of God or His bidding; he just felt that he was utterly unusable and unworthy and that God was making a mistake in desiring him to preach. He would cry and cry.

Wayne asked his mother what it felt like to be called to preach. His mother said, "Wayne, honey, all I know is that it is just a heavy burden. That's all I remember about your daddy when God called him. It was just a heavy burden."

Once, a preacher came to his house, and in conversation, Wayne showed him all the trophies he had won as a ball player. The preacher stepped back and asked him a question that shook him to his core, and he never forgot it! He said, "Where are all your trophies for God?" That struck a chord deep down in his soul that began to resonate with his very being. From that moment, he started to visualize and work to attain trophies for God, win souls, and do God's will. Those are the only ones that will last! When we get to heaven, we want trophies for the Kingdom.

Wayne had decided to quit baseball after the end of ninth grade when he was changing schools and entering high school.

However, when Wayne's freshman year at Garinger High School came around, peer pressure was very present. All his friends were going out for the Junior Varsity Team, so Wayne decided to join them and made the team.

During practice one day, the coach of the Varsity Team came over to Wayne and told him, "We want you to be a part of the Varsity Team." Being invited to play in this elite group was exceptionally unusual for a first-year student. In fact, Wayne was one of only two freshmen with this distinguished honor!

But one night, after a church service, at a time of consecration, he was rolled up under a pew about halfway to the back of the auditorium, and God called to him again. He spoke directly to his heart. This time, it was not a gentle nudge as before, but it was an ultimatum. "Tonight, you choose ME or BALL. I have plans for you, but it does NOT include baseball." God needed and wanted Wayne's complete allegiance. If he were to do what God wanted him to do, be what God wanted him to be, go where God wanted him to go, and achieve what God wanted him to accomplish, he could not be double-minded in any way. God wanted 100% of his love and commitment.

Brother and Sister Sechrist

Wayne said, "All right, God. I think You are making a mistake, but if You want me, I will do what You want; I will preach."

About that time, Brother Sechrist said, "Where's Wayne?" Someone pointed under the pew where Wayne was lying. Brother Sechrist said, "Come on up here to the platform. Wayne has something to tell the church." Thank God for a pastor who knew God had called him and had him confirm God's calling.

He doesn't know *what* he said that night; almost all he could do was cry. When he opened his eyes, the altar was full of people praying. God established His calling and His leading hand in his life by the word of his testimony.

So, he conceded to the Lord. It was just one week before the first Varsity game. With his ball uniform tucked under his arm, he walked purposefully into the coach's office, and with apprehension, he laid it on the coach's desk and said, "I quit."

Coach Tamanchek was big and boisterous, and Wayne was half afraid of him. The coach exclaimed, "What! Why?" Wayne told him that he felt his call to preach, that he could not be divided in his allegiance, and that he needed to quit. The coach said, "I understand."

Wayne walked out and never looked back, knowing that was the right and best decision. From that moment on, Wayne has always given God one hundred percent of himself and his effort to God's Kingdom.

While everyone else was worshiping and praising during church services, Wayne would be travailing in prayer because of this intense burden on his heart. Wayne made a pact with the Lord. "Okay, Lord, I will do my best to preach and follow You and do Your will, but that's all I am going to do. I will not learn another trade or have any other career. I am not my own; I'm Yours, for whatever, whenever, and wherever You choose."

He recently returned to the little church building on Howie Circle (which has not been a United Pentecostal

Church for some years) in Charlotte, North Carolina. He stopped and went up to the front porch, tried

the door, and oddly enough, it was unlocked. He went in, and a picture was taken of Wayne pointing to the spot under the pews (the same pews, by the way) where this spiritual pact was made.

Wayne has never been sorry that he chose the spiritual over the carnal, the godly over the fleshly, or the eternal over the temporal. God has paid him back over and over again in every way. God will not be indebted to us.

At one time, a young preacher named Brother Bob Anderson, his wife, and their baby were trying to start a church in Hickory, North Carolina. They must have come down to Charlotte to fellowship with the saints on Howie Circle. They had a very tough struggle financially.

Wayne, as a young person, wanted to help. He desired to buy milk and diapers for their baby, so even though he and his mother had many needs, they wanted to share their meager goods with them.

Wayne vividly remembers the day the Andersons stopped in Charlotte on their way out of town. The car was loaded with their few worldly possessions. Having fought the fight as long as they could, they were leaving Hickory for good. Wayne remembers thinking, *"But what about those few saints left in Hickory? Who will pastor them?"*

Wayne was very saddened for those sheep without a shepherd. With no animosity toward Brother Anderson, Wayne purposed in his heart that if God ever allowed him to start a home missions church in North Carolina, he would come to town, knowing that he would stay, of course, with the help of God.

Over fifty years later, while Wayne was ministering in Mississippi, a man approached him after a church service and told him that when he was a baby, he and his parents had come to Hickory for some time. Wayne realized that 'this man' was 'that baby' of over fifty years ago whom he had felt to buy milk and diapers; the circle of life goes round and round.

So, it was then that, while we were still evangelizing, once while preaching in North Carolina, we took a "day trip" to Hickory to look at the town, feel things out in the Spirit, to see if God would give us the go-ahead to relocate there and try to start a church. We spent the day there, walking the streets, looking at buildings, and even making contact with someone we had heard about. A person who used to be a committed Christian lived there, and we went to her house and told her what we were doing and thinking about.

When we returned to Texas after our visit to North Carolina, Wayne and I attended a district service in Houston at Brother O. W. Williams' church. Papa Eurial McClain (Wayne McClain's father) found me in the church building after church and was frantic. He told me to get Wayne because he had something to say to us both. We located Wayne, and he grabbed both our hands and declared, with tears in his eyes. "I don't know what you children are thinking about doing, but *don't*. It's not time yet."

We thanked him and God for giving us the sign we needed to ensure we didn't make a mistake. We didn't know it was not time *yet* because God was saving the *best place in North Carolina for us,* the capital city of Raleigh.

We *knew* Hickory wasn't for us. However, we continued to pray for that beautiful city, and some years later, on Valentine's Day, 1981, God answered our prayer — and others, I am sure — and sent Wayne's brother, Gerald, and his wife, Susan Snyder Huntley, to pastor that group of saints. God didn't send us, but he did send Wayne's brother!

Gerald and Susan Huntley moved to Hickory in 1981, when their son, Marcus, was just ten months old. They built a beautiful building and worked for Jesus for many years. They retired in 2014, and their only child, Marcus Gerald, and his wife, Tonia Gubic Huntley, along with their two girls, Macy and Mila, have taken over the pastorate there in Hickory.

Uncle Bill Padgett told Wayne, "If you are going to preach, you need to go to Bible school. I was never privileged to go, and I feel you need it. I read in the *Pentecostal Herald* (a magazine periodical of the UPCI) an advertisement for scholarships offered to the different Bible schools. I will help you apply, and you can win it."

He did apply, and he won the scholarship to Texas Bible College. One day, Wayne came home from school, and lying on the kitchen table was a telegram addressed to Wayne from Tom Fred Tenney, Conquerors' president (Comparable to the youth president today), telling Wayne that he was the 1968 Texas Bible College Scholarship winner. This was the inauguration of the Bible college scholarships. Going to Texas changed his life forever, and mine for good.

His mother told him that he had to save $500 to go. (I think she was secretly thinking, hoping, and wishing that he would not be able to achieve it.)

In 1968, that was a LOT of money. He had saved $250. He achieved this by working at an A&P grocery store.

He had first worked at Park-n-Shop grocery, which was within walking distance or a short ride on his bicycle from his house. After this first job, his friend Raymond helped him get a better-paying job at the A&P grocery store. By that time, he had saved and purchased a car. He had driven it around in his backyard while he continued to work and save for insurance. One day, as he was driving to work, minding his own business and doing everything right, at an intersection, an off-duty police officer ran a red light and hit Wayne, who was driving his 1953 Chevrolet that he had purchased for $225.

Of course, it scared him to death because the officer wore his police uniform. The officer didn't want him to call for a police report, as it might be bad for his work record. It was just a little fender bender. He told Wayne to take his car, have it appraised, and he would pay him cash. Wouldn't you know it was appraised at $250, the exact amount he needed to complete the $500 savings his mother required!

Teasingly, Wayne has said many times throughout the years, "Back when I was in the grocery business," this or that. We laugh because he was just a bagger or a cashier, or sometimes he worked in the bottle room, sorting the Coke bottles that were returned for a deposit. Yes, we used to have to pay a deposit on the glass bottles, and we could take them back to the store for a refund. Thus, we have found bottles on the side of the road and anywhere else where people would leave them. We collected and returned them for five cents per bottle. It even got up to ten cents before that nonsense stopped.

One day, his cousin, Ray Padgett, called him to his house because he had something for him. Ray had attended Bible school for a short time but had since stopped attending church.

When Wayne got there, Ray had laid out on the table a *Thompson Chain-Reference Bible*. Wayne surely could not afford this fantastic kind of Bible. Ray said, "Wayne, I don't need this Bible anymore. I thought you could use it as you prepare to become a minister; I wanted you to have it."

Thankfully, Wayne received this most precious gift with much gratitude and has always used a *Thompson Chain Bible* from that time. It's his Bible of choice. He brought it home, took a pen, crossed out the name Ray Padgett, and wrote instead, "Wayne Huntley." There is always someone to take our place if we decide not to follow Jesus and do His bidding.

Wayne gave this, his first preaching Bible, to Huntley Starr, our first grandchild. Each of our grands has been given the latest Bible, from which he was preaching when they were born. The Bible is our greatest treasure, holds the key to life and eternal life, and is worth more than silver or gold.

It was nearing the time of Wayne's departure to leave home, sprout his wings, and fly to Texas. On numerous occasions, Wayne looked up as he and his

48

mother and brother sat at the dinner table, and tears flowed down his mother's face. He would say, "Mama, what's wrong?"

She would say, "Nothing." She was anticipating that her son, the one she leaned on, who took care of his brother, was her strong arm to rely on; that son was leaving North Carolina and going to Houston, Texas, over one thousand miles away. He had never been away from home or flown on an airplane. This was the day before cell phones. You had to use pay phones. She would have no way to contact him unless she called the Texas Bible College office.

She knew things would never be the same again, and they surely were not. Wayne's life would forever be changed. He would meet me, his sweetheart, there and start a ministry lasting fifty-plus years.

Johnny and Peggy Garrison

He had never seen a large Pentecostal church. He had only seen small churches. His home church often consisted only of him and his brother as the youth department. His cousin, Peggy Padgett Garrison, and her husband, Johnny, provided the foundational strength and encouragement that helped him remain in the church as a young person, along with Dottie Rambo records. He still likes Rambo songs to this day. They take him back to much simpler times when he was being called by God and learning to lean on the Lord. He feels that he would not be in the church if not for the Garrisons and their concern and impartation of love into his life.

49

When he received his call to preach, his pastor was William Harvey *Sechrist*. (Odd, isn't it that my pastor's name was William Harvey *Davis?*) Brother Sechrist had Wayne leading the congregational singing and being the master of ceremonies, along with being the Sunday school director, all while he was still in high school. This was great training. Brother Sechrist knew that Wayne had a special call on his life.

Finally, the day came, and Wayne and two friends, Ronnie Nelson and Gary McLain, flew from Charlotte, North Carolina, to Houston, Texas.

Wayne's school pictures

Texas Bible College, September 1968

What a time of enlightenment for Wayne. As previously stated, he came from a district with not many churches; most of them were very small. He had never seen large churches with a powerful move of God, influential preachers, pastors, and evangelists. People whom he may have previously just heard about, he is now meeting and getting to be in their presence.

Teachers who were pastors in the Houston area opened Wayne's mind to God's greatness and what He was doing and wanted to do. And to think, Wayne Huntley could be used by God to fulfill God's plan and be a part of it.

Brother Fred Foster (and his lovely wife, Pat, whom many people in those days thought I favored, and for me was a very high compliment) was the president of Texas Bible College.

Wayne had no idea, at that time, that years later, when both would be pastoring in North Carolina, Brother Fred Foster's oldest son, Mark, would become his best, lifelong "fast friend."

Wayne settled into the routine of college life: classes, schoolwork, church services, chapel services, prayer meetings, vesper services, hamburgers cooked at the Student Union Building (SUB), meeting new friends, and playing ball.

Wayne often worked the third shift, staying up all night, and would get off just in time for class. As soon as class was over, he would head to his dorm for much-needed sleep, only to have his buddies come and shake him awake to get him up to play ball. They needed him to play ball with them on their pick-up team, so he half-heartedly — not! — dragged himself up to play. Lots of action and movement kept him awake until it was time to go to work that night on the third shift. He would head to work as a janitor at some municipal buildings in downtown Houston and immediately go to the restroom and wash his face with cold water to wake himself up.

Sometimes, this went on for two or three days. That's youth for you! Young and ignorant! When you get older, you learn better and find that IF you CAN sleep, you'd better do just that. There comes a time when it's not as easy as it once was, and it's not a punishment for someone to say, "Go take a nap!"

General conference time came in the fall, and one of Wayne's fellow students, Sam Dougherty from Gainesville, Texas, asked him to attend his home church for the weekend to preach and sing, while Pastor Garth W. Landtroop, my oldest brother, attended the conference. This was a very significant event for Wayne! Little did he know at the time just how important and intertwined the Landtroop family would become in his life for the rest of his life.

DeWayne and Loretta Landtroop, my nephew and niece, who had not attended the conference with their parents, met and fell in love with Wayne before I did. They loved him first, but the rest of my family, down to the very last one (including me), followed suit as soon as they met him.

Well, if the truth be known, for my dear mother, it was not love at first sight, like it was for me. When Wayne first came home with me from Bible college, she asked me, "What in the world do you see in that little ole boy?" It didn't take long for her to see exactly what I saw in that 'little ole boy.' She loved him very much until the day she died. She indeed found out just what it was that I saw. Mr. Wayne certainly gained a whole new family to love him, and they all have respected him through the years and made him their unappointed spiritual leader, mentor, and guide.

Wayne, 1968, Gainesville, Texas

At one chapel service, Wayne was praying when he heard a loud voice behind him, so he turned around to see who it was. No one was there, but the voice had said, "I have called you, and I will provide for you."

He received a note from Sister Lucille Galbraith, a female instructor, stating, "Great privileges require great responsibilities."

That Christmas, in 1968, Wayne went home for the Christmas holidays. He only had a couple of suits and shirts. He had learned the hard way that you don't wash tennis shoes (especially ones you had been wearing while working as a hired hand roofer) with your white shirts; yes, as unthinkable as this sounds, that's just what he did. He had to wear white shirts with specks and blobs of tar on them and keep his suit coat on to hide this hideous mistake. The school of hard knocks is a tough way to learn, but learn you do! When he got home, his daddy took his suitcase (which just happened to have all his meager belongings inside) to a pawn shop to gain a few dollars for a drink. Wayne had to find out where he had taken it to retrieve it.

While he was home for that Christmas visit from Texas Bible College, he was asked to speak to some of the students at Garinger High School, giving his testimony and telling of his ministerial training in Texas.

One woman who came to church testified one night when Wayne was home and said, "We are so glad to have 'Fonald Eugene' home from TBC."

This was so funny because she had just gotten his name completely wrong. After Wayne and I married, and I heard about this incident, I started calling him "Eugene" as my pet name. To this day, after over fifty years of marriage, even if we are in a large group of people, I can call out loudly, "Eugene," and he will look up immediately because he *knows it's ME!*

The freshman class was exceptionally large and had several hundred enrolled. Sad to say, many of the young men were dodging the mandatory draft of the day. You were exempt from that draft if you enrolled in a ministerial preparation college. It was the time of the Vietnam War, and many were there for no other reason than simply to avoid being drafted.

But this certainly was not the case for Wayne. He was there to consecrate, dedicate, and grow his ministry. He learned to pray and listen to the voice of God during his TBC days. He spent many hours in the prayer room there on campus, invoking God to lead, direct, and use his life. Many of Brother James Kilgore's classes began with a prayer that lasted the whole time. Students would lie on the floor, leaving big puddles of tears. Brother Kilgore would admonish the students, "Somebody needs to sell out; somebody needs to sell out." Those prayer meetings showed Wayne things he had never seen, and he was formed into what he had never been.

Chapter Three

Wayne and Patsy
January 1969

I was so excited to arrive in Houston, Texas, at Texas Bridal, I mean, Bible College. I had loaded my little 1962 Granada Gold Chevy II with all my "stuff," along with my best friend Rose Milam, who also planned to go to TBC. She only stayed a few days and decided to return home, but I was finally there.

In January of 1969, Wayne and I had our *informal* introduction. It was not face-to-face or one-on-one. Wayne was preaching in one of our chapel services. It was the custom that the preacher, for the day, would introduce the person who was to sing before they preached. So, he had a paper with the person's name to sing on this particular day–someone new to the campus this semester. It read, "Patsy Landtroop, singing, 'I'll Regret.'"

When I finished, Wayne said to himself, "She sure will," but I never have!

I knew who Wayne Huntley was on the TBC campus; everybody did. He was well-liked, friendly, consecrated, and dedicated. He could play a mean game of basketball, and he sure wasn't bad on the eyes, either. But we had never been officially introduced.

That fateful Sunday afternoon, April 20, 1969, I entered the school cafeteria for lunch and passed by a table where Wayne and the rest of his "evangelistic team" sat. As I walked by, he said to them, "Ask Patsy; she has a car." Somebody, not sure who, but not Wayne, asked me to drive the team to Highlands, Texas, where Brother and Sister Johnny Wilhoit pastored. His church was about thirty minutes from the school campus. Wayne's team had a service that Sunday night, but no one had a car to transport them. How did *he* know that *I* had a car? I don't know, but he had noticed! *Yes!*

That afternoon, in the Student Union Building (SUB), we all practiced singing and playing guitars, while I played the accordion. Getting ready to leave for church that evening, the back seat of my little car quickly filled up with students. Another girl was in the front seat along with me. This was the day when automobiles had front-bench seats. There was no bucket seat, and the gearshift was on the steering wheel column. So, three people could easily sit in the front. Everybody was in the car except Wayne. I drove to the circle to pick him up and his *Yamaha* guitar.

(How sad it is that, many years later, after we had moved to Raleigh, North Carolina, this special guitar, purchased for him by his parents and used by us for the seven years we evangelized, was stolen from our little church building on Loop Road in Garner.)

I thought the only nice and polite thing to do was to let him drive so that he wouldn't be sitting in the middle between two girls. I shifted to the middle, and he climbed into the driver's seat. On the way to Highlands, every time I glanced up at the rearview mirror above my head, Wayne was looking at me!

The same thing happened after church on the way back to campus. I was lost in those luscious brown eyes. It matters not if you do or do not believe in *love at first sight*; it happened to *us*!

That week, Wayne received a call from Brother Johnny Willhoite. He had a revival scheduled, and for some reason unknown to us, the evangelist couldn't come. What a fateful ordering of our steps by God.

Brother Willhoite told him to ask *"me"* to help with the singing, and of course, I had "the car." Our revival was on Sunday, May 4, a few days during that week, and Sunday, May 11.

Other than the will of God and the hand of God orchestrating, that rearview mirror on my little Chevy II might just have been what brought Wayne and me together. God works in mysterious ways! In the Bible, He used a donkey; I guess He could use a car. I just know that in my little car, traveling to and from Highlands, I fell deeply and completely in love with Wayne Huntley.

Neither of us had any *idea at all* where our road of life would take us. What an exciting journey our "wonderful life" would be!

So, as the *will of God would have it,* Wayne and I conducted our very first revival *together!*

We drove back and forth from TBC to Highlands each evening of the revival. It was a little town, six and a half square miles, located north of Interstate 10 and west of Farm to Market Road 2100 in Harris County, Texas.

It was just a small town, but it had a great church and such a profound impact on Wayne as a preacher and on us as a couple.

To get there, our route took us down Interstate 10, where we had to drive past a huge, lit-up sign of an eagle flying. It was on the top of the

Anheuser-Busch corporate office building, which was several stories tall. It could be seen for a long way. It was beautiful and quite a landmark of the day.

Thus, we began our journey talking, talking, talking, and talking—all the way there and all the way back, each day of the revival. Our spirits soared, along with that eagle flying high in the heavens.

Wayne with Robin Smith Brannan

At that time in history, not very many people received the Holy Ghost in revivals, but we were so excited that we had eight, one of whom was Robin Smith Brannan, the eight-year-old little sister of Susie Smith Cecil. Susie's husband, Terry Cecil (although they were not yet married), was one of Wayne's good friends from North Carolina.

On Sunday, May 4, Wayne and I were riding in the back seat of Brother and Sister Willhoite's car. We entered the dimly lit Washburn Tunnel. Construction was completed in 1950, and it connected Galena Park and Pasadena. The tunnel was 3,791 feet long, plenty of time for Wayne's sweet lips to somehow find mine for the first time. I remember that kiss so vividly. Even to this good day, over fifty years later, it still is the sweetest, most precious kiss I have ever experienced. It was not a lustful kiss but a gentle, tender, and protective one. It made me feel completely loved and respected.

Since that day, all I have ever wanted is to be with Wayne. Some couples may act like they need a break from each other occasionally, but we have never felt that way. We truly enjoy each other's company, and when we are separated, it's out of necessity, not because we want to be!

Sunday afternoon, May 11, 1969, we spent the day with the Willhoites. We went to the San Jacinto Monument, which stands regally at 575 feet (twenty feet taller than the Washington Monument).

While waiting in line in the car to ride across the Lynchburg Ferry, which has been in operation since 1888, some people came up beside the vehicle, selling crepe paper roses dipped in wax. They were quite beautiful and were a mere twenty-five cents for three. Wayne bought me flowers, the first of many, many flowers to come, for so many occasions, and some for no other reason except to say, "I love you."

We rode with the Willhoites to see his parents, who attended Apostolic Temple, pastored by Brother Wayne McClain. We had yet to meet the McClain family, but we would soon. Oh, what an intricate part of our lives these precious people would become.

On that Mother's Day Sunday afternoon, May 11, at the elder Wilhoit's home, we were asked to sing and were prophetically introduced as Mr. and Mrs. Wayne Huntley.

Brother and Sister Willhoite could see our connection and pushed us together. They encouraged us as a couple. They could sense that we fit together and worked together like a horse and carriage, like peanut butter and jelly, or hand in glove.

After church that night, we found ourselves at Kip's Restaurant, close to the school. Before we went inside to eat, Wayne said, "I know everyone has been taking it for granted, and so have I, but *Will You Marry Me?*"

Of course, I said, "Yes!"

Kip's Big Boy Restaurant

We went inside and called my mother for Mother's Day. Amazingly, we found a penny on the floor by the pay phone, which I still have. If there *is* such a thing (which there really is not), we have had *"good luck."*

It was May 12, 1969, and time for the end-of-the-year banquet. "Reach for the Stars" was held at the Shamrock Hilton Hotel. Sitting at our table were Randy Cappadona and Beverly Campbell, Dennis Whitt and Linda Presley, Wayne and me, and another couple whose lives would also be intertwined with us down through the years: Sam Doughtery and Thelma Fisher Doughtery. That's how she signed her name that night on my banquet program. 'Thelma Fisher (Dougherty).' She was prophetically speaking because they did get married.

As I have already stated, Sam Dougherty had asked Wayne to go to Gainesville, Texas, with him to preach a weekend at his home church in the fall of 1968, which was pastored by my brother, Garth. Sam married Thelma Fisher, whose younger sister, Joyce Fisher, married DeWayne Landtroop, my nephew. DeWayne and Joyce were married for many years till she was taken from us in an untimely death at the way-too-young age of fifty-six. God did smile a second time when He brought Barbie into his life and our family four years later.

May 15, 1969, was graduation day, and the school year ended. May 16, it was over!

On Sunday, May 18, we went to Bethel Tabernacle, pastored by Brother Orlin Ray Fauss. Later that day, we helped hold a church service at St. Thomas Rest Home, where Wayne played his guitar and sang "Born To Serve the Lord."

We decided to stay an extra week to have a good time before going home to Waco. May 19 to 23 found us all over town, doing this and that. I stayed with some girls who had an apartment at Arrowhead Apartments, and he was with some guys. I don't even remember who they were, but they would spend the summer in Houston and not go home between school years.

We spent the week traveling around Houston with our good friends, Ronnie Nelson and Kathy Saul, who later got married. We rode the bus downtown, toured the Gulf Building, went to the zoo, played Putt-Putt Golf, and went window shopping at Foley's Department Store. We ate at Frontier, Kip's, and Vallian's restaurants and enjoyed a picnic. We had a week of fun, but it passed too quickly and came to a close. It was time to head to Waco, Texas. Wayne would drive me safely home in my little car to meet my mother and church family.

My brother, M.C. Landtroop, invited Wayne, Mother, and me to Carthage, Texas, for a weekend. This was when Wayne met them for the first time. Dennis Ray Landtroop, my ten-year-old nephew, began his lifelong admiration of Wayne Huntley. Everywhere Wayne went, Dennis (or Denny Ray, as we called him then) was nearby. He seemed to idolize Wayne. Many years later, in 1980, Dennis would come to Raleigh to be an apprentice, or intern, to Wayne. He called Wayne and asked his opinion on whether he should or should not go to Bible school. Wayne told him that if he came to Raleigh, he would teach him all he knew, and he could also have a "hands-on" experience of starting the church in Raleigh.

So, he was in Raleigh when we were in the formative years of revival and the building of our new church facility on Lake Wheeler Road from 1983 to 1985. He put much blood, sweat, and tears into Raleigh, North Carolina. He was the son we never had, our son 'by another mother,' and Christy's brother. He remained with us until 1987 when he left to evangelize and marry sweet Christine Fritzenschaft.

That summer of 1969, Wayne and I decided we didn't want to wait to get married. We were ready, "now!" We picked July 19.

Brother and Sister Bill Davis kindly invited Wayne to stay with them for almost two months until the wedding date. He gave Wayne twenty dollars a week and room and board, which was a tremendous blessing for Wayne. Sister Karen Davis treated him like a son, washing and ironing his shirts. Brother Davis allowed Wayne to emcee and lead the worship services and had us sing together.

Wayne on the morning of our wedding

We Said, "I Do." July 19, 1969

Our wedding was such a special event. The kind people in my home church provided it. Wayne and I didn't have two nickels to rub together, so we planned to go to the justice of the peace. We just wanted to get married.

Several concerned ladies of First Pentecostal Church, Waco, Texas, would not have that. They said, "You know we want to give you a wedding shower, so why don't you just have Brother Davis marry you at that event? That way, all of your church family can attend."

That sounded good to me. Then, Sister Frankie Dennard said, "You know, you only get married once, and I want you to get married in a white wedding gown. My daughter,

The wonderful ladies who planned my wedding

Janine, recently married David Milner, and I want you to try on her dress."

Sister Ruth Gideon said, "My daughter Sandra's dress might fit you, so try it on, too, and see which one you want to wear."

I tried them on and decided on Janine's. My mother made a few alterations, and it turned out beautifully. I was so excited.

Sister Frankie said, "I will have a photographer there for you. After the wedding, the vows are said, the cake is eaten at the reception, and the lights are all turned off; all you have left are memories, so you need pictures."

Myra Hennigan said, "My mother, Sister Rice, makes wedding cakes. I will buy all the ingredients, and she will make yours." It turned out lovely, and the cake style was used for my twenty-fifth and fortieth wedding anniversary celebrations. Myra also delivered the cake to the church for me, which was not an easy task.

Sister Neeper said, "If you are gonna get married in a white wedding gown, have a bridal party, and have a photographer present, then you need some flowers." So, I had Sister Davis come with me to Reed's Florist on Austin Avenue, downtown Waco. I picked out gladiolas and one large chrysanthemum to be placed on my Bible as my bridal bouquet. Sister Neeper provided all these.

Reed's Florist

Sister Georgia Lee Heath worked as a seamstress in a lingerie factory. She brought a catalog home for me to choose a beautiful white gown and robe set for my wedding night. I felt like I was clothed as rich as a queen! These five ladies and Sister Davis helped orchestrate the wedding, shower, and reception.

My brother, Ken, was living in California at that time and could not attend our wedding. Right before the ceremony began, we received a telegram from him congratulating us on our marriage and expressing regret that he could not be there. He was there in heart, even if he couldn't be there in person.

Mother and me

Gary Gideon and Gary Dennard lit the candles at the altar. As Myra Rice Hennigan began the bridal march on the Hammond C-3 organ, the same one I had played in church as a teenager, I started down the aisle on the arm of my oldest brother, Garth, my surrogate father. Just in these few steps, from the back door to the altar, and just by Wayne and I repeating a few words in front of the preacher and a company of friends and family, I was changing from one world to another, from single to married, girlfriend to wife, and from a college student to a minister's wife.

I kissed my mother's soft cheek as I passed her, seated in the second row. After I heard my brother say, "Our Mother and I," in response to Brother Davis's question, "Who giveth this woman to be wed?" I looked

Patsy and Garth

at my sweetheart waiting for me, with love shining in his eyes. I could not wait to become his wife.

Finally, we stood at the altar with my bridesmaid, Portia Heath, my matron of honor, Rose Milam Webb, and the groomsmen, Gilbert Bessent and Leon Webb. After David Hennigan sang "I Love You Truly," and my brother, Malcolm (M.C.), prayed the prayer of blessing, the unity candle was lit, and we proceeded to the part where we pledged our love, "forever, till death do us part," Brother Davis pronounced Wayne and me "husband and wife." With adoring love in my heart and with all my soul, I sang to my love,

"Whither thou goest, I will go.
Wherever thou lodgest, I will lodge.
Thy people shall be, my people, my love.
Whither thou goest, I will go!"
Earl Chalmers, 1954

I did go, and go, and go, the first many years of our marriage. I must admit that it got harder and harder to keep that promise when my sweet grands

started arriving. Now, I tell him that I will "keep the fire burning and the supper on the stove," ready for his return from traveling.

But, back to our wedding. Excitedly, we exited the church, and as we got to the foyer, one of us proclaimed, as we grabbed each other in a big bear hug, twirling around, "We did it!" The reason I said, "one of us," is that I don't remember who. That was over fifty years ago, and we have been ONE for so long, I just don't know.

I became Patsy Sue Landtroop Huntley and, more importantly, MRS. Wayne Huntley. Oh, how sweet the journey has been since that sizzling hot day in Waco, Texas, on July 19, 1969, when there were over thirty consecutive days with a temperature of 100˚ or higher.

So, to put it in a nutshell:

We met: April 20,
Got engaged: May 11,
We were married: July 19,
   All in the year of our Lord 1969!

What a year—it was a very good year! Fast, huh? We have never wished we had waited. It worked for us–maybe not for everyone, but for us, yes! I had prayed all my life for the right person, and when I met Wayne Huntley, I knew! I literally would have married him the next day if he had asked me!

Patsy, Wayne, Bill Davis, and M.C.

Wayne and Patsy's marriage license

Chapter Four

Mr. and Mrs. Wayne Huntley

We left the church in my little 1962 Chevy II Nova with the words "Just married" painted all over it with white shoe polish. Someone had pulled a spark plug, and the car would hardly run. After a short jog along Austin Avenue, the "drag" in Waco, we returned to the church. My brother, Garth, put the spark plug back on, and all was well; we were again on our way.

We drove to Pizza Inn on Valley Mills Drive, stood in line, and purchased a pizza "to go" to take to our honeymoon hotel.

Brother and Sister William Harvey Davis paid for *our luxury suite* at the Best Western, "Flamingo Motor Hotel," much like a Motel 6, but we didn't care; we were finally together as husband and wife forever! We did not have to say goodbye to each other every night anymore!

Flamingos played a vital part in the decorations fifty years later at our Golden Wedding Anniversary celebration, many years and miles down the road (See Chapter Ten: "The Golden Years").

It seemed Brother Davis was always one to enjoy embarrassing someone.

Because he paid for our room for a couple of nights, he felt that he had the right to come to our room the next day, Sunday afternoon, and bang on our door. He thought that was so funny. I was not very much amused, but I guess the old saying is true: *"You must pay the fiddler!"*

Honestly, though, we are still indebted to many people, Brother and Sister Davis included, for the unselfish blessings they have bestowed on us.

We were very dedicated Christians and knew that we should go to church that Sunday night… after all, we had missed Sunday morning! We came in and sat in the back row of the church, where, approximately twenty-four hours earlier, we had become Mr. and Mrs. Wayne Huntley. Nothing would do for Bro Davis, except that we *had* to come up and sing a special. I have no idea what we sang, but sing we did!

July 20, 1969, was when Apollo 11 landed on the moon. Wayne and I were *"over the moon"* in love. We still are. He makes my heart pitter-patter, even after fifty-plus years of marriage.

When you are young,
You are making deposits into the bank of "Old Age,"
So that when you are old,
You can withdraw from that increase!

Astronaut Buzz Armstrong declared as he placed the first human foot on the moon, "That's one small step for man and one giant leap for mankind."

That's how it was for the Huntleys. We made seemingly small steps by joining the spaceships of our lives with each other and launching our life's journey. But for the many lives that would be intertwined with ours, it was a giant leap.

On Monday, July 21, we boarded Delta Airlines in Dallas, Texas, and headed to Charlotte, North Carolina. I had never flown in an airplane, but I was excited to be introduced to my new family for the first time! Yes, that's right. I had never met them before.

We stayed with Wayne's parents for about six weeks between the first and second school years. There was dinner at the fish camps, carp fishing at Wallace Lake, the trip to Boone and Chimney Rock, rides on Tweetsie Railroad, tubing down the mountain streams, and so much more.

One day, I was sitting in the car next to Wayne, close together, in the same kind of straight seat that I had in my Chevy II. There was no bucket seat or gear shift in the way. My father-in-law said, "Aw, I'll give you six months, and you won't be doing that." I am so happy that we proved him wrong. Even many years later, we are still so much in love, still holding hands, kissing, cuddling, and generally enjoying being close. We love to sit on the back porch of our country cabin at the *Non-Typical Family Farm* in Tillery, North Carolina, Halifax County, and have a cup of hot coffee or a white chocolate cappuccino while watching the corn, cotton, or soybeans grow. We are complete in each other's presence and company. If you work at it, you can indeed have a love that lasts a lifetime.

> *"A person's face can change over a lifetime,*
> *But the heart can stay true forever."*
> **The Inheritance**, by Louisa May Alcott

Between school years in North Carolina, Wayne worked for the rest of that summer for Pastor W.W. Gilmore's church in Gastonia, North Carolina. This was a relatively new church that was being established at the time. Brother Gilmore had a thriving plumbing business and needed someone to work for the church. So, he hired Wayne to do door-to-door visitation during the week and preach a revival on the weekends.

It was decided that the first week of September, right before we were to leave North Carolina, we were to hold our second revival together, the first revival after our marriage, right there in Gastonia, North Carolina, for Brother and Sister Gilmore.

Then, it was time to return to Houston and Texas Bible College for Wayne's second year.

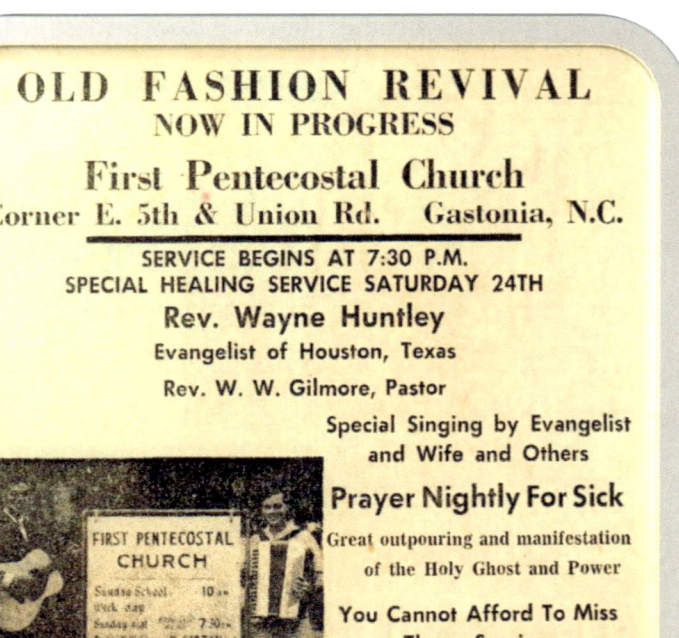

Texas Bible College 1969-1971

It was so much fun playing "house." We opened all our wedding presents that had been packed away after the wedding until we moved into our apartment at Patricia Manor, located a few blocks from the Texas Bible College campus. I loved cooking for my husband and was genuinely so very glad to be Mrs. Wayne Huntley. That just has a ring to it. I love it!

I worked for Star Steel this year, and Frito-Lay Company employed Wayne.

We were so excited to purchase our own Christmas tree at Christmas time. I bought it from "Globe Department Store," sort of like K-Mart or Walmart. It cost ten whole dollars. Believe it or not, I still have that tree, and I put it up most Christmases, along with the tree topper I purchased at the same time for a measly thirty-three cents. Nowadays, it is adorned with unique ornaments that our sweet Christy, our nephew/son, Dennis, and our grandchildren have made through the years, plus special ones given to us by our TOP family. We were so fortunate that it was not on location at our house that was burned in 2016, but it was in our country home in Tillery, North Carolina, and was spared. I'm so grateful.

Our first Christmas tree

Wayne was voted in as junior class vice president. Wayne and I mostly attended Bethel Tabernacle, pastored by Rev. Orlin Ray Fauss. Rev. Oliver F.

Wayne and Patsy married six months

Fauss, Orlin Ray's father, who pastored Bethel Tabernacle before his son, was still vital to that congregation. It was an honor to be in the presence of such prestigious people, who were an influential part of the beginning of the United Pentecostal Church International.

Bro Orlin Ray Fauss's son, David, played his electric guitar expertly. On a couple of occasions, he would travel with us when we would go out to preach. We became lifelong friends. Although there were a few years our paths didn't cross that often. But after we renewed our old acquaintance, we are closer now than before. Now, we enjoy blessed fellowship with him and his sweet wife, Cathy, in the beautiful Hill Country of Texas or at our individual 'happy places' (The Branson, Missouri, Arkansas hills, or the deer hunting Non-Typical Family Farm in Halifax County, North Carolina). We are so blessed!

Right before his second school year ended, Wayne got a call that his father was in the hospital in serious condition. He had been coming off a drunk and had so much dry heaving while vomiting that he had pushed his stomach up into his body, dislocating it. We quickly left and drove our little Toyota Corolla to North Carolina, stopping at York, Alabama, on the wrong side of town, at a little "roach motel" to sleep. We felt so uncomfortable and frightened that we pushed a chest of drawers in front of the door, but God was with us, and we left the following morning without incident.

We arrived in North Carolina, and thankfully, God touched Wayne's father, and he recovered. However, because of this trip, we were in North Carolina. Wayne was able to meet with the District Board to apply for and receive a local ministerial license with the United Pentecostal Church International. This was about May, and his license came through in November of that year, 1970.

Another year came and went, and it was time for his third and final year at TBC. This year, he was voted in as senior class president. If I remember correctly, he was the first married person to have this distinct honor.

Brother Keith Clark would go to the Champion Paper Products plant once a week to have a church service at lunchtime. The men would come and eat their lunch while students sang and preached. Keith was a senior in Wayne's second year, so Keith bequeathed the "pastorate" of Champion Paper to Wayne for his third and senior year. We had some anointed services there.

Rose, Martha, and Patsy

Rose Milam was my best friend as a teenager in the Waco church. She sang in a trio with me and her sister, Martha Milam, who played the piano, organ, or sometimes accordion. Martha taught me some chords and helped me with music. Martha married Jack Wellborn, and Rose married Leon Webb. Rose was the matron of honor at my wedding.

We were all devastated when Rose was diagnosed with leukemia. We were still in our twenties–too young. Rose was living in Houston and had not been attending church faithfully. Wayne and I had driven by a church named Apostolic Temple in Pasadena, close to where Rose lived. We were not acquainted with the pastor, but we got to know the McClains in the ensuing years. We took Rose and Leon to church, and we met the wonderful people who would become such an essential part of the rest of our lives. We became like family. The McClain name is woven all through the tapestry of the story of our lives.

Jessie Alexander from Apostolic Temple helped me get a job this last year. I worked at Dr. Kenneth Mathis and Dr. C. D. Henderson's office in Pasadena, Texas.

Wayne had many after-school jobs. He would be working and get an invitation to preach a revival. He would quit his secular job in order for this to happen. There were so many weeks that I would go to work on Monday morning, get off at 5:00 p.m., and leave immediately from work to travel to out-of-town revival services. We would drive home after the service that night and get home late. I would have to go to work the following day, while Wayne *might* sleep through the first one or two classes (laugh). This would happen the whole week, from Monday through Friday, but someone had to make a living, and that someone was me! I have told him for many years that I worked and put him through Bible school. Some people graduate from college and have thousands of dollars in school bills owed. I never let him live down the fact that he was sleeping while I was working. Years later, this has proven to be quite handy information to be used whenever it was convenient for me, and, laughingly, I say, he will <u>never</u> get those school bills paid! Seriously, though, God worked and conveniently provided those places for us to hold revivals during the third and final school year. That's why Wayne came to Texas Bible College to launch his ministry; these places were so important to accomplish this.

On several occasions, we would go to Carthage, Texas, to preach for my brother, M.C. Landtroop. We always enjoyed visiting with family and eating good cooking prepared by his wife, Dorothy. She was an exceptional cook. One particular time, we were on our way there for the weekend, and we knew their family had moved since our last visit. Remember, this was before cell phones, and we did not know their specific address but had an idea of the general vicinity. As we got close to Carthage, passing through Tenaha, Texas, only about seventeen miles from our destination, we realized we didn't even have ten cents to make a pay phone call. Driving through that little town of less than one thousand people, we looked up on the sidewalk in front of a storefront building, and there was our answer. Two *returnable* soda pop bottles stood at attention by the door, on the brick ledge, just waiting for us to snatch them up, which we quickly did. When we arrived, we drove to the church, and then, down the road about a block away, there were their cars. We had found them *without having to redeem the pop bottles.* On the way home to Houston Sunday night after church, we decided to return the pop bottles to their original location, on the ledge of the storefront building, just in case taking them would be considered stealing. They just may have belonged to someone, and since we did not actually need them, we gave them back.

Brother and Sister Huntley, and Brother and Sister Wayne McClain

In our third year of TBC, we continued to attend the Apostolic Temple with the

McClains. It was a great church with such a powerful move of God. They had us sing sometimes during the Sunday evening services. "I've Found a Better Way" became one of our "go-to" songs. Brother and Sister McClain took us under their wing, and we had much-blessed fellowship with them and their three children, Darla, Orlin, and Gayla. At this time, Brother McClain became our pastor. Growing up, Wayne did not have "one" pastor; he had had several, so we put ourselves under his leadership and direction, and he never led us wrong. We always did as he advised. There were times that, maybe fleshly, we did not totally understand, but we always submitted our spirits to the man of God. We always came out of all situations much the better for listening and obeying the leadership over us.

> *Everyone needs a pastor.*
> *Even preachers and pastors need a covering*
> *of someone that you're submitted to,*
> *and who has veto power in your life.*
> *"If you are gonna lead…*
> *You must be led!!!"*

Brother James Kilgore was the college's interim president at this time. He certainly made an impression on Wayne. Wayne knew no one, had no Pentecostal heritage, and was just one of the many TBC students. If memory serves me correctly, there were somewhere close to three hundred students in the freshman class.

When Bible school students were walking the sidewalks and Brother Kilgore happened to be there talking to some preachers who were much more important than the students, he would still stop, make eye contact, and say hello to the students. Wayne was so impressed by this. Someone of Brother Kilgore's caliber would stop talking with influential people to say hello to lowly students. He always remembered this when many folks in the years to come would feel that *he* was too important to talk to or take time with them. He *always* takes time because he *knows* how important this is to many people, and he *always* has time for kids. He adores children, and they love him. He is like the "Pied Piper," and kids are automatically drawn to him.

A pastor would often call the school, wanting a student to preach on the weekend. Brother Kilgore would send a note to Wayne in class, and he would get the honor, and we would have a weekend revival. Many, many weekends were spent preaching out, which we loved! Most of the time, the pastor seemed to like us and would ask Wayne for a revival. Consequently, when this third and final year ended, we had about a year's worth of revivals lined up and ready to go (which was and is unheard of).

We have been abundantly blessed throughout the years, and we do not take the blessings of the Lord lightly or for granted. We have been given high privileges way beyond what we deserve.

Graduating from Texas Bible College in May 1971 was such an exciting day. Wayne's mother, dad, and his Huntley grandparents had driven from North Carolina to be in attendance. That was a grand day of accomplishment and one that his parents, uncharacteristically, were able to attend, enjoy, and be a part of the celebration.

So, Wayne graduated from Texas Bible College. We had no idea what path our lives would take; we just knew we were ready "to go!" The good Lord usually doesn't give you a roadmap for the rest of your life; He simply whispers in your ear what "next" step to take. So, with that whispering, we headed headlong into the will of God for our lives, the beginning, baby steps, of this most precious journey to the TOP and beyond.

Wayne's graduation from Texas Bible College

Chapter Five

Rev. and Mrs. Wayne Huntley
North Carolina District, United Pentecostal Church International, 1970

The North Carolina District was newly formed in 1969, the same year Wayne and I married. It previously had been the Atlantic District and contained several states on the Atlantic Coast of the United States. Later, it was the Carolina District, which included North and South Carolina. In 1969, North Carolina became a district when it separated from South Carolina.

It is interesting to note that many years later, Brother Tom Fred Tenney told us he had been the UPCI Headquarters' representative at that district conference when the North Carolina District of the UPCI was formed. When the district was setting up its financial bank account, Brother Bill Padgett, Wayne's uncle and pastor at one time, had given twenty dollars to open that account!

Brother W. J. Daigle was the

Evangelist and Mrs. Wayne Huntley

district superintendent, and Brother Jesse Williams was the district secretary. Brother Stanley Wilt, Brother Ray Hayes, and Brother W. W. Gilmore were presbyters, and possibly a couple more, but I don't remember who they were.

The day Wayne received his local ministerial license was quite a momentous day. He has always appreciated and loved the United Pentecostal Church International and all its constituencies.

I always accuse my husband of being a politician, not because he *is,* but because he *would* make a good one! He speaks to everyone, shakes hands, acknowledges everyone, truly loves everyone, and wants to ensure he does not overlook anyone. This *can* be problematic when getting from point A to point B at a general conference. *I'm just saying.*

This church organization has always been so good to us; we have nothing but positive things to say about it. We are UPC to the core! Wayne has held several positions and had numerous opportunities in this great organization over the years.

- Youth President of the North Carolina District—1979–1982

- North Carolina District Section #4, Presbyter, 1982–1995

- Southeast Regional Director for the Home Missions Department (now called NAM, North American Missions)

- South East Regional Executive Presbyter (as a pastor)—1986–1988

- South East Regional Executive Presbyter (as a District Superintendent)—2020–2022

- North Carolina District Superintendent—1995–1997 and 2014–2025 (As Ashley Landtroop Morris, our niece, called it as a little girl, "Super-District-Attendant.")

North Carolina District Board

- Texas Bible College Board of Governors, 2022–present.

- "Distinguished Alumnus" in 1985. Texas Bible College certainly has given honor and double honor to a most appreciative but unlikely candidate.

"**Texas Bible College**

1985

Distinguished Alumni Award

Rev. Wayne Huntley
Class of 1971

*Presented by:
Texas Bible College and its alumni association for outstanding dedication and service to the Kingdom of God.*"

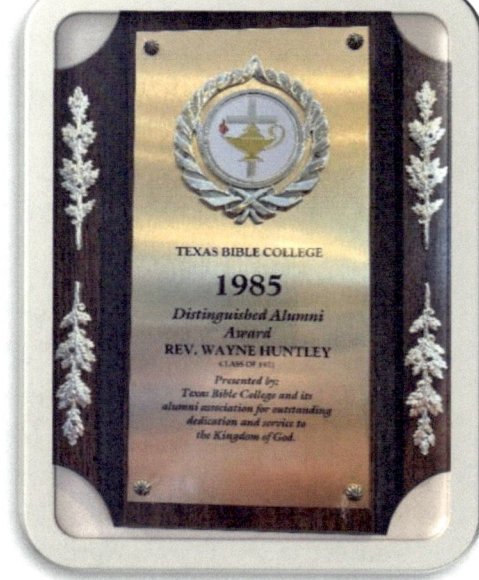

- In 2023, he was invited to speak at the Texas Bible College graduation ceremony. This alone was a privilege beyond expectation, but the board of governors decided and agreed to bestow on him, that same year, an "Honorary Degree of Bachelor of Arts in Theology."

He had gone three years and received a "diploma" in 1971; the four-year degree was not offered at that time. This honor was above and beyond our most extraordinary imagination, from being a scholarship recipient in 1968 to receiving the two highest awards possible.

Honorary Degree of Bachelor of Arts in Theology

- Urshan Graduate School of Theology annually holds the "Urshan Pulpit Conference." They award a preacher whom they feel has made a significant impact on the Apostolic Church through a commitment to Apostolic preaching. In the spring of 2024, my husband was the honored recipient of the "Urshan Pulpit Award."

"The Urshan Pulpit Award 2024 – Wayne Huntley

In recognition of the generational impact made on the Apostolic church through a commitment to Apostolic preaching.

Urshan College, Urshan Graduate School of Theology, and the Urshan Pulpit Award Committee honor this great man of faith."

Also, in the spring of 2024, my husband was privileged to be interviewed by Brother Darrien Sparks with Truth Radio. They tell the stories via video of some ministries they call "Living Legends," whom they feel have been influential in our Apostolic movement. It was such an honor for Wayne to be among that select number.

In 2021, Wayne's name came up for Assistant General Superintendent of the Eastern Zone at the General Conference in Indianapolis, Indiana. He may or may not have been elected if he had left his name in the running, but he didn't. This was the second time that he had withdrawn his name for consideration. The first time was in 2005 in Richmond, Virginia. Of course, Wayne consulted our pastor, Brother Wayne McClain, about what he should do. He gave my hubby a particular scenario, indicating that he should pull his name. That precisely happened, so he withdrew his name.

However, in 2021, he withdrew his name in this manner: "Given my age, which is seventy-one, I know that my time of leadership is limited. I thank you for your vote today, but I want to devote what time I have left to the North Carolina District, which I love deeply."

He went on to serve four more years as district superintendent until election time 2025 at our North Carolina District Conference convening in Wendell, North Carolina. He felt that this was the time to withdraw his name from the voting. Almost everyone "leaned on him" not to do this. However, he told them that he felt just as strongly that it was the will of God for him to go out as it was the will of God for him to go in as district superintendent.

Entrances are brief, but exits are eternal.

At his last district board meeting, the board voted for him to become an *"honorary board member."* Then, at the last business meeting where a new district superintendent was elected, the constituency voted him in as *"Honorary Bishop of the North Carolina District UPCI"* for the rest of his life! This honor had never been given before and was above and beyond every expectation.

His last time to address the church body of North Carolina as their district superintendent was on Thursday night, June 12, 2025. His title was *"An Observation That Became a Revelation."* The thought that God does not bless churches, but He blesses ministries. So, a church is blessed according to the blessings of God upon its pastor. He wanted his last message to be an encouragement to our wonderful North Carolina ministers and pastors.

Dennis Landtroop introduced Bishop Huntley to preach that night. An edited copy of that presentation is below.

"So much of my life is interwoven with the person I am blessed to call my pastor, and Uncle Wayne. It would be easy to enter a nostalgic state of mind and regale you with personal experiences that have shaped my life.

I must first say, 'Thank you,' to First Lady Sister Huntley. Without Aunt Patsy, I would have no Uncle Wayne. My love, admiration, and respect for him are immense. To catalog his accomplishments would be time-consuming.

How do you introduce one of the greatest Apostolic Pentecostal preachers of this age? How do you introduce the authority of adjectives? Who also happens to be the king of content and the instantiation of inspiration, one whose unique insight into the Word of God and singular ability to convey that insight is unmatched.

His powerful ministry illuminates the obvious and underlines the overlooked. My vocabulary, verbiage, and verbosity are not enough. My words fall woefully, wailfully, and wishfully short. What deserves to be said is something most difficult to formulate, articulate, communicate, enunciate, or even insinuate. Fortunately, for all of us, there are his own words. Messages like 'Abraham's Last Trial', 'How Wise Were the Wise?', 'The Second Dimension of Spiritual Deliverance', 'The Miracle Is in the Add-On', and 'The Audacity to Ask' are just a smattering of his preaching.

Long before God's Word was written and read, it was spoken and heard–Wayne Huntley has mastered the art of speaking for God.

The impact of his ministry of preaching in the UPCI is practically immeasurable. Not just in preachment but in personal conversation in times of sadness and loss, joyous occasions and celebrations, words of greeting before a service, personal words of encouragement after a moving message, or phone calls at just the right time.

The great blessing of my life is that I have shared time up close and personal with this great man, and that greatness exceeds far beyond the platform and pulpit to every area of his life. I have been privileged to hear him from the high-rise seats of a convention center at general conference to a comfortable recliner in his home. From a camp meeting to a campfire. From the baptistry to the bass pond. From the pulpit to the Bar-B-Q pit. He is just as real at each.

Life moves faster when Wayne Huntley is around. It's guaranteed more smiles per hour.

A man came to our church and heard Wayne Huntley preach. He went home and evidently looked him up on social media. He came back to church that night and exclaimed, 'Wow, Uncle Wayne is worldwide!'

Actually, Wayne Huntley is 'world-class' and is among the best in the world when it comes to Apostolic preaching and godly men.

He is a world-class man—he has character that matches his charisma.

He is a world-class leader. He holds in balance all of the most desirable Christian traits. He has many Christ-like qualities.

John 7:46 '...Never man spake like this man.'

Had I the soul of a poet, the mind of a sage, the skill of a virtuoso, and the tongue of an angel (none of which I possess), I might be able to say what needs to be said. But what I do have is the heart of the grateful. Not just personal gratitude, but the appreciation of family, friends, ministers, pastors, the district of North Carolina, and the fellowship of the UPCI.

Thank you for all you have said and done and for all that you are. Your words and life have uplifted us, convicted us, saved us, and blessed us.

While this will be the final message as the district superintendent of North Carolina, it will certainly not be the last we hear from him.

Ladies and gentlemen, brothers and sisters, would you please rise to your feet and rise to this moment of destiny for the people of God this day?

I bring you the man of God for the hour with the Word of God for this moment– The Reverend Wayne Huntley."

None of those positions identified Wayne. He was happy to serve, but his highest calling is "servant of God," along with "minister, pastor, bishop, and preacher." And, of course, his most significant personal privilege was that of "husband, father, Grandbuddy, Grandbuddy the Great, son, brother, uncle, and friend."

Waco First Pentecostal Church Choir Recording featuring Wayne and me singing "I Found a Better Way."

Chapter Six

Evangelist and Mrs. Wayne Huntley
June 1971–December 1977

We were so excited to be on the road. Most of our revivals were in Texas. Many people thought that Wayne was from Texas, but he was always quick to say, "I love Texas, but North Carolina is home. I hope to go there one day and, if the Lord will allow it, start a church somewhere."

One of our first places to preach was in Daisetta, Texas, with Brother and Sister Gary Sylvester, who pastored there. They were so very kind to let a novice preach for them. They allowed us to come on several occasions, first in Daisetta and later in Buna, Texas.

Brother Sylvester was a true cowboy. I had known Sister Becky Hosch Sylvester since childhood. Although we hadn't kept in touch over the years, it was good to renew an old acquaintance. She and her family had pastored the First Pentecostal Church in Waco when I was around four. I remember their last Sunday in Waco before they moved to another city to pastor. Her father, Brother L. J. Hosch, handed out nickels to the children, and I was privileged to receive one. That was a "big deal" to me. That's probably why I remembered.

Patsy, in the front row, Lenda behind Patsy, and Josie in the center wearing the white hat

A few years later, when Christy was one year old, we preached for the Sylvesters in Buna, Texas. One Sunday after the morning service, Sister Sylvester and I were in the kitchen putting the finishing touches on lunch, and man, could she ever make a mean roast beef!

The children, Gail, Clint, and Christy, were outside playing on the front porch, where a wooden, two-person swing hung. A little step was beside the swing, leading to an unused entrance door. Christy sat down on the little step, and one of the other children got up on the swing. Children have the uncanny ability not to see danger. As they started to swing, Christy decided she wanted to "get up." When she did, the corner of the heavy swing struck her right in the upper lip and made a hole through to her gums. Thankfully, it just made a hole and left her lip intact on the lip line. Brother Sylvester got us in the car and drove one hundred miles per hour to the emergency room.

When we arrived, they took her in to administer sutures. They had to roll her in a blanket with her little arms inside. Standing outside the door, we could hear her crying, "Jesus! Jesus!" She knew where her help would come from, even at just one year old.

Gerald, Wayne's brother, affectionately told Christy that she was trying to be like her Uncle Gerald by having a split lip. He was born with a cleft lip and cleft palate, so he had a scar on his upper lip, much like Christy.

Brother Wayne McClain had taken Wayne to introduce him to the Texas District Board in session in Lufkin, Texas. He had never actually "heard" Wayne preach but had us fill in for him at his church, Apostolic Temple, in Pasadena, Texas, numerous times while he was away. He "knew" him by the "Spirit." He told all the board members they needed this young evangelist to preach for them.

When Wayne and Brother McClain left the meeting that day, Brother Jack DeHart followed them out and asked us to come to Irvine, Texas, for a revival.

Brother DeHart had not been pastor there for very long, and this was to be his first revival. When we arrived at the beautiful city and began the revival, my husband was "stressed" about something happening in each service. Brother DeHart realized that Wayne was "uptight," so he took him aside and said, "This is God's church. He wants to bless as much as you want Him to bless, or more. Just relax and know that sometimes, during the service, God will move. When that happens, flow with it. You have done your part to prepare, and God will do His part at the proper time."

During that revival, from time to time, Brother DeHart kept saying that the church was:

"A place where good things always happen."

Wayne thought, "When I pastor, that will be my church motto." Some years later, in 1978, when we went to Raleigh, North Carolina, that indeed was our church motto for many years.

Also, we had a most unusual and frightening event during the revival in Irvine. We were not scared easily; we had stayed in other churches and were never afraid. In this particular church, there was no outside entrance to the evangelist's quarters. We had to come inside and walk down a hall to get to the evangelist's quarters. But that was okay. One night, around 2:00 a.m., we were sound asleep. We both were awakened at the same time by a loud noise. It sounded like an army of people marching up and down the hall right outside our bedroom door. We sat up in bed, terrified. The noise stopped after a bit, and we lay back down and went back to sleep.

"I will both lay me down in peace, and sleep:
For thou, LORD, only makest me dwell in safety."
(Psalms 4:8)

July 19, 1971, our second anniversary, found us in Mont Belvieu, Texas, with Brother Frank and Sister Pat Davis. We had precious fellowship with these sweet people.

They had saved for a week of revival before we arrived. The revival was going so well that everyone wanted to extend it to the second week, but Brother Davis was concerned about finances. Wayne said, "Let's just go on; whatever comes in the offering will be fine." Of course, more came in the second week than in the first week.

*"If it's God's will,
It's God's bill!"*

Something funny happened there. Wayne had an ingrown toenail that was very painful and giving him fits. Brother Davis showed him how to push cotton "under the toenail" on the ingrown side and keep it there. He would redo it every so often until the toenail grew out. This cured his ingrown toenail, and he has never had it since.

The fall of 1971 brought Wayne and me to Richardson, Texas, just north of Dallas. Brother and Sister R. E. Johnson's revival was certainly one of which we have fond and fun memories.

When we arrived, Brother Johnson asked, "Brother Huntley, do you drink coffee?"

"No."

"Well, we can't have revival if you don't drink coffee!"

"Then, give me a cup."

"Alright, what do you want in it?"

"Cream and sugar."

"I asked if you wanted a cup of coffee, not a milkshake!"

So, we started drinking coffee, but we still added cream and sugar.

One night, my husband was going to preach a particular sermon, and he planned to use Brother Johnson's cane as an illustration. Brother Johnson had his cane hanging on the pulpit during the preliminaries. Unusually, he left it hanging there as he returned to his seat. My husband felt that was a sign to him that he was indeed to preach the sermon.

Another night after church, Brother Johnson began talking to Wayne, telling him what a great job he had done preaching that night. But he said, "Would you let me help you?"

"Please, do."

"If I were preaching that sermon, I would have saved my best illustration for last instead of first; it would have had a greater impact."

My husband did not take it personally or offensively, but he appreciated his input and began to apply the wisdom of a great camp meeting preacher to his own preaching.

During this revival, people began to notice that I was in the family way; I was expecting; I was pregnant!

Daddy and Mother, 1971–1972

We had been traveling on the evangelistic field for a little over a year when we began to think that we would love to have a sweet baby of our own.

In October, I realized that I was indeed about three months "with child." We were so ecstatic.

I had no problems whatsoever except when we were preaching a revival for my brother, Garth, and Bobbie Landtroop in Gainesville, Texas. About two o'clock in the morning, I woke up hungry! I shook Wayne and whispered, "Are you hungry?"

Groggily, he said, "No, I'm sleepy!"

I said, "I am. Let's go eat."

Christmas 1971

So, as any good husband would do, he got up, and we sneaked out of our room and out the front door. Because the car lights would shine straight into their bedroom window, we turned them on after we were on the road. That was in the old days when you had to turn your lights on manually. We went to an all-night truck stop, ate, came back, and sneaked back into the house, and they were none the wiser!

My brothers were always so good to have us preach for them. It was such a blessing to us. We had many a good time with Garth and Bobbie and their children, DeWayne and Loretta. Garth was always the surrogate father in my life.

We would go fishing on a small stream that fed into a larger body of water near the small town of St. Jo, Texas. We called it the "Mighty St. Jo River."

Many times, we would ride to the UPCI General Conference together. Oh, what fun we had. We trekked across the United States from Texas to Anaheim, California, for the conference there. As we crossed the desert, I think we blew out every tire on our Mercury Marquis. We were running "re-tread tires, or re-caps," which was all we could afford. These were usually fine, but the desert heat was too much for them.

While we were in California, we took in the sights. We went to Disneyland, Knott's Berry Farm, and Universal Studios (where Wayne made his debut as an actor, playing a policeman in a little scene they did there). Then, when we were almost home, we went to Six Flags Over Texas, just for good measure.

Another time, the conference was in Miami, Florida. We left Gainesville, Texas, and Wayne, Bobbie, and I begged my "truck driver" brother to stop and let us sleep. But, no, he said we could make it all the way, and we did, but we were dying—everybody but him!

This generous brother of mine did not have much in the way of earthly goods. They did okay financially, but they didn't have much extra. He gave us one of his credit cards and said, "This is for emergencies. Just in case you are out on the road and need something and don't have any money." I don't remember ever using the card, but it felt good knowing it was available should the need arise.

Things like this have not been forgotten, and we have tried to make it up to him with a bit of help in his senior years.

Because I had worked for Dr. C. D. Henderson during Wayne's senior year at TBC, we decided to have him deliver our baby when the time came. He gave us a discounted price of $250 for his doctor's fee, which was a mighty blessing. This was not the only blessing we received for our child's birth.

During my pregnancy, we had stopped in Pasadena, Texas, to visit with our precious "bosom friends," the McClains. During a conversation, Brother McClain told Wayne that he wanted him to begin sending him all his tithes. As evangelists, we could pay tithes to the churches we were preaching at or to our home church. Sister McClain was dismayed that he would ask us to do such a thing. But, of course, we began to obey our pastor. After Christy was born, he wrote a check to the hospital to pay off the hospital bill. What a blessing that was to us.

There was also the time we came to Pasadena for a doctor's visit, and when we drove up in the driveway, Brother McClain was outside. He approached our automobile, and as I got out of the car, he said, "Patsy, you go on inside; I want Wayne to drive me somewhere." I got out, and he had Wayne take him to a tire shop. He told the proprietor to install four new tires. As we had driven up their driveway, he noticed our slick, balding tires and told Wayne, "You can't evangelize and drive all over Texas with tires that may blow out any moment."

We have been blessed by these unselfish and giving people numerous times and in many places. Mere words cannot begin to show our thankfulness.

About this same time, when I was in my first trimester, we had a day off and went to Waco to visit Mother. She was babysitting a little child, and I played with this baby girl, probably thinking about my baby being formed inside me at that very moment. When we got to our next revival in Cisco, Texas, Brother and Sister Thomas, my mother, called with not-so-good news.

The baby girl that I had been playing with was diagnosed with rubella, German measles. I was devastated. My doctor told me that the mother does not necessarily have to have symptoms of measles for it to affect the unborn baby. Congenital disabilities can be numerous and life-altering, such as deafness, heart defects, intellectual disabilities, and liver and spleen damage, among many other things.

I was so worried and afraid. I spent the better part of three days of my waking hours inside the church sanctuary praying, begging, pleading, and trying to have faith that my child would be born healthy.

On the third day, Brother Wayne McClain called and told Wayne, "Tell Patsy that everything is

March 1972, Nacogdoches, Texas

going to be okay." I got up, dried my eyes, praised my God for hearing my prayer, and never worried about it again. And, of course, Christy Renee Huntley was born healthy and beautiful, one hundred percent whole and well, even though at that time, there were over 100,000 children born each year with congenital disabilities caused by the rubella virus.

I have often prayed with vigorous thanksgiving that God heard that "one prayer." If *this* prayer had not been answered, our precious girl could have had a debilitating life. If she had been born deaf, we would have never heard all the hundreds of songs she wrote because she could not have heard them to write them. If she had been born with mental disabilities, we would not have our son-in-love, Bryan Starr, our pastor of the Temple of Pentecost, or the "*crown of our old age*"–our grandchildren. We could have had a "forever child." Instead, we have a daughter who is an accomplished woman. Oh, the prolonged effects of just one answered prayer. God has answered many, many prayers for me through the years, but none is more significant or far-reaching than this one prayer.

But let's get back to the "happenings as they happened!"

Arriving in the Dallas, Texas area, at the O. C. Marler home for the first time to preach a revival, Tim Marler, the pastor's five-year-old son, met us at the door. He swung it open wide, gesturing with his arm with great flash and flare for us to enter, and vehemently announced, "Welcome to the clubhouse; we play golf and praise the Lord!"

Tim had been learning songs at school. Our bedroom was next to the kitchen, and while Tim was getting ready to go to kindergarten each morning, he would sing all the little kids' songs that he knew to the top of his voice; of course, sleep was entirely out of the question.

I was pretty far along by this time, expecting our sweet Christy, and he knew another song.

*"Country roads, take me home,
To the place I belong,
West Virginia, Mountain Mama
Take me home, country roads."*

John Denver

At this point, he pointed to me and said, "You're the *Mountain Mama!*" We laughed and laughed about him.

I think he is best known for this little incident. One night, after a church service, he was heard to make this comment while he was alone in his darkened bedroom. "God, I know You are in here, but *don't You move,* 'cause if You do, it will scare me to death."

Brother Marler always called me Laverne. He said I reminded him of a relative by that name.

The last revival before our baby came was with Bob and Christine Sharp in Batson, Texas. We stayed in the house with the Sharps and their three children, Daniel, Kerry, and Christi. Later, they had another child, but they only had three at that time.

It was a small house with only one restroom. That was no problem; I only mentioned that because of Sister Sharp's words to me. There I was, eight and a half months pregnant, waddling around, huffing and puffing, feet swollen, and after a few days, she said to me, "You are *not pregnant* because you do not go to the restroom enough!" That was so funny to me.

I was still playing my accordion and singing in church services just days before her birth.

Wayne took me to Pasadena from Batson — a little less than seventy miles on Thursday, April 20, 1972.

He left me in Pasadena, returned to Batson to preach that night, and returned after church. We were to go to the hospital the following morning.

While Wayne was gone that night, I had a little prayer meeting at the McClain's home. I was, of course, apprehensive about giving birth. The Lord spoke to me with a *word*, especially for me. God always knows where we are and what we need at the moment.

"Am I a God at hand, saith the LORD, and not a God afar off?"

(Jeremiah 23:23)

Christy Renee Huntley
5:01 p.m., April 21, 1972

Early Friday morning, April 21, 1972, Wayne took me to Southmore Hospital in Pasadena, Texas, to be induced into labor. Dr Henderson decided to induce my labor because he was planning a trip away about the time I was due, the first week of May. We were out of town preaching most of the time, so it made sense to have a specific date.

My mother and sister had come to Pasadena for Christy's birth. Sometime during that long day, Mother and Wayne were in the waiting room and overheard a group of people talking about the Holy Ghost, speaking with tongues, as is recorded in Acts, the second chapter.

One woman, who seemed to be the self-appointed spokesperson for the group, spoke up in her most "hoity-toity" voice as if she really had an understanding of the Word.

"Well, we know that the Holy Ghost is not for us today and was only for the disciples and those in the Bible days."

My husband, always and forever listening to *everybody's* conversations going on all around him, perked up and began to run scriptures through his mind, disputing this subject, trying to quickly decide just how to start to set them all straight. All of a sudden, he had the quickest and best answer.

Leaning toward the group, he cleared his throat, indicating that he was going to say something. "Well, I've got it!"

Before anyone had time to retaliate in any way, my mother leaned in, piped up, and exclaimed, "Me, too!"

That ended that conversation because you can't argue with an experience. You can't say, "It's not for us," when we have it.

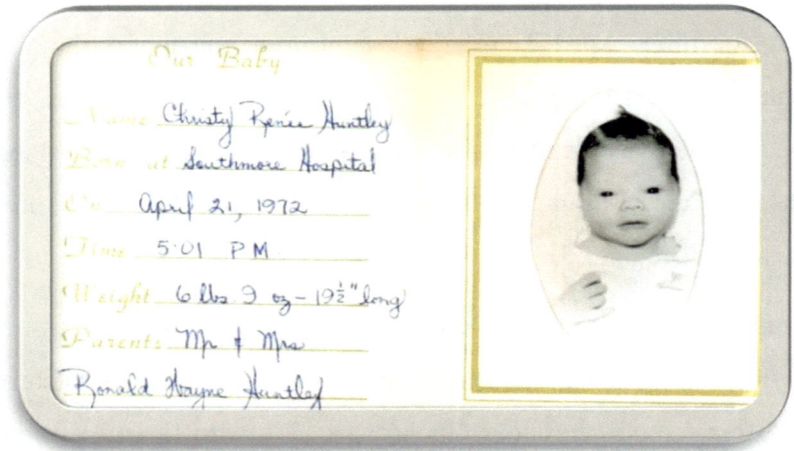

Friday was a long day, but at 5:01 p.m., Christy made her entrance into *the* world and *our* world. Oh, how our lives were changed forever, for good, by this precious, sweet, and perfect little girl. She was so very beautiful, and that has never changed. As a baby and a toddler, people always stopped me and talked about how gorgeous she was. Of course, *we* thought so.

Dr. C. D. Henderson, who delivered her and for whom I worked our last year of Bible college, told us how pretty she was at our six-week check-up.

He said, "She is a pretty little thing, isn't she?"

I said, "We think so."

He said, "Well, what you think doesn't count because you would think she was pretty, even if she had a horn growing out of her forehead, but she *is* pretty."

For some reason, all the time we were expecting, we both felt we would have a boy. I don't know why. Some people just seem to know if they are having a boy or a girl. It didn't work for us. Our perception antenna was totally off! We were so wrong. God is so awesome to give us what we need instead of what we "think" we want. We didn't "plan" on having just one child, but there never seemed to be another time that we felt it was the right time to have another.

We were so convinced that our baby was a boy that the first time Wayne looked through the nursery window and saw this beautiful baby with a head full of very dark hair, he said, "Looks like the first thing we're gonna have to do is get "him" a haircut."

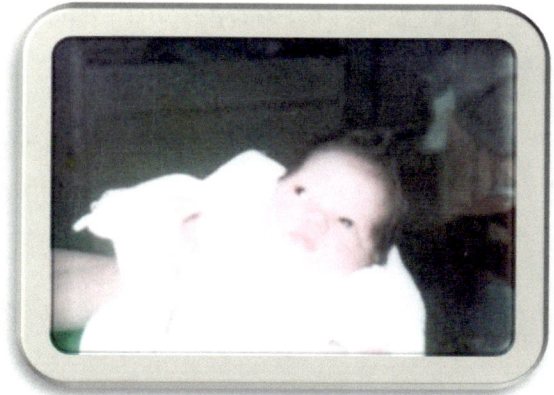

Christy's first picture: 4 hours old

Oops! It's a "girl," and she doesn't get haircuts. No, she doesn't.

As a young person, I made a covenant vow to the Lord that I would not cut my hair! I passed this covenant along to my daughter, who has kept that vow. Now, she has passed that covenant vow along to her sweet daughter, Christyana, and praise the Lord, the covenant goes on! I reminded our Lord of this covenant in the fall of 2018, when I really needed a prayer answered for my darling daughter, and I am thankful that He heard and answered this prayer, too! (See Chapter Nine: "Bishop and Mrs. Wayne Huntley" for that story.)

We are so thankful that we had a "girl." We didn't realize just how much. With just one child, we needed Christy Renee! There's an old saying that says,

*"A 'boy' is yours, 'til he takes a wife,
But a 'girl' is yours all her life."*

We needed an "all her life" child!

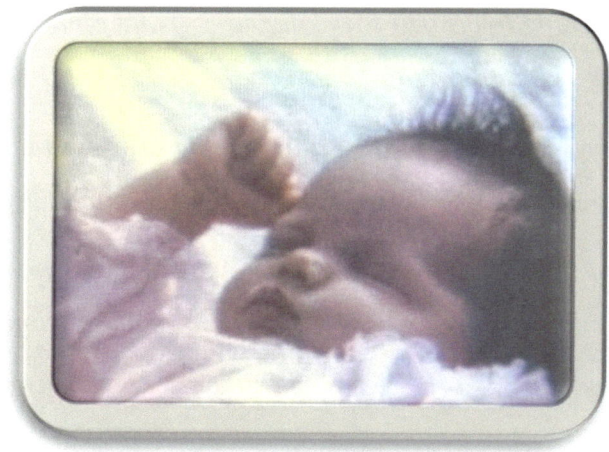

Emotions of a Mother

This was edited from a talk I presented at the Mother-Daughter Banquet in May 2001, in Fuquay-Varina, North Carolina.

I feel so sorry for any mother who <u>only</u> has <u>sons,</u> because there is just something special about a mother and her daughter.

For me, something special started the moment that she was born, and she came out winking and blinking her beautiful blue eyes in the bright light of the delivery room, and Dr. C.D. Henderson said, "You have a GIRL!"

That was B/G (before my girl), and her Dad and I were expecting a boy. We thought we wanted a boy.

So, I said, "Are you Sure…???You'd better check again because we were expecting a boy."

Thank God for unanswered prayer. Well, we really didn't pray for a boy; we just thought that was what we were having.

Oh, what fun I had dressing her in all the frilly fru-fru girl stuff. She wasn't as excited as I was, and when they did not feel as comfortable as they could have, she would exclaim, "I'm not 'hump-ta-ble.'"

She was so much fun when she was little. We have beautiful memories of her learning to crawl by rocking herself and plunging forward on her face. Or when she was learning to 'walk' <u>on</u> the bed in the trailer. It had a wall on three sides.

When you showed her a picture of a house and asked her "what" it was, she would say, "Trailer." She thought everyone lived in a trailer.

She was so bright. By the time she turned two, she was fully potty trained and could say anything she wanted or repeat anything you asked her to.

We rode bicycles and flew kites.

I have always loved gazing at her beautiful little face. I still do. I've never outgrown that pleasure. Only a mother can understand the emotion that comes when you look into your child's face or hear their voice.

When they are little, you don't know how or what they will turn out to be.

The most important thing that you can do for your children is to pray for them.

"… for I know whom I have believed, and am persuaded that he is able to keep that which I have committed unto him against that day."

(2 Tim. 1:12)

He is able to keep that which we commit unto Him in prayer, and when we dedicate them as babies or children.

Pray for them. Don't be ashamed to let the hot, salty tears flow from your eyes and fall unchecked onto their precious faces as you rock them.

Pray! That sounds so simple. But let me tell you, prayer is work. Remember, prayer is the key to heaven.

Every night, we prayed before bed. But I'll never forget the first time she acknowledged that she felt the Spirit of God at the age of about three. We were, as usual, praying before bed, and all of a sudden, she started sort of hollering out, "Thank you for my clothes. Thank you for my food. Thank you for my toys." I'm so glad that her first real prayer was a prayer of thanksgiving to God for what he had given her, because one of the great sins of the end time is unthankfulness.

I can tell you that much praying for her and with her took place all through her life.

There are many chapters in the Book of Life and Parenting. Being a guide to them is a vicious circle of holding on and letting go. Only God knows the right balance of when to hold on and when to let go, and it's not the same for all children. There does, indeed, come a time that, as parents, we must let them go.

We have done our part in raising them right! If you do not "let" them go or help them cut the apron strings, they will rip them out of your hands and will rip your heart at the same time. It is going to happen, one way or the other, and it's much better to help them cut them than for them to be ripped.

"Prayer is what gives you the perfect key for each child."

After Christy's birth, we went home from the hospital to our intimate friends' home, the McClains. They were so very kind to us. As evangelists, we did not have a home. As I mentioned earlier, I had worked in the insurance department at Dr. C. D. Henderson's office, located in Pasadena, Texas, and he delivered Christy. The McClains provided us a place to "land" for a few days during and after her birth. The ladies of the Apostolic Temple gave us an unbelievable shower. She was clothed like a little princess.

Christy, playing her first piano on her one-year birthday.

Evangelist and Mrs. Wayne Huntley and Christy–1972

The Huntley family

Christy and her cousin, Andrew

Our very first revival after Christy was born was in Bryan, Texas, with Brother and Sister Virgil Castolenia. Christy was just nine days old. I had thought that I would stay with the McClains for a few days while Wayne went to revivals, but when it came down to it, I could not let him leave without us. So, we packed up our new little girl and all her "gear" and headed back on the road.

This was definitely a new experience, but how happy we were to be Mommy and Daddy!

The Huntley family

While in Bryan, Texas, Brother Castolenia took Wayne fishing. Evangelizing, we were poor as the proverbial "Job's turkey." Out on the boat, Wayne noticed Brother Castolenia's fishing equipment. He had a first-class rod and reel, and Wayne was quite impressed. He kept commenting on how nice it was, bragging and bragging and complimenting Brother Castolenia.

Brother Castolenia said, "You don't like it that well, or you would have one by now."

Wayne said, "I can't afford one."

"If you really wanted one, you would have one!"

"No, really, I would love to have one; I just can't afford it."

"If you really, really wanted one, you would get one the same way I got this one. Save for it. Save two dollars this week, five dollars next week, and maybe only a dollar the following week. Just save what you can each payday, however long it takes, until you have enough to buy one. No, you really don't want one."

111

Wayne learned a valuable lesson on saving money for a specific purpose.

Brother and Sister L. S. Marcus (my pastor when I was a teenager) had us come for a revival in Baytown, Texas. Christy was only six weeks old. Actually, Christy Renee Huntley was named after this remarkable woman of God in my life, Christine Marcus.

Garland, Texas

We stayed in their home. I have memorable silent Super 8 home movies of Brother and Sister Marcus making her laugh out loud. These are precious memories. I would not have them because of our house fire in 2016, had my son-in-law not transferred them to digital files before that time. Thank you, Bryan, for this great treasure.

15 months old

Something very encouraging and exciting happened in that Baytown revival.

One night, a young boy, about nine or ten years old, born in this country and never learning any language except English, received the Holy Ghost between the pews. As he prayed, hands raised, with tears flowing down his innocent face, he began to speak in tongues so clearly, not just one or two words, but fluently. You could feel the Holy Ghost in his speaking. All of a sudden, the Spanish lady praying beside him got so very excited.

She said, "He is speaking in fluent Spanish!"

"What is he saying?"

He is saying, "Jesus, I love You. Jesus, I praise You. Heaven is a beautiful place where angels are always rejoicing."

Christy at 3 years old

We were privileged to return to Baytown at another time when Christy was about three years old, and let me tell you, she was quite the talker. At two, she could repeat anything and spoke in complete sentences; by three, she was "fluent."

We had been having a great revival with some young hippy people of that day, receiving the Holy Ghost. They really seemed to be getting a good experience, as the old-timers often said. We all know there are no bad experiences with the Lord, but I know what they meant. They were making it more than just a tongue-talking glossolalia experience; they made it a lifestyle.

There was a certain young man named James who had received a glorious experience and was coming to the revival every night. One night, on our way home from the revival service, Wayne and I talked in the car. Christy was standing between us in the front seat—before the days of mandatory car seats—listening intently, in fact, a little too intently.

Her Daddy, who was just making conversation and actually being complimentary to Brother James, said, "Brother James is doing so well. I'm very proud of him, and he is making progress in each service. He needs to get a haircut, but I'm sure that is in his near future."

The very next night at church, Brother James randomly sat on the second pew next to Christy. Christy, tugging pretty firmly on his arm, asks this question.

"You *are Brother James, aren't you?*"

"Yes, I am."

"Well, *my daddy said that you need to get a haircut!*"

Christy and Daddy

It just so happened that he had gotten one *that day.* After church, he looked us up and laughed so hard. He told us, "I love that little girl, and I hope one day, when I have kids, I have a little girl *just like Christy."* Well, this learning experience taught us a lot. We discovered that children have big ears and sometimes even bigger mouths. Thank the good Lord that no harm was done, and we avoided disaster.

This time is also when Brother and Sister Marcus, along with another couple from their church, took Wayne and me on an exciting trip to Matamoros, Mexico. Oh, how thrilled we were. It was our first pleasure trip flying and our first trip to Mexico. We felt like we were *hot dogging it*. Brother Marcus, always a very generous man, paid for our trip. (We would not have been able to go otherwise.) On that trip, Brother Marcus purchased a beautiful bone china figurine of a woman playing the piano for Sister Marcus; how I loved that piece. When Sister Marcus was much, much older, and Brother Marcus had already passed away, I told her that I wanted her to leave that piece to me in her will! There's nothing like just asking for something! She kindly wrapped it up ever so nicely and sent it to me by my husband when he was once preaching near her. It has a special place in my dining room hutch to be cherished and looked at, remembering the times shared with our mentors and friends.

We had an extraordinary revival with Brother and Sister Gerald Perry in Whitesboro, Texas, when Christy was six months old. They were so kind to us. We stayed in their home as we did quite often in those days. Brother Perry was also working a secular job as well as pastoring, and every morning, he had a ritual that he did to get ready for work. As soon as he got up, he would put a full kettle of cold water on the stove to boil for coffee. He would turn it on a certain level of heat and pray until the kettle whistled, which was about thirty minutes. Wayne began to get up with him and pray on those early mornings.

I have silent Super 8 home movie films of street meetings there in Whitesboro, where I was playing my accordion and singing "Only Jesus Can Satisfy Your Soul" (Lanny Wolfe), and Wayne was preaching. Revival began to happen. We had quite a few receive the Holy Ghost. The church was doubled when we left to go to our next meeting.

The winter of 1972 found us in Cleburne, Texas, with Brother and Sister B. E. Moore. Christy was around eight months old. She was learning to crawl by getting up on all fours and lunging forward, falling on her face. She finally learned to move her arms and legs, thus saving her "beautiful face."

Brother Moore drove us about eighteen miles from Cleburne to Alvarado, Texas, to a tie factory where we bought ties for fifty cents. We loved that.

We purchased our first *home* while in Cleburne. It was an astounding 22-foot travel trailer. (No, that is not a typographical error; it was 22 feet.) We certainly lived in a *tiny house before* they were so sought after! You could stand in the kitchen and brush your teeth in the restroom, but we were ecstatic – it was the first home that we owned!

Oh, how happy I was to get my "own" little place. A place to put our clothes in a *drawer*, not in a suitcase, and hang clothes in a *closet*. We could cook and eat what we wanted, when we wanted, go to sleep, and wake up on our own schedule instead of someone else's. No matter where it was parked, no matter what city or state, when I would lie down at night, my house looked the same. When I awakened each morning and opened my eyes, it was to the same ceiling. It was ours.

Our first home

Quite regularly, at night, right before I fell into a peaceful sleep, I would whisper a prayer of thanksgiving to my sweet Jehovah Jirah. "Thank you, Jesus, for our trailer."

Since then, I have done that many, many times. I just say, "Thank you, Jesus, for our home!" I have been blessed with wonderful, peaceful homes filled with love, mutual respect, and appreciation for each other.

This is another one of the times, during the writing and editing of this book, that as I read the written words from my heart, I have had to stop

The Huntley family

and wipe my tears as they flowed unchecked from my eyes in thanksgiving before I could continue. We serve a great God who always takes good care of us.

First of all, an apartment in Patricia Manor, from 1969 to 1971, in Houston, while attending TBC, was our first "together home."

We were so blessed with our travel trailer, from which we evangelized from 1972 to 1978.

As the new pastor of the First United Pentecostal Church, we purchased our first starter home, a small one-thousand-square-foot home at 401 King Arthur Trail, Garner, North Carolina, that, by the way, seemed huge in comparison to our 22-foot trailer.

The miracle home that God gave us in 1986, a three-thousand-square-foot home at 6979 Cornwallis Road, Garner, North Carolina, is another story I will tell later in Chapter Seven: "Pastor and Mrs. Wayne Huntley." The home we live in now is the one that insurance built after the 2016 fire.

I have been so thankful for all my homes; I know God gave me each one! I plan on going up in the rapture or to heaven from my current home, but then, I also had planned on going from my last home; God had other plans. More on that later in Chapter Nine: "Bishop Wayne, and Your Bishopness, Patsy Huntley."

That Christmas in 1972, my sweet husband went to Zales Jewelers in Waco, Texas, and purchased a watch for me. Of course, we didn't have the cash to buy it, so he bought it on time. Seven dollars a month. I don't know how many payments we made, but dividing $7 by $120 plus interest was quite a lot, but my darling wanted me to have it. It was "mine" until I decided to give it to a very special person–Christyana! More about that in Chapter Seven: "Pastor, and Mrs. Wayne Huntley" – Gramommy and Grandbuddy.

In June 1973, at the Texas Camp Meeting in Lufkin, we stood talking to people on one side of the tabernacle. Wayne looked up to see a man approaching us from the other side of the auditorium. A dapper-looking man of small stature walked toward him with purpose in his stride and eyes.

He walked right up to Wayne and said, "Young man, are you a preacher?"

Wayne said, "Yes, sir, I am."

"Are you an evangelist?"

"Yes, sir."

"Well," he said, "God just spoke to me and told me to come over here and ask you to preach a revival at our church."

This is how we met Rev. Marvin Cole, the pastor of the Apostolic Church in Beaumont, Texas. Oh, how Brother Cole has influenced our lives! Brother Cole could pray like no other. It was as if he were reciting the Book of Psalms or Proverbs. But it was rolling out of his "own" heart and soul.

Many years later, Wayne was asked to return to Beaumont to participate in Brother Cole's eightieth birthday celebration. He had Brother Cole lay his

hands on him and pray for him. That precious moment was captured in a photo. How awesome it was to be able to have this great man of God impart spiritual power!

By the time we got to Beaumont to preach for Brother Cole, it was early 1974. We had a wreck on the way to the revival. We were on Interstate 10, headed to Beaumont from the Houston area, pulling our little travel trailer. We had pulled off the interstate to get gasoline at Winnie, Texas, making a right-hand turn onto the service road. A man driving a pick-up truck passed us on the right-hand shoulder and hit us broadside on the passenger side of our car.

God most certainly had His hand on us. He hit the very center of our car, right on the edge of the front seat where I was sitting, and pushed it, and me, forward instead of hitting it just a bit further toward the front, which would have thrown me "into" the impact instead of forward "away" from it. Of course, the door window shattered and cut my arm and leg. Not bad, just little cuts. Two-year-old Christy began crying and saying, "Look at 'h-our' car! Look at mommy leg! Look at 'h-our' car! Look at mommy leg!"

We were able to have our trailer towed to the revival and set up while our car was being repaired. So, we came into Beaumont with a bang.

One day, my husband came to the trailer for a break. He had left his legal-size yellow tablet and pen lying in one of the classrooms on the church property, where he had been praying. Brother Cole came looking for him, and when he didn't find "him," he wrote a note on Wayne's paper tablet, something that has had such an effect on him and so many others that he has shared it with all through the years. Wayne also still has this paper in his memorabilia. Brother Cole wrote:

The True Definitions of Prayer

*Grasping the Word of God by Faith, and
Pleading it before Him, saying,
'Lord, do as Thou hast said.'*

Bradley and Brenda Honeycutt were in the Apostolic Church. Brother Cole had commissioned them to take care of us while we were there in revival. They took us out to eat after church services, as the Coles didn't care to eat then and wanted to go home. Bradley and Brenda were young and full of energy. Well, at least Brenda was, ha-ha! We instantly fell in love with them and have always had a special place in our hearts for them through the years. When we left that revival and headed to the next place, we had a miracle from the good Lord.

We didn't realize it, but when we wrecked in Winnie, Texas, and were hit broadside while pulling our trailer, we were unaware that the impact had weakened the attachment of our trailer hitch to the car.

As we were driving along late one night on those small Texas two-lane highways, suddenly, the car jolted and lunged around. We had no idea what had happened. We stopped; Wayne got out of the car and walked around, looking at everything. It all *looked okay,* so we took off and went to our destination. When we began to unhitch the trailer from the car, we found that the hitch was completely loose in the main middle part. Only the two sidebars were attached. The impact of the collision had almost broken it off, and while driving, it completed the task. You might think that the car couldn't pull the trailer in this condition. Well, probably not… *but God!*

He must have had an angel to hold it together until we reached our destination. Otherwise, the trailer would have disengaged from the car, and we would have surely wrecked again. Most probably, the trailer and maybe the car would have overturned.

I'm reminded of a line in one of the songs Sister Joan Ewing wrote and Brother Murrell Ewing sang: *"Have you counted the angels that kept you from harm?"* This is genuinely one of many times to thank God for being our protector and keeper and for "The Feast of Purim." (The Jewish feast of thanksgiving for "what did not happen" when Haman's scheme to have Mordecai killed and the Jews annihilated was foiled.)

We preached several revivals for Brother and Sister Jerry Green in Porter, Texas. We always enjoyed being with them and their boys so much. We became close friends with these wonderful people and have remained so ever since, feeling more like family than friends.

The Greens had five boys: Curt, Mark, Tim, Steve, and Kerry, and *no girl!* Wayne and I loved their family dynamics. Their boys were well-disciplined, but love was all through the fiber of their relationships. Growing up, neither Wayne nor I had a father leading in our homes, and we loved this about the Green family. Since they did not have a girl, we told them that, should something unforeseen happen, and Wayne and I both should die, we wanted them to have Christy to raise.

Many years later, God did give the Greens a *Christy*, an adopted daughter. I told them that I was happy they *got their Christy,* but glad it was not *our* Christy.

One such revival, Brother Green told Wayne that he was going to fast for seven days during the revival. Wayne told him he would join him. At that time, he had never fasted for seven days, but he had always wanted to. I tell you this because something extraordinary happened during those seven days.

Wayne had always suffered from allergies and asthma since his youth. In fact, when he was young, he and his brother, Gerald, shared a bedroom, and

Gerald would holler to his mother in the other bedroom, "Mama, make Wayne be quiet; I cannot sleep." This was because Wayne was wheezing so loudly that it was bothering him! Of course, Wayne couldn't help it, but Gerald sure didn't know that either. Many times, Wayne would suffer and not be able to breathe until dawn, when something seemed to change in the atmosphere, and he could go to sleep.

The Porter revival was several months behind us when, one day, Wayne realized that he no longer had asthma and allergy problems. It was during that seven-day fast that God had healed him, and he hadn't even asked. It was just an added blessing that the good Lord did for him.

When Christy was two years old, on Easter 1974, we were in Clute, Texas, with Brother and Sister L. L. Stevens. There was a lady in his church who was an excellent seamstress. She made Easter dresses for Christy and two other little girls, one of whom I believe was her daughter or granddaughter. They were absolutely stunning, but the material was sort of rough and uncomfortable to the touch. Christy would cry and say, "I don't want to wear my 'stick' dress." I tried to help the situation by putting a whole slip under the dress, but evidently, it didn't help much. I'm sorry, Christy, for every time I made you wear that old, sticky dress. That just was not right! See, I'm just an old person trying to get right by repenting for every wrong thing I can think of. You did look beautiful in it, though.

Dibol, Texas, pastored by Brother Elzine Strong, was a church we knew well, although we had never preached there. We had driven through Dibol many times on Highway 59 when we drove from Houston to Carthage and back to preach for my brother, M. C. I remember one night in particular as we traveled after Sunday night church. We were exceptionally drained and sleepy, but we had to return to Houston for work and possibly (lol) TBC classes the next day. We had driven approximately one and a half hours and still had about two hours to go. Of course, we had no money for a hotel room or the time to spend the night. As we drove through Dibol, we pulled into the church parking lot, located right there on Highway 59. We were going to try to catch "forty winks" of sleep, but really couldn't because we were so tense. We had no idea such an important event would transpire a few years later when we would return for a revival in this church.

We were staying in the back of the church in an evangelist's quarters. One night, after we had gone to bed, Christy woke up from across the room on her little cot, terrified of something unknown. She tended to have an oppression of the spirit of *fear*. This had happened on numerous occasions. That night, we had had enough. Wayne picked her up and sat her in his lap. She was hiding her eyes and would not even look up. We began to pray. "Devil, you take your hands off our little girl. We rebuke this spirit of fear that has overtaken her. We cast it out and away from her. She is covered by the blood of Jesus through her believing parents. We will not have this anymore in the name of Jesus, we pray." From that time to this, she has been delivered from that horrible spirit of fear. God IS a present help!

Christy was about five years old when we found ourselves at the church in Texarkana, Texas. Brother Bobby (G. R. to Wayne and me) and Sister Elaine Edwards were pastoring there at the time. Their son, Lamar, was just a little guy. We had known Bobby at TBC, and both of them as evangelists. Now, they had taken the church in Texarkana. We love them dearly and have remained close friends throughout the years.

Wayne didn't get to see his family or his beloved North Carolina very often. Once, we were preaching our last revival (the place will remain anonymous to protect the guilty) before taking a trip "home" to be there for the district youth camp and camp meeting. They were combined in those days. It was like youth camp during the day and camp meetings at the night services. We were counting on this paycheck to get us there and help us with money to pay bills in the future because we *knew* all the churches were small in North Carolina, and they did not have much in the way of finances to give us. Something happened that was very distressing, but it was definitely a time of "lesson learning." We are not proud of our reaction, but God taught us a very valuable lesson.

Sunday night, after the service, the pastor gave us our weekly check. In our minds, we reasoned that because his son was also a full-time evangelist, he would be more generous and apt to pay better than most, or at least as well as he had in the weeks before. When my husband opened the envelope with anticipation, he took one look and actually threw the check on the floor in dismay. Normally, we never thought much about pay, but this time, we were *counting* on it. The check was only about half of what he had paid in previous weeks and much less than we were expecting.

After we arrived in North Carolina, we went to the camp meeting. One night, after church, Brother Jerrol Wallace, the then pastor of the church in Winston Salem, approached my husband and said, "Brother, I have been saving some of my tithes for a little while to give to a preacher, and God spoke to me tonight and told me that I was to give it to *you*!"

It was more than we expected from that last revival in Texas, and we repented very thoroughly with much sorrow and realization that we need never worry about finances, especially "where" it would come from. God uses people and places you never expect, and has everything under control. He alone will supply, often not from the place or person that "we" think. Just because a church is big does not mean that it pays better. Small churches sometimes have a bigger heart to bless others. God taught us a most valuable lesson.

We do not work for churches, or pastors, or people;
We work for God, and He alone is our employer!

We had exceptional revivals in many churches during our evangelistic tenure. We mainly preached in Texas; therefore, most people thought Wayne was from there. But Wayne knew, and his heart was constantly yearning toward North Carolina. It's as if Texas was his learning ground for what was his *always-present calling:* to start a church in North Carolina.

The Huntleys in Paris, Texas

Chapter Seven

Pastor and Mrs. Wayne Huntley
First United Pentecostal Church
105 Yeargan Loop Road,
Garner, North Carolina, 1977

It was Thanksgiving Day, 1977. Wayne, Christy, and I were at my mother's little duplex apartment at 518 North Twenty-second Street, Waco, Texas. All my family was gathered to have a delicious meal together. Early in the morning, the men went to the woods to hunt rabbits while the women made final preparations.

I received a call from North Carolina that Raleigh wanted us to consider taking over the church's pastorate there.

How ironic! When Wayne was in high school, his father was incarcerated at Central Prison in Raleigh. After getting his driver's license and first car, he drove his family from Charlotte to Raleigh to visit him one weekend.

They attended church with Brother and Sister John Paul Hughes, who gave many years of their lives and sowed seeds of Truth into this great city.

The Hugheses were ever so gracious and kind to them. My husband never dreamed that years later, God would allow him the privilege to come and work for the Kingdom here. He came first in the 1960s as the *son of an incarcerated alcoholic.* Approximately ten years later, in the 1970s, he would arrive *as God's specially called son*, an ambassador of Truth to the 144,000 plus souls (most of them lost) living in this impressive city. He would become the pastor and later the bishop, but would always be a home Bible study teacher and a called, burdened minister of the Gospel to those needing salvation.

Oh, how God works and weaves the threads of life in ways that we cannot see or comprehend. He takes the most unlikely and makes something we cannot imagine.

After Thanksgiving, we loaded up and drove to North Carolina to check things out. Brother Bill Brooks was pastoring in Raleigh then and felt it was time to move on.

On our way, we stopped off to preach for Bobby and Elaine Edwards in Texarkana, Texas. They were so kind to us. (God always cares for us and has often used our precious friends.)

They let us use their van to travel in, gave us a special offering, and paid our expenses to North Carolina. We owe them for

Patsy, Christy, Wayne, and Josie

helping us get to the place on earth we would love the most–Raleigh, North Carolina.

Over forty years later, in 2021, my husband thought it was *time*! Time for what, you might ask? Time for *payback*!

With Pastor Bryan Ballestero's permission and approval, we asked the Edwards to come to Raleigh for a weekend service. We had them on the platform and told the story of their unselfish contribution in helping us get to Raleigh. We gave them a check to repay those expenses, gave her a dozen roses, and had the

Temple People shower them with appreciation. We must never forget how we got to where we are and the friends who helped us!

In the fall of 1977, we went to preach for a little group at the First United Pentecostal Church on 105 Yeargan Loop Road in Garner, North Carolina, a suburb of Raleigh. My husband preached, "The Son Is Rising in Raleigh."

After church, my husband gave people time to ask him questions. Brother Vernon Lawson said (not with a wrong attitude, but with sincerity, wanting to know the answers), "What will you do when the revival doesn't come? How long will you stay, and will you get discouraged and leave when it doesn't happen?"

Later, he told us he was worried about our family because it seemed that the church had not been productive, no matter what they had tried in the past. He knew my husband had to provide for me and our five-year-old daughter.

My husband assured him that if he decided to come, he would come to stay, and as long as there was one sinner left in Raleigh, he would not get discouraged.

Brother Lawson would remain a trustee and my husband's greatest encourager and supporter the whole time of my husband's pastorate and well into his promotion to Bishop. In fact, on one Sunday, the first year of our pastorate, when our little church was filling up with guests, Brother Lawson stood at the back of the

Vernon Lawson and Brother Huntley

church, watching the people flow in, all the while jumping up and down, pumping his fist in the air, and shouting, "Hallelujah!" He got so excited, as did we all!

While we were waiting for the pastoral election, Brother and Sister Johnny Godair invited us to preach for them in Durham, North Carolina. My husband sought the Lord for His will. Mickey Godair became my most loved and special friend and confidant for many years. Our daughter, Christy, became so close to Lisa and Cindy Godair that many people thought her name was Christy Godair! She spent many happy general conferences running around with those sweet girls and bunked with them in their hotel rooms. They were the sisters Christy never had, and their bond went very deep. I remain so thankful that they loved her and took her into their lives.

During that time of seeking the Lord, one night in particular, while in Brother and Sister Godair's home, Wayne stayed up most of the night praying and listening for the voice of God. In the early morning, God spoke after a night of wrestling with the facts of the reality of our lives. We had a full schedule of revivals to preach. We were just about to branch out to California after preaching almost entirely in Texas for nearly seven years, with only a few revivals in North Carolina and Ohio. We had the security of scheduled revivals instead of going to a small church with only two or three families and complete uncertainty. With a wife and daughter to support, leaving behind the security of two years of revivals for the promise of nothing was not an easy decision.

God's Will will never take you,
Where His power cannot keep you!

God always has a unique way of speaking His will if you listen. This time, He used a song!

*Learning to lean, learning to lean.
I'm learning to lean on Jesus.
Finding more power than I ever dreamed,
I'm learning to lean on Jesus.*

John Stallings

The Lord assured Wayne that if he would lean on Him, He would care for us and provide. He did, and He always has!

Wayne emerged from that night of prayer, knowing it was God's will for our lives to come to Raleigh, North Carolina. He said he would take the church if he only got a simple majority of the vote. But guess what? We got one hundred percent of the vote.

During the waiting, many couples who were part of the church and had come to help Brother Brooks in the church in Raleigh decided to leave and go back where they had come from. So, all five (yes, five) voting members wanted us! Johnny and Linda Atkinson, Vernon and Elizabeth Lawson, and Alice Nine all wrote "Yes" on their ballots, and we were now the happy and excited new pastors of Raleigh, North Carolina. There may have been only five voting members in the church at that time, but there were 144,000+ people within the city limits and 286,000+ folks in Wake

The Huntleys and the five people who voted for us as pastor in 1978

County for whom we were becoming pastors. To fulfill the "Great Commission" of Matthew 28:19, we must go into "our" world and preach the Gospel to all nations.

We had just moved into our new church facility when one of our men came to the church to pray early one morning before work. To his dismay, someone had taken spray paint and painted racial slurs on our brick building and our church vans. Someone didn't like it because we welcomed "all" people to worship with us. Thankfully, they had used cheap paint, and the walls and van were wet with dew, so the paint came off quite easily!

Not long after this, we held a Sunday service focused on children. The mayor of the city, Tom Harrison Fetzer Jr., was invited and was present. He noticed that our church was very diversified and integrated with people of all colors and nationalities. He asked my husband, sitting on the platform, "How do you get all these different people to worship together?"

My husband exclaimed, "I tell them that if they don't, they will go to hell!" He may have been a little crude and even rude back in the day, but it was true. Heaven will be filled with all nationalities, and if we can't worship with them down *here*, how can we do it in heaven?

Yes, we were called to every soul living in our fair city…
red, yellow, black, and white, and everything in between.

By the color of their church members, some seem only to be called to one group of people. But the Bible says:

"For the son of man is come to seek and to save that which was lost."
(Luke 19:10)

All lost people!

We are to be His hands,
His feet, His voice,

*and most of all
His heart of love reaching
to "all" the lost people,
of the place God called us.*

We returned to Texas for Christmas 1977, packed up our belongings, and returned to the best place in the world–Raleigh, North Carolina. Oh, how this one turn of events changed our lives!

We rented a U-Haul truck, which our nephew, Mike Landtroop, drove. Wayne pulled our 22-foot Brougham travel trailer, which we had been living in while evangelizing.

We had been preparing for this move and felt a change coming. We knew that we were still in the will of God evangelizing, but we just knew that a change was in our not-too-distant future. For two years, we started paying off bills and saving money. We sold a Mercury Marquis that was a gas guzzler, so we would not have a car payment. My brother Ken had some used cars for sale. We went to his back lot, raked off dirt and dead leaves that had fallen on a 1970 Chevrolet, and drove it away for $250. This was the car that, when it rained, your knee would get wet because the windshield leaked. It was also the car that, when we were almost to Charlotte, North Carolina, on our journey from Texas to Raleigh, the driver's sideview mirror on the outside of the door just fell off while we were driving down the road. Brother David Elms said it was a sign. "No turning back!" We never did!

LaFern and Ken Landtroop

We rolled into Raleigh around 11:00 p.m. on a rainy Saturday night, January 7, 1978, via Highway 70 East Business. In those days, Interstate 40 was not finished in our fair city, so we had to travel right through downtown. When we pulled into 105 (Yeargan) Loop Road, Garner, Brother and Sister Atkinson were there to *happily hand over the church keys*.

Thus, we began this epic experience, our journey to the TOP–the happiest and most fulfilling time of our lives.

We had no income except to live by faith, which we had already been doing while evangelizing. Our home was a 22-foot travel trailer that was not hooked up to a septic system, so we had to make late-night runs, filling a trash can and emptying it in the commodes in the church. We tried not to make that excursion often. But the church was so cold and had no heat during the week that it was way more often than we wanted. We had a car that dripped water on your left kneecap when it rained, and there were only five members in our church, but there was a city of lost people who needed what we were bringing to this place. God was just about to open up the windows of heaven with a revival that would astonish us and astound the one in Texas who told my husband, *"If you go to North Carolina, your ministry will die, and you will never be heard of again."* God heard that! Yes, He did, and quite the contrary, Wayne's ministry flourished and was just beginning.

The following day, Sunday, January 8, 1978, was our first service as pastor of the First United Pentecostal Church. We had fifteen in attendance, and we were indeed excited.

Our first service on January 8, 1978

On Monday, January 9, while my husband was outside setting up our small travel trailer, someone from the little house next door to the church came out into the yard. My husband introduced himself to the man, told him he was the new pastor, and invited him to church the following Sunday. The man's name was Robert Strickland. He was the boyfriend of Lois Finch, who lived in that house with her son, Mike Finch, her mother, Mrs. Alice King, and her sister, Shirley King. Robert said, "I'll be there."

My husband saw Robert again sometime during the week and said, "Don't forget this Sunday."

Robert said, "Preacher, I told you I would be there, and I will." And he was! He brought his girlfriend, Lois Finch, and Lois's friend, Elizabeth Wade.

That Sunday, January 15, 1978, these three returned to the evening service. While my husband was praying for that service, he felt the Lord impress upon him that three people would get baptized that night. As he was preaching Sunday night, the Holy Ghost was moving, and my husband told everybody what God had impressed on him that afternoon. Robert, Lois, and Elizabeth came to the front, and Robert said, "That's us."

Robert and Lois both received the Holy Ghost right then and there. Since we didn't have a baptismal tank yet, we traveled to the Durham church to baptize them. Elizabeth came up out of the water, speaking in tongues.

The revival was well underway! When you get the right man, at the right place, at the right time, with the right message, you will have revival!

The Formula for Revival is:

The Right Man,
At the Right Place,
At the Right Time,
With the Right Message!

Our daughter, Christy, wrote the dialogue below and tells some of her memories of God's significant provisions to us and our church in our early beginnings. The first lady mentioned is Lois Finch Strickland's mother, Alice King, who lived in a little house adjacent to the church property. (Maybe just beyond the church boundary, but not beyond God's reach.)

Thank you, Jesus!

"I wanted to bring breakfast to my pastor." The petite, aged hands accustomed to a full day's labor proudly extended the warm plate of homemade sausage biscuits. "And I wanted to pay my tithes," she said. How could she have known the new pastor in town, residing in the 22-foot travel trailer beside the church with his wife and five-year-old daughter, needed propane for their little heater? It was one of the coldest winters in The Old North State, and the pastor had more dreams than dollars. His calling exceeded his currency, but that has never been a deal-breaker for our God.

That same pastor's family was blessed to move into their first house a few months later. Oh, the excitement! Their budget wouldn't allow for brand-new furniture, so off to the second-hand store they went. The young pastor's wife found a beautiful bedroom furniture set. It was perfect and within their price range. A few weeks later, as they were riding downtown, something caught the eye of the wife. In the front window display of a fine, elite furniture store was the same bedroom furniture set they had purchased at the second-hand store! They could almost hear the voice of God speaking: "I will take care of you. I will provide you with the best. I will give you the desires of your heart!"

The road-worn 1969 Toyota Corolla sputtered into the gas station. The pastor and his family were heading to a district meeting. The pastor filled the gas tank, thinking his wife had cash. She thought he had the money. What a surprise for both of them! They began searching every nook and cranny of the vehicle, looking for extra cash. They even checked their little girl's purse, hoping to borrow a few dollars she possibly had tucked away. It was to no avail. The embarrassed pastor went inside to explain to the attendant that they would have to pay on their way back. "You've been paid in full," the attendant stated. He pointed toward the front door. "You see the gentleman there? He paid for your gas."

The pastor went to the gentleman and humbly expressed his appreciation for this incredible generosity. "Well, you see, my brother is a pastor on the West Coast," the gentleman explained. "I know pastoring can be a challenge, but I hope that if I show kindness to you, someone may show kindness to him."

"We would like you to receive the offering at the coming district meeting." It was time to raise funds for Sheaves for Christ (SFC).

The pastor and the congregation were in the thick of a building fund drive, so money was sparse. The pastor felt so convicted trying to generate funds from others, and he seemingly had nothing to give. "Lord," he prayed, "if you bless *me with $5,000.00, I'll give it to Sheaves for Christ." Two or three days later, he went to the mailbox. There was a check for $5,000.00! Somehow, they had overpaid for their new sanctuary pews! You better believe he gave it in the SFC offering!*

These stories are the real-life happenings of Bishop and Sister Huntley. That little girl? "Yes, it was yours truly." This is the financial foundation upon which this church was built. That's why I don't question His Divine provision. Even in an economic upheaval, He is faithful. Even in political distress, He is faithful. Even during a worldwide pandemic, He is faithful!

The widow's mite has always carried out His work, and a handful of meal, a few drops of oil, and a little boy's lunch.

Christy Huntley Ballestero

Our workforce in the beginning was small but tenacious! We had the Atkinsons, Lawsons, Alice Nine, Eva Garrett, my husband, and me. (Eva Garrett's granddaughter, Candace Bradley, would become our great-niece by marriage when she married Jeffrey Landtroop after they grew up!)

We were blessed to have a church building acquired by the former pastor, Brother Bill Brooks, right before we arrived. We were actually to make the first payment, three hundred and something per month, which might as well have been three thousand. We had to make some money in some way. So, of course, in those days (and some even today), the means of choice was making peanut brittle!

The church didn't have a cook stove, so we went to the second-hand store and found exactly what we needed. The cost was $100. My husband and I invited the proprietor to church. He and his wife came! And would you believe they put the one-hundred-dollar check we had written them in the offering plate that morning? That stove cooked thousands of patties of peanut brittle, made thousands of dollars, paid many church payments, and put much money into our building fund for the next phase of our journey: building a new church in 1984–1985.

People began to come, and God began to fill them with the Holy Ghost. Between the time we had "tried out" for

Sister Lawson and Sister Huntley making peanut brittle

the church and the actual time we arrived in town, the church had dwindled to five voting members. The North Carolina District board ruled that Raleigh would be a new work (so that we could receive new work advantages). Other ministers, Brother and Sister John Paul Hughes and Brother and Sister Bill Brooks, had come to Raleigh to work, plant seeds, and water with tears and prayers for quite a few years. Their labor and prayer did not go unnoticed by God or us.

One particular Friday, Brother Wayne McClain called our home and said to me, "I have purchased plane tickets to Houston for you and Wayne. The tickets are waiting at the airport counter. You are coming to Apostolic Temple to preach our weekend services."

"Yes, sir. Let me contact Wayne, and we will be on our way." When your pastor tells you something, you don't question it; you just do it.

Sunday night, after the service had come to a close, Brother McClain was talking to the church. He said that Wayne Huntley would begin traveling more and preaching out from Raleigh. I was somewhat dismayed at this thought.

All of a sudden, Brother McClain exclaimed, "I see luggage. I see luggage. Yes, Brother Huntley thinks he's settled down in Raleigh and has given up traveling. He is about to travel more than he ever did while evangelizing, and Apostolic Temple will buy them a new set of luggage."

His prophecy indeed came to pass. Right after that, Wayne Huntley began his preaching ministry all around the country and some out of the country (although this was not his first choice). He began to preach in more and more places, including meetings, camp meetings, and conferences. I tell him he never quit evangelizing. I did, but he didn't!

Once, when he returned from an out-of-town preaching event, we went to the airport to retrieve him. Brother and Sister Marshburn were with us. The men greeted each other, talked, and laughed as they stowed Wayne's luggage in the trunk. We were probably talking about where we would eat, as that is always foremost on Wayne's mind at any given time. He has commented, *"If you don't like to eat, you cannot be my friend."* We left the airport, and a few days later, Wayne began to prepare for a radio broadcast.

Wayne had several radio broadcasts during our formative years in Raleigh. He had a thirty-minute broadcast for a while, as well as a five-minute program. He declares the five-minute program is much more complicated than the thirty-minute one because, as he jokingly said, your opening remarks as you come on could be, "So I see that my time is just about gone!" He also feels that it would be good if every preacher had a radio broadcast, as it is the best training on how to limit our speech and get something said within a short time limit. It teaches you to keep within a time frame, something many preachers struggle with!

Wayne began to prepare for his radio broadcast, and needing some sermon notes, he realized he did not have his tan Samsonite briefcase that contained the paper copy of every sermon he had ever preached in his entire preaching career, which was probably around ten years at that time. He always took them all with him on his trips away to preach in case he needed notes from a particular sermon. This is when he realized he had left his briefcase at the airport. He called, and they told him they did not have it.

Wayne preaching on WPJL radio.

On Friday night of that week, we had a district meeting, and Wayne was telling Brother Jesse Williams, the pastor from Fayetteville, North Carolina, about what had happened. Brother Williams's eyes burst into tears, and he grabbed Wayne's hand, exclaiming, "Brother, this cannot happen. Your sermon notes are too valuable, and we are gonna pray, and God is gonna bring them back to you." They did precisely that, praying and imploring God to restore them. The next day, Saturday, Wayne was praying and had a vision. He is not given to this, but it happened, nevertheless. He saw his briefcase sitting parallel to a wall, and he just had the understanding that it was in the lost and found at the airport. Sunday after church, as we were preparing to leave the church to go to a restaurant to eat, Wayne said,

"Let's go eat out by the airport."

I, always wanting to know *why* about everything, asked why we were going there, as this was not our customary direction to have our Sunday afternoon meal.

He said, "Afterward, we are going to the airport to pick up my briefcase."

"Well, you already called, and they said it was not there."

"I don't care; it *is* there, and I will pick it up."

We drove to the airport and parked out front, as you could still do in those days. As Wayne exited the car, he saw a security woman walking towards him.

"Ma'am, I am here to pick up a tan Samsonite briefcase that you have in your lost and found."

"You know, I believe you are right; I think I saw one there."

Wayne went with her, and sitting on the floor, parallel to the wall, exactly as God had shown him, sat his Samsonite briefcase. Hallelujah! Won't He do it?

Shortly after this, Brother Williams helped us set up a computer with all of Wayne's sermons entered, so this would never happen again.

His traveling became increasingly extensive as time went on, to the point that when Christy was about ten years old, during the Christmas season, she and I were out shopping. I was trying to help her find a present to give to her Daddy. I told her that, within reason, she could pick out any gift she would like. We found something extraordinary that depicted this particular time in her life. It was a Norman Rockwell figurine. A little girl was running down the steps of her home, arms outstretched toward a man dressed in a suit, coming in from a business trip, who had dropped his briefcase on the sidewalk; his arms were

Christy and Patsy

also extended toward his young daughter. The caption read, "We Missed You, Daddy."

When Wayne came in from a trip or working in our town, she would exclaim, "Daddy, put on your jeans." These were play clothes, not work or business clothes, and meant that he was home for the evening and not going anywhere else for the day, which could be her special daddy-daughter time.

We had been in North Carolina for only a month or two when the UPCI Home Missions Department (now called North American Missions) held its annual meeting. At that time, Brother Johnny Godair, one of the regional directors on that committee, had encouraged Wayne to fill out an application to receive a monthly check. With his excellent recommendation, we were approved for full support for one year, totaling $300 a week or $1,200 a month, stipulating that Wayne would be working full-time and could not hold a secular job.

That was fine with him because he had made a pact with God many years ago when he first accepted His call to preach. He told the Lord, "I don't feel worthy to accept a call to preach, but if You want me, I will give You my all. I will not seek any other career or money-making schemes. I will do as the Bible says."

"Even so hath the Lord ordained that they which preach the Gospel should live of the Gospel."
(I Cor. 9:14)

He has never told others that they should do that; he just felt he should. God has always taken care of us.

The following year, when it was time to apply for "Christmas for Christ," my husband filled out the application and mailed it in. It was customary for the second year to request half of the support, which would be $600 per month. That is what he did.

At the Home Missions Board Meeting, they had finished with their allocations. Brother Godair said, "We haven't allocated money for Brother Huntley in Raleigh." They looked around, and his application was nowhere to be found. Several of them knew that they had seen it. Someone spoke up and said that they knew things were going great in Raleigh, so let's give him what we gave him last year–full support. (It had never been done at this time.) They voted and decided to do just that. We received full support for two consecutive years. That was such a blessing, and we were able to accomplish more without financial pressure. God has just always done miracle after miracle for us. We are thankful.

We received just under $30,000 for those two years, and the First United Pentecostal Church gave back that much several times over to the annual "Christmas For Christ" fund drive for the Home Missions Department of the United Pentecostal Church International, giving $30,000 each year for several years.

We have always appreciated the UPCI for giving us this financial support. My husband took it seriously and worked for the church eight hours a day, visiting, talking, praying, visiting the local restaurants to meet people, hospitals, and funerals, seeking out sinners, and teaching home Bible studies. Anywhere, there would be people in need of salvation.

He feels that a person should work for God,
with the same fervency and passion as
a person who works for "gold" or more!

The increase will come if you put the time and effort into God's work. You cannot sit at home all week and then expect people to flood into the church on the weekend. If my husband didn't work, we would have no people. So, he worked and worked and worked, and God gave the increase.

We were happy in our 22-foot travel trailer, which had cost $3,000, but we began to look for a home shortly after we arrived. We found our dream starter home on 401 King Arthur Trail, Garner, North Carolina, for $33,000. By this time, we were receiving the "Christmas for Christ" monthly check, which allowed us to obtain a loan. We didn't have much for a down payment and needed just a bit more. Would you believe that the real estate agent loaned us the little bit more we needed and took it off what he was to make on the sale? God can work things out if we let Him "take the wheel."

In May 1978, we were the proud owners of our first starter home, just over 1,000 square feet. We had put down roots; we were here to stay, which made our church people feel safer knowing we were not leaving.

We had a house and no furniture, just a few odd pieces. As any frugal penny-pincher would do, we began looking at second-hand furniture stores. We returned to the one where we had purchased the electric stove to make peanut brittle. They had a beautiful bedroom suite that we bought for $400. It was a light cream color, with just a hint of a line of gold and blue trim.

I had always wanted a canopy bed for our little girl's bedroom. I told the proprietor of the second-hand store what I wanted. He told me to come back the next day because he felt he knew where to get one. We returned the next day, and there it was–a beautiful, white canopy bedroom suite for $300. God supplied exactly what we needed and wanted for the prices we could afford.

Not long after we made those furniture purchases, Wayne and I were driving in downtown Raleigh. We had stopped at a traffic signal. I was looking around and just happened to look to my right, out the side door window, straight into a furniture store showroom window. I *could not believe my eyes!* I told my husband to pull over; I jumped out and ran to look in the window. There, sitting featured in the window for everyone to see was my exact bedroom suite, priced at $1,500. Look what the Lord did for us. The Lord was saying to me, loud and clear,

> *"You may have gotten your bedroom suite at a junk store,*
> *and paid junk store prices,*
> *but I didn't provide you with no junk.*
> *I gave you beautiful furniture worthy of being featured*
> *in the front window of a downtown furniture store."*

Wayne was always on the lookout for people who were hurting and needed a pastor. Once, when he had gone to Wake Medical Center to pray for someone, he noticed a person crying in the foyer. He approached her and introduced himself as Pastor Wayne Huntley of the First United Pentecostal Church, asking if she had someone in the hospital who needed prayer. She confirmed that this was so.

Wayne offered, "May I go to your husband's room and pray for him?"

"Sure," she said, "I would appreciate it."

So, Wayne went and prayed for him, and God heard and answered his prayer. They came to church and knew we had just moved into our home. They wanted to get us something for our new home, so they purchased custom-made drapes for our living room window.

God has a way of doing beautiful things for His people. We have learned to trust God, pray, and wait! If you don't get in a hurry, be patient, and at the proper time, God will bring the desires of your heart right to you!

Remember, the coin is in the fish's mouth!

Because we were approved by the Home Missions Department and received a "Christmas For Christ" monthly check, we could attend the Home Missions Seminar for home missionaries held that year in Fort Smith, Arkansas, at Brother James Lumpkin's church.

It was during one of Brother Jack Yonts' sessions, where he was teaching "How to Teach Home Bible Studies," that my husband kept punching me in the arm, saying, "That's it. That's it. That's what we are gonna do. We can do that."

I must pause here to tell how much Jack and JoAnn Yonts personally meant to Wayne and me. They also took us under their wing, and we had many, many good times of fellowship together. They were a bit older than Wayne and me, but they were young at heart and so much fun to be around. We took several trips together.

One trip was to visit and tour the beautiful city of Charleston, South Carolina. I read a book by Gwen Bristow when I was just a teen entitled "Celia Garth." It was then and remains my all-time favorite fiction book. It was centered around Charleston, South Carolina, 1775–1776, during the Revolutionary War, or the War of Independence. I had always wanted to visit and explore. We did that with them, and what memories we still enjoy now! We spent time in each other's homes. Brother Yonts had Wayne preach everything that he had a say in the choosing!

A funny thing happened in our home. They came downstairs one morning,

Brother Huntley, Brother Jack Yonts, and Patsy

and Brother Yonts exclaimed, "Jody has me looking and feeling like a lobster this morning."

"Why, what happened?"

"Well, somehow, the electric blanket controls got mixed up. I was hot; I kept turning mine down. She was cold, and she kept turning her control up. So even though I was hot, I kept getting hotter, and although she was cold, she kept getting colder."

I don't guess they figured it out until morning. Sorry, so sorry!

Another benchmark of privileged opportunity came in October 2013, when Brother Yonts asked Wayne to preach at the incomparable Jody Yonts' funeral. Because they were so inseparable and close, Wayne said during the funeral, "Brother Yonts, I can't help but almost preach yours and Sister Yonts's funeral at the same time. You will get to be present for yours. I cannot talk about her without talking about you!"

Later, we were sitting in the family car with Brother Yonts at the end of the emotional funeral, waiting for the imminent procession to begin from the church to the cemetery. As the pallbearers came out of the church bearing the casket, laden with the sacred relics of what was left of the humanity of sweet Jody, Brother Yonts emotionally and lovingly exclaimed, as I am sure he did thousands of times when she was alive to hear, "My Baby!" They will never be forgotten as long as _we_ live.

I genuinely do believe that the Raleigh revival was actually *born that day* in my husband's heart during that one Home Mission seminar session. That's when Wayne got his answer to how and what we needed to do in Raleigh to reap the harvest and grow the church in our great city. A year later, there were about one hundred souls filled with the Holy Ghost because my husband and I had the privilege of teaching them a home Bible study using this method. What a fantastic Biblical tool! Everyone who came to the church was a potential home Bible study recipient. At one time, my husband had seven in progress. That is not really encouraged, but it *was* my husband's job. He worked eight hours a day for God. He arose each morning, adorned his suit and tie, and went out into the city to *find* the lost that would be receptive to this great Gospel. He was like a wild man, going to hospitals, restaurants, and any place where there would be lost people. No one was safe because he was looking for, witnessing to, and talking with every single person that he came in contact with.

To this day, we are always looking around to see who else we can teach a home Bible study. With this tool, we have genuinely reaped the harvest and grown the church. It has been the foundation and the making of our church. Many, many people have been formed into stable, upright Christians through this excellent means of discipleship.

In the beginning, we put signs all down the walls of the church that read, "100!" We started pushing for attendance. In just six short months, this dream became a reality, and we saw this come to pass.

On one particular Sunday, we had 99 in attendance. At the end of the service, my husband told some of the men, "Go outside and down the street and get one more. We are not leaving till we have 100 today."

There was a man at a gas station across the street from the church who agreed to come to the church long enough to be counted. What an exciting day to tear the posters off the wall with the extra-large letters exclaiming "100!" We had accomplished that goal. Through the years, our church always seemed to be able to set a goal and then watch it come to pass. Of course, it didn't just happen; it came about by excitedly being promoted, with much passion for every little goal we set. My husband has never lacked passion and has the unusual ability to promote a project.

Being involved with a choir has always been my love and joy. I directed our church choir for a short time when I was a teenager. Christine Marcus was my mentor and pastor's wife, and she affected me like no other person. I wanted to be just like her. She had such anointing and the power of God on her singing and choir directing, and always looked like an angel. Since that time, I have enjoyed singing in choirs and solos, and I love directing our choir.

When we came to Raleigh, one of the first things I did was to start a small choir. We used this means to establish a church standard of holiness and godly living. We had a *choir covenant* that members were required to sign to be involved. We did the best we could with just ordinary people. We had no great singers or musicians who were accomplished, but we knew how to worship. How God moved during our choir singing, and what a blessing it was to our church! However, we had a tenor section that couldn't sing tenor. I worked and worked and then worked some more, trying to teach them their part during one particular choir practice. As long as I was singing their part into the microphone, and they were singing alone, they sang just fine. But sure enough, just as soon as we started putting all the parts together, you guessed it, they jumped right back onto the soprano part.

That particular day, I stopped everybody and said, "Okay, I've had enough. Everybody on your knees."

I prayed a short, simple prayer that went something like this: *"Lord, You see these tenors. You know they really want to sing tenor; we want our choir to sound good and have all the parts because 'God is not the author of confusion...' (1 Cor 14:33). We want to glorify You with our praise. Please, Lord, help our men to be able to hear and sing their part.*
In Jesus' name. Amen."

When everyone got up from their knees, I am here to tell you that from that good day until now, our tenors have been singing tenor. It was indeed a "miracle." It was not an answered prayer where the men started doing better and better; it was a miracle. They started singing tenor right then and there. God heard our prayer to the point that a few years later, Dan Dean, a great singer, songwriter, and choir director, came to our church for a weekend choir clinic. He, not knowing *anything* about our prayer that fateful choir practice, said after practicing with our choir, "Man, I know people that would kill for a tenor section like this one." God is a God of miracles.

Our little choir went from that humble beginning to becoming a choir of one hundred-plus members years later, with the privilege of being invited to sing at the UPCI General Conference 2005 in Richmond, Virginia, and also at the 2008 conference held in Greensboro, North Carolina. Who would have thought it? Surely not me, nor them, I'm thinking.

2008 Richmond, Virginia, UPCI General Conference

Josie, also known as Granny Landtroop

Mother turned sixty-five in May 1978 and retired from working. I never thought she would leave Texas, but when your baby lives in North Carolina and you have no other family living in Waco, Texas, it gives you that extra push to pull up stakes and move a thousand miles away.

So, before Christmas in 1978, Mother became an adopted citizen of North Carolina. She fell in love with North Carolina and its people, especially the church folks. They loved her and treated her as if she were the *queen of heaven*.

It seemed that we were inundated with people who were a few "French fries short of a happy meal" in those days, and some of their "elevators didn't go all the way to the top." We do welcome all people, but we seemed to be overrun with them at that time. We felt that the devil just sent so many of them to us early on to try to discourage us. It worked to some degree, as you will be able to see in the stories below. The precious people's names have been left off because they are God's creation, have souls, and are important to God and us. I never would hurt or embarrass them.

For instance, one Sunday, a person approached us and proclaimed, "Today is my birthday!"

"Wow, that is so exciting. How old are you?"

"Well, I'm forty-five or thirty-five, I'm not sure."

Duh! Ten years is a significant gap to not know.

Another time, my husband was taking a little couple home after Sunday service who had no car or way to get to church. They lived in the downtown projects known as "Halifax Court." There is absolutely no shame in either of these facts. My husband and I found ourselves in this same dilemma when we were young. But as the couple walked away from the car, down the sidewalk to their apartment, my husband noticed the lady had something flapping down below her dress and between her knees. Looking closer to try to figure out what was happening, he could tell that as she walked, the crotch of her underwear was slipping down, and you could see it waving around as she walked. Bless her heart. They were souls, and we didn't care how or who they were; if they were a warm body and could fill a pew, we would get them to church.

We had one lady, a little on the heavier side, in a wheelchair, who had a cute personality. My husband was trying to get her wheeled into her little house, straining to get her up the ramp and onto her porch. As he huffed and puffed, strained and pulled, she looked over her shoulder at him and exclaimed, "Too much of a good thing, huh, Cap-m (Captain)!" She had a physical problem with her kidneys and bladder. The wooden pew where she sat in the church had the paint peeling, and the ammonia smell reeked so strongly that it was almost more than could be endured.

One sad little lady with no apparent family had grand mal seizures and had several during the services. It totally disrupted the service, and if you know anything about those debilitating seizures, she was left completely disoriented.

As a result of these incidents, and so many others not written on these pages, I reiterate the following. One night, after church, we were in the car, heading home. As we pulled out of the church parking lot, my husband stopped in the driveway, pointed, and said, "Do you see what that says?"

I said, "Our church sign, First United Pentecostal Church, Pastor Wayne Huntley?"

He said, "I'm getting ready to change it to First United *Nut House, Warden Huntley.*"

With that, he drove out the driveway toward home! Not long after that, during a sermon, he told our people that we did accept people with brains, and we didn't have a sign on the door that read, "No brains allowed."

However, we have found out through the years that if you love people that no one else loves, God will love and bless you. If you care for those that others seem not to care for, God will care for you!

*"If you will reach those that no one wants,
God will give you people that everyone wants!"*

My husband's philosophy of life:

*"If you will make <u>God's</u> business, <u>your</u> business,
God will make <u>your</u> business <u>His</u> business!"*

We were incredibly blessed with great revival, so much so that we have always said we would not want to start another church because we just felt that it would not happen the second time like it did the first. It was a God thing. It was miraculous. We are just thankful that He let us be a part of what He wanted to do in Raleigh.

So, the revival began in Raleigh. It was fast-moving, exciting, and exhilarating, and it kept us going. My husband worked like a madman. Day and night, that was all he had on his mind. He spent hours knocking on doors, teaching Bible studies, and praying. God rewarded him, and people began to come.

We could not have done it without Johnny and Linda Atkinson and Vernon and Elizabeth Lawson (the two couples who had been four of the five that voted us in as pastors). Alice Nine, a new convert, had just received the Holy Ghost and needed them as her examples. They were our rocks, our firm foundation on which everything else was built. When new people arrived, they observed what they were doing and mimicked their lifestyle. These great people were at every church service, Saturday morning visitation, and weekly peanut brittle-making. They gave over and above finances to the church. They gladly lived by the standards of holiness and godliness preached by Pastor Huntley. This gave new folks a perfect example of what they were trying to achieve in their own lives, making it so much easier to teach and train these new Christians in their new way of life.

Mark Foster and Wayne

We had a revival with Mark and Paulla Foster in 1979, whom we had first met at Texas Bible College while attending there. We knew each other on campus, but our circle of friends did not intertwine with theirs on a close basis. We four had no idea what path our lives would take that would form such a close-knit bond, to the point that we would become fast friends, best friends, and even *deer friends*. In fact, Wayne and Mark would become like brothers, and all of us, like family. Wayne said that Mark taught him how to *be* a friend. We have shared many, many happy times and a few sad times, and had numerous heart-to-heart talks through the years. Our grandchildren call them "Uncle Mark and Aunt Paulla."

But in our church's infancy, my husband had seen Brother Foster at a General Conference and felt quickened for them to preach us a revival. So, my husband went up to Brother Foster and said, "You need to come to Raleigh and preach a revival."

"I will pray about it," he said.

"No, I have already prayed about it, and it's the will of God."

The next day, he saw him, and Brother Foster said, "I will come."

So, in October of 1979, they came. We had such a tremendous revival. One Sunday, Brother Foster preached from the roof of our little building. We had a record-breaking number of 313!

During these exciting times, we conducted various Sunday school promotions. Come and see the longest dog!! The longest dog was a hot dog made on a table with hot dog buns lined up, connecting end to end to create an extra-long dog!

There was the tallest man, when Brother Billy Rogers wore stilts that he used for hanging drywall, and he could reach the ceiling wearing these stilts.

We had the mystery man. My husband went out into the community and got a well-known businessman (maybe a particular person that you would really like to visit your church) to commit that, should someone from our church ask him to come to Sunday service, he would not let them know that he was the mystery man, but that he would agree to come. The church person asking and the mystery man both would get a monetary prize. We gave $100, which was a reasonably good prize in the 70s.

We made flyers using the (now, not then) antique mimeograph machine, a stencil duplicator that works by forcing ink through a stencil onto paper. The copies were primarily purple. They were widely used in the late 1960s and continued into the 1970s, but became largely obsolete with the development of xerography and other photocopiers.

At that time, we met Ronny King, a young man who was twenty-seven years old. Gerald Blake, a young boy about twelve years old, had been riding our Sunday School bus. He asked Brother Huntley if he would go to the hospital and pray for his uncle, Ronny King, who was gravely ill with cancer.

Ronny, quite the fisherman and hunter, was neither a churchgoer nor religious at all. But God can take our dire circumstances and use them for our good.

My husband did visit him, and Ronny told him, "If I get out of the hospital, I will come to church."

He did get out, and he did come to church during the Foster revival. His sister, Billie Batts, brought him and practically had to carry him into the building. At the end of the service, he was helped to the altar. A chair was brought, and sitting there at the altar, with his sister by his side, God gloriously filled Ronny with the Holy Ghost. He was baptized in Jesus' name, and just a few days later, he passed from this life, only having been able to come to one church service. What a testimony of the great mercy of our God.

This was the first funeral we conducted at our little church building. It was packed tight with this big family of sinners. They were good people, but they didn't know God. My husband preached, *"When God Takes the Enemy's Tool of Destruction and Makes It an Instrument of Salvation."* Our little choir sang, *"Soon and Very Soon, We Are Going To See the King."* We had a powerful anointing of the Spirit of God in that little church that day. My husband presented Ronny King's mother, Alice King, with his baptismal certificate. Ronnie was buried in the clothes in which he received the Holy Ghost, that he had purchased to come to church.

From one person, a bus kid, Gerald Blake, who didn't even have the Holy Ghost himself at this time, there was a mighty family revival birthed. This family, who now are many, has been a part of the church all these years.

Every Saturday was visitation day! So, after Ronny King's funeral, on several occasions, we visited James and Billie Rose King Batts on Oak Road in the Carolina Pines Community. One particular Saturday, James said to my husband, "I am going to start going to church, but it will *not be to your church*!"

He must have just been under conviction to say that because the next day, or shortly after that, James woke up on Sunday morning and started getting ready. His family said, "Where are you going?"

He said, "I'm going to church." They were surprised.

Contrary to what he had said, 10:00 a.m. found him at the little block church building that looked like "green slime" on Yeargan Loop Road. At the altar call, Wayne walked back to where he was sitting with the intention of just shaking his hand and thanking him for coming.

James and Tommy Batts, and Brother Huntley

When Wayne reached the end of the pew where James was sitting, he shot out into the aisle, fell on my husband's neck, and started making his way to the altar. It looked as if his legs were made of rubber; he could hardly stand on his feet. Before he got to the altar, he was speaking in tongues. He never wavered and was a faithful member until the time of his death, September 15, 2022, when he had just turned eighty years old. He served as the church's official door opener and closer for many, many years and was the head usher. You cannot judge a book by its cover or by what a person says. Sometimes, it's just a cover-up for what's really inside the heart.

Billie Rose Batts was our faithful church secretary for many, many years. She was the first person who helped me with the bookwork and then went on to become a full-time secretary for the church. We owe her a lot because the finances were not always "easy peasy," and many times, there was a lot of pressure. She handled it with grace, poise, trustworthiness, and professionalism. She was intelligent and just precisely what we needed. Bills were always paid in a timely manner, on time! She was so responsible and dependable.

Now, James and Billie Rose lie in waiting in Montlawn Cemetery, close to her brother, Ronnie, and mother, Alice, and just a few paces from our TOP cemetery plots to await the "trump of God" to sound, to be caught up to meet Him in the air. (I will write how we acquired these TOP plots further on in this chapter.)

These are just four of the souls that will now be in heaven (and we know that just one soul is worth the whole world) because God called a man to bring the Gospel to a great city. How privileged we have been to share this great Gospel with people who had never heard it, and now they will be a part of that great body of believers that will rise first at the rapture.

James and Billie's son, Thomas Ray, received the Holy Ghost at the age of fifteen, standing side by side with his first cousin, Gerald Blake, at the 1981 North Carolina Youth Camp in Fayetteville, North Carolina, held at the Methodist College. They were both called to preach and went on to receive their minister's license with the North Carolina District of the UPCI.

Tommy has been such a tremendous help to my husband and me through the years. He told my husband that God had spoken to him and said that he was to take care of Brother Huntley in his later years. He has certainly done that. All we have to do is hint at something that we need or want, and he is "Tommy" on the spot. We have and do trust Tommy with *everything*. Business-wise and financially, he has been our representative and power of attorney. This means we were not even present when we purchased the land for the "Non-Typical Family Farm" or at the closing of our modular log cabin for that land. Tommy was there to represent us. He is the mediator of our hunting lease in Halifax County: all this and everything in between, even purchasing two vehicles. Tommy is our go-to guy. If we need it, Tommy does it! This is how much we lean on him and know that he is a man to be trusted.

For this, we say a big, big "Thank you" from the bottom of our hearts. His sweet wife, Kim, is so precious that Tommy is allowed to take time away from her to take care of us.

Shelly Strickland was a young girl of about twelve years old who had ridden our Sunday School bus. She came and received the Holy Ghost. Shelly became a Bible quizzer in 1980, and this particular year, the study material was the Book of Acts. Her mother, who was not coming to church at the time, had to help Shelly study, as she quoted all the scriptures on how to be saved. Shelly came alone faithfully for about three years, and finally, the scriptures did their work. Of course, Anne had watched Shelly live for God and be faithful in all that God wanted her to do and be.

So, when Anne came and received the Holy Ghost, she immediately began to live as an Apostolic. She received the Holy Ghost on a Sunday, and on Monday morning, she started out the door, adorned in her usual pants to go to work at J.C. Penney. When she got outside, she said to herself, "I just don't feel right." So, she turned around and went back and changed into a dress. She never wore them again. When she arrived at work, her coworkers looked at her and exclaimed, "Why, Anne, you do have legs!" They had never seen her in anything except pants!

Anne lived for God for many years, and her husband, Jimmy, watched her, even as he and Anne had watched Shelly. One day, he also came and received the Holy Ghost and was baptized. He served the Lord and was a part of our great church until he was planted in the sod at our church cemetery in Mont Lawn to await the rapture with the rest of the saints buried there. (Further on in this script, I will tell more about how the great blessing of this church cemetery came about.)

Some saints had a burden for Mexican immigrants who lived in a commune outside of town, where they worked mainly in the tobacco fields. They brought several of the young men to church. One of them was Elpidio Guerra. One night, during a service, I glanced over and saw him with his hands lifted and tears flowing down his cheeks. I got my husband's attention, and he went and laid his hands on his head, and Elpidio began to speak. It was evident that he was not speaking English or Spanish but was speaking in tongues as the Spirit gave him the utterance. We had no idea this was the fledgling beginning of a worldwide revival among the Spanish-speaking people.

More and more of these precious people began to come, and we tried to communicate with them, but the language barrier was definitely a hindrance. We continued to do our best, working with them in any way we could for several years. We eventually had Elpidio positioned in the sound room with a microphone that transmitted the interpretation into headsets to those sitting in the back rows of the church. By this time, he knew English fairly well, but so much of the power and anointing was lost from the one in the pulpit to the interpreter to the listeners. Even though it was difficult for them, we had between twenty and thirty men coming anyway because they were so hungry for God. They were being transported by bus and van by dedicated drivers: Brother Tom Phillips, Sister Judy Stephens, and Brother Russell Farmer. We tried our best to minister to them, but we didn't have very much success in them receiving the Holy Ghost. We needed someone who could relate to them through their language.

My husband was speaking with our good friend, Brother Scott Smith, from Columbia, South Carolina, and one day he mentioned that we needed a Spanish pastor in the worst way. Brother Smith said, "I may have your man. Brother Sergio Vitanza, who is from Honduras and fluent in Spanish, is in my church. He has a call to preach but is currently selling insurance. If you'd like, I can arrange for you to meet, and you can talk, have him come for a weekend, and see if all of you are a good fit." So that indeed happened.

Brother Vitanza and his family moved to Raleigh and actually started the Spanish church in 1992. Thus began a fantastic revival. Brother Vitanza prayed and asked the Lord to help him fulfill the dream in Brother Huntley's heart, to put the same heart in him as Brother Huntley had for revival. They had services, first in our prayer room, then after we built our Jesus In Ministries (JIM) Building, they held services in the youth room. By the time they moved off our church property in September 2010, they were running between 250 and 300 and had multiple services to handle the crowd. God gave them a miracle building, a 1000-seat auditorium, in Wendell, North Carolina, that was in foreclosure. Because of their work ethic and generosity, God has helped them not only to survive but also to thrive. At this time, they have never been late on any payment, although the payment is very steep.

Together, the Vitanzas (Sergio and Rhonda) pastor and have started three other churches. Along with their children, they labor tirelessly for the Kingdom. They have been instrumental in assisting other pastors in North Carolina with establishing Spanish congregations. Many saints in different countries, such as Honduras and Mexico, got their start through their ministry. Brother Vitanza has been the National Spanish Ministry Director for the United Pentecostal Church International and has traveled extensively for this department around the country and world.

161

Brother Huntley and Brother Sergio Vitanza

On several occasions, when my husband was preaching out of state, he would meet some precious Mexican man who would say, "I received the Holy Ghost at your Spanish church in Raleigh while I was there working. I now live in Texas or Illinois (or wherever), and I am a preacher, or I am a pastor, or my family and I attend a UPC church." God has undoubtedly given the increase.

Elpidio married Ann, a lady in our church. They had two boys, Paul and Mark. Unfortunately, Ann left this life way too soon, but her son, Mark, married Stacey Rogers, and they have two girls, Chloe and Riley. They have been with us almost since the beginning.

One of the home Bible studies we taught was held at Earl Kirk, Jr.'s home. He, along with his wife, Pauline, and several of their family members,

Mark, Paul, and Elpidio Guerra

were in attendance. Their daughter, Lisa, was another one who had come to church on our Sunday school bus.

Brother Kirk was a lay preacher at a Church of God. He thought the Bible study was for his family, and it was, but it was for him, too. We had the Bible study chart set up in the living room, where everyone sat for the study. He sat in the attached dining room at the table with his Bible open in front of him, studying along with everyone. He saw the truth of Jesus' name, baptism, and one God. In fact, when he first started coming to our church, my brother, Garth Landtroop, was visiting us from Texas. During a church service, he and Wayne were standing on the platform, and he looked back and saw Brother Kirk. He told Wayne that the Lord had just spoken to him and that Brother Kirk would be one of the pillars of our church.

He did, indeed, become one of our strongest supporters. In fact, the day he passed away, he had been painting at our new facility on Lake Wheeler Road. He went home for lunch and passed away while at home. He died with his boots on. We named our conference room the Earl Kirk Conference Room in his honor!

When another one of the Kirk's daughters, Brenda Dolen, came to our church for the first time, she exclaimed, "This is it. I had a dream about being in a church by the railroad tracks, and I didn't know what church it was until I came here. And this is it!"

One evening, we were having a drama practice at the church. Suddenly, a woman shows up whom we had never met before. She walked in and up to my husband, who was not dressed as the pastor, and said, "You *are* the pastor, right?" Her name was Barbara Eason, and she had been reading the book *The Late, Great Planet Earth* by Hal Lindsey. It had scared her so badly, and she was praying as she drove past our little church on the other side of the tracks.

The Lord spoke to her and said, "Pull into that little church; they have what you need to be saved in there."

So, she did. My husband, Brother Dennis Landtroop, and I took her into the office and basically told her in a nutshell what the Lord wanted her to do. We knelt beside a straight chair in that simple little, no-fanfare office, and what praying she did! She prayed and began to repent passionately. In just a minute, she stopped and said, "I'm sorry. May I take off my shoes? I would be much more comfortable."

We said, "Of course."

She took off her shoes, set them neatly beside her, and began again to pray fervently. In just a few short minutes, my husband laid his hands on her head, and she began to speak in tongues and glorify God. She jumped and said, "This is it. This is it. This is what I wanted and needed!"

My husband quickly told her, "Yes, this is that, but there is more! You need to be baptized in the name of Jesus to make your salvation complete."

So, she was baptized and went home, rejoicing that she had found perfect peace with God. God had indeed answered her prayers.

A little later on, Sister Barbara Eason told us that her daughter, Anita Biggerstaff, and her husband, Ricky, were living in the mountains somewhere, but she didn't know where or how to get in touch with them, as she had had no contact with them in quite some time. She wanted to tell her daughter about her conversion, her change of heart, and what God had done in her life. My husband told her that we were going to pray that God would quicken Anita's heart and that she would call her mother. Before that week was out, Anita had called, and shortly after, she and Ricky came to Raleigh. Both were filled with the Holy Ghost and baptized in Jesus' name.

Barbara's life was cut short in a horrible car accident that left her incapacitated for quite a few years before the Lord called her home.

Ricky and Anita Biggerstaff have been strong and faithful Christians and members of the First United Pentecostal Church, also known as the Temple of Pentecost, for many, many years.

One bit of encouragement and instruction that found its way to many people just receiving the Holy Ghost is a short bit of advice from me.

> *"If you live for God EASY… It's HARD.*
> *But if you live for God HARD… It's EASY."*

If new converts live for God according to this concept, they will have no problem living for and loving the Lord.

When trying to win people to the Lord,

> *"We need to be an INTERESTED person,*
> *Not an INTERESTING person."*

Because,

> *"People do not care how much you KNOW,*
> *Until they know how much you care.*

Rilla Anderson was a wonderful lady who started coming to our church from Fuquay-Varina, a suburb of Raleigh, about twenty minutes away. She had been attending a Trinitarian church. Her son had come and received the Holy Ghost and had taught her a Bible study, and on occasion, she had begun to visit our church services.

One day, my husband felt a nudging from the Lord to call her. He thought, "I'll just call her and encourage her and tell her I'm glad that she started coming to our church." He called her phone number, and she picked up the receiver.

"Hello."

"Sister Anderson, this is Brother Huntley."

On the other end of the line, he heard this sort of scream/yell. Then he heard shouting, and in a thunderous voice, speaking in tongues that would shake any person to the core.

In a minute, it stopped, and Sister Anderson said, "Brother Huntley, thank you for calling me. I was praying this morning, talking to the Lord, and asking Him what I should do. Is the First United Pentecostal Church where I need to go? Do they preach the Truth there? Is this what I need? Lord, if this is the true church and it's where I need to be, and if Brother Huntley is a true man of God, have him call me today."

Thank God Wayne called her. We surely need to be listening to the voice of the Lord to lead and guide our every move. Sister Anderson did, indeed, keep coming. Many of her family have come and have been filled with the Holy Ghost and baptized in Jesus' name. She had prayed for many years for a church to be built in Fuquay-Varina, the city in which she lived. God answered that prayer, and before God took her to Glory, she got to be a part of that daughter church, started by DeWayne and Joyce Landtroop, now an autonomous church pastored by their son, Rodney Landtroop.

We were teaching a home Bible study at John and Edna Moore's home in Apex, North Carolina, where the Pinkerton family, who were friends of the Moores, attended. Many of their family members came and received the Holy Ghost and were baptized. Another neighbor of the Moore's, Lindy Blalock, just happened to come in at the time they were just about to begin one of the studies. He sat down to listen. He had plans to be baptized in his church that weekend. Would you believe that night's lesson just happened to be on baptism in Jesus' name? Sure, you would! It was no accident. God had it all orchestrated just right.

Lindy came to church, received the Holy Ghost, and became such an intricate part of the happenings and doings of the church. (More about Brother Lindy a little farther on.)

It was the first, or maybe the second, Christmas season that we were in Raleigh (1978 or 1979) that my husband got the grand idea to advertise our church in the Raleigh Christmas Parade with a float. The parade has been a beloved community event since it began in 1939, only being put on hold during WWII before resuming in 1945. It is the largest parade between Atlanta, Georgia, and Washington, D.C. The city would have thousands of people lining the streets on the Saturday before Thanksgiving, with thousands more watching it on live television. In fact, in 2022, over 250,000 tuned in on live television, with over 80,000 watching in person on the streets. It has always been, and continues to be, a well-attended, monumental event in our fair city.

Wayne went to the Greater Raleigh Merchants Association and spoke with Mr. Walter Williams, the parade coordinator at that particular time.

Mr. Williams said, "The parade is not really about *Christmas* as much as it is the grand opening of the Christmas shopping season. We have never had a church in our parade, so I will need to consult with the committee to see if we want to allow it.

They decided to allow us in, the very first church ever in the parade. Since we initially entered our non-professional float that year, many more churches have participated.

Someone was supposed to have a big truck to pull our float. For some reason, that did not materialize, and we had to use a small truck that was so small that the float came down the road very, very wapper-jawed, leaning down heavily in the front. It didn't look exactly as we had hoped–neat and cool like we had it all together, but instead, it seemed somewhat pitiful, as if we didn't know exactly what we were doing. My sweet husband got his finger caught under the hitch somehow as they were hooking it to the little truck, and some of the guys thought maybe we should abort the idea altogether! But my husband was determined not to let the adversary steal our victory.

Even though it was not a professional float, the float itself looked terrific. Brother and Sister Lawson designed and put it together themselves. It might not look totally up to par as it came rumbling down the parade route, but it indeed sent a message to all those thousands of people that day.

On the trailer was a huge, white, wrapped package, a very, very large red ribbon and bow, and on the side, big red letters proclaimed that the box was filled with "The Holy Ghost." A tag attached to the box stated that this was a gift: "From God To You." Overhead, a banner flew announcing that this was "The Perfect Gift."

Our Christmas float

Once, we were having a revival, and we had seen the local fire department advertising some event they were having by placing a very long sign on an overpass that strung across two lanes of traffic on the busiest local highway, Highway 70. Sometimes, it's easier to get "forgiveness than permission," so we just did likewise. After a few days, we got a message from the city asking us to take it down. We did and told them that we supposed that if the fire department could do it, so could we. Sorry, fire department, you were never able to advertise there again.

I remember how the burden of the souls of this great city seemed to settle on my own heart, personally, and I could feel the weight almost like it was something tangible. Any time I was out and about, where there were people walking the streets or maybe a place like the Christmas parade, the people's spirit seemed to reach out to me. I seemingly could feel their souls reaching, and I could, through the Spirit, hear them saying, "I need God. I want God. Please help me find God. Please take me to God." It would always bring tears to my eyes, and I would whisper a prayer.

Because of the vast growth in population in Raleigh, there are more lost people in this city and county now than when we first arrived in 1978, although we have had many, many souls that we have been able to "take to God." Although our work sometimes seems to be an effort in futility, we thank God for every soul that we have had the privilege to help save.

The story of the "Starfish" comes to mind.

An old man was walking on the beach one morning after a storm. In the distance, he could see someone moving like a dancer. As he came closer, he saw that it was a young woman picking up starfish and gently throwing them into the ocean.

"Young lady, why are you throwing starfish into the ocean?"

"The sun is up, and the tide is going out, and if I do not throw them in, they will die."

"But, young lady, do you not realize that there are many miles of beach and thousands of starfish? You cannot possibly make a difference."

The young woman listened politely, then bent down, picked up another starfish, and threw it into the sea.

"It made a difference for that one," she smiled.

Adapted from the original by Loren Eiseley

I'm so sorry that we cannot save them all. Just one of their souls is worth more than the whole world. (This is something else I remember reading in a significant Book.)

In 1981, our church and people were featured on the Home Missions Filmstrip. (Do you know what that is? If so, you are not young. Ha! Ha!) In this filmstrip, people told their personal stories of how they came to the church.

One picture I remember vividly was of us kneeling at a grave and apologizing for not getting to Raleigh in time for them to hear the Truth. This was an actual story.

Brother Arthur Jones, an older man, came and received the Holy Ghost and was baptized. He was such a sweet old gentleman who had loved the Lord a long time, but he just didn't know the Truth. Unfortunately, his wife, Sudie Jones, had died before we made it to Raleigh and to Brother Jones with the Gospel. We are so sorry, Sudie Jones, for being too late for you and thousands more. However, we did make it in time for your beloved husband and many, many others, for which we are so thankful.

That same year, at the Home Missions Service during UPCI General Conference, our church, under the direction of Brother Lindy Blalock, presented a drama based on Don Francisco's recording, *I've Got To Tell Somebody*.

Lindy wanted to be a blessing to Pastor Huntley and the First United Pentecostal Church, so he took night classes in drama. My husband had a dream of great professional dramas, and Brother Lindy fulfilled his dream. He became our drama director, and after we built our new facility, he oversaw fabulous productions, which initially took place on our church property as outdoor dramas.

Behold He Cometh and *The Day He Wore My Crown* had live animals, Roman soldiers riding in horse-drawn carts, and Jesus riding into Jerusalem on the back of a donkey. We had beautiful costumes created by the ladies of the church, involving complete families from our congregation. Fathers, mothers, and all the children were a part of these remarkable events. Some of these productions had up to two hundred church people involved. The people willingly gave their time, many times during the Christmas holidays, to sponsor these events. Our children have fond memories of being in our church dramas. Several of these events took place at the historic Dorton Arena, which was built in 1952 and is located on the North Carolina State Fairgrounds. This is an unusual saddle-shaped building that boasts the world's first cable-supported roof system. Literally, thousands came and heard the Gospel through the means of drama.

Lindy Blalock and Shelly Strickland married and became part of the backbone of our church throughout the years.

One interesting thing happened through Acy and Janice Childers's home Bible study. One day, she was out in her yard, and the Lord spoke to her and said, *"Ye shall be filled with the Holy Ghost, not many days hence."*

At the next Bible study, she asked Brother Huntley if he knew what that meant. She did not even know that it was a scripture in the Bible. Well, she was filled with the Holy Ghost not many days after that. In fact, they both were filled, and she has always called my husband *"My Moses."* On several occasions, the Lord has spoken a very significant word to her for us.

Quite a few years later, Sister Childers's brother and his wife, Paul and Mae Henson, received the Holy Ghost and were baptized. Brother Paul went on to his reward, loving Jesus and the church. Just a short time before he passed away, my husband went to his house and asked Brother Paul who he would like to speak at his funeral. Our number three grandchild, Christian, who was only around five or six years old and could not read or write very well yet, had befriended Brother Paul and was loved by him so very much. So, Brother Paul said, "I want Brother Christian to speak." It was so sweet and cute. A small, child-sized pulpit was placed on the platform, and he spoke. His mother had to help him write it so he could read it. He did a really great job and just told us that Brother Paul was his special friend. He is probably the youngest person to speak at a funeral!

As already stated, in one year, my husband and I had won over a hundred people through home Bible studies. It works because it is biblical.

"... I kept back nothing that was profitable unto you, but have showed you, and have taught you publickly, and from house to house,"

(Acts 20:20)

In 1984, a newly married young couple named Doug and Caroline Douglas moved to Raleigh from West Virginia because of work, as did many people during this time.

We all jokingly said that West Virginia was sliding off into North Carolina; it was not a very happy time for West Virginia.

Doug and Carolyn Douglas quickly molded into the First United Pentecostal Church as if they had truly been *born into the family* here. They took Pastor Huntley's vision and desire for revival in Raleigh, North Carolina, which included raising our children to be champions for Christ and involving them in the work of God and the church at a very young age. Our greatest desire for our children was for them to be used by the Lord in whatever way the good Lord saw fit.

Even when, at one time, his employment played out, they chose to remain in Raleigh because they wanted to keep their children in our church, even though it cost them very much financially, and they had many personal hardships. They felt it paid off in the end, and they were able to achieve their ultimate goal, which was for their children to grow up and never leave the church but to stay faithful to God all their lives. We know that our kids will make mistakes, but we trust they will remain steadfast.

Brother and Sister Douglas had four children. Jay, Kristen, Caleb, and Joshua. All four of their children are grown and married, with children of their own.

For many years now, we have had a service once a quarter on Wednesday nights, which we call *Heroes in Training*. Our kids actually do the service. They take the prayer request and the offering, sing on the worship team and specials, and do the preaching and speaking.

We also have a kids' church service called Kids Hour of Power, which is geared toward them receiving the Holy Ghost and meeting their particular needs.

We named our children's choir "The Little Saints Choir." It's not original with us, but it's a name I love. They were privileged to be asked to sing at the Sunday School Service at the UPCI General Conference in Richmond, Virginia, in 2005. They indeed are not just the church of tomorrow but the saints, although young, of *today*. Many times, I think we lose a very significant workforce by not involving our children more. I looked at our "Little Saints Choir" singing at our recent Christmas Musical Drama and thought, "Most of those precious children singing on that platform are our spiritual great-grandchildren." Their grandparents are the people we won years ago. This is one of the great rewards for growing older!

After forty-plus years, we have come full circle and have seen our children grow up in the church, never leaving the church, working for the church, and being a part of the church. They are now our leaders and key people at the very core of our church family.

Brother Wayne Mitchell, pastor of the church in Molene, Illinois, had practiced this principle, and he was known for saying:

"Save an adult, and you save half a life;
Save a child, and you save a whole life."

Brother and Sister Douglas have been our Christian Education Directors for many years, taking over from me and moving it forward with the greatest of burden and efficiency. In the meantime, he has become the principal of a secular school, earned his doctorate, and has written a book titled *Building a Fence: Keeping Our Kids in the Church,* all the while raising his children and being a significant part of the Temple of Pentecost. He has also been on our church's trustee board for quite a few years.

We had a sweet lady named Brenda, whom Wayne and I were teaching a home Bible study, along with her sister, Joy. Brenda worked with Marvin Williams. She got us a Bible study with Marvin and his wife, Candy. Marvin and Candy both received the Holy Ghost and were baptized. They were faithful Sunday attendees for several years. Candy didn't move as fast as Marvin, and it took her a few years to come to the fullness of being Apostolic. My husband preaches a sermon called *Carrying Cripples Until the Miracle Comes.* We loved and carried Candy until she came to the place where she decided she was ready. One day, she just made that decision: "I am saying yes to everything God wants of me." She never looked back. Marvin became one of our church trustees for many years until they retired and moved to Florida.

Marvin worked with a man, Jim Turner. Marvin arranged for Wayne to teach a Bible Study with Jim and his wife, Frances. One Bible study leads to another.

Jim and Frances were upright members of another denomination. Jim taught Sunday school, and they lived for Jesus to the best of their knowledge. When they heard the Truth, they received it with gladness. Both received the Holy Ghost the same night, standing side by side at the altar. They were both baptized.

Our little church building was overflowing. It would only seat about 165 on the hard wooden pews, and we were consistently running 250. We had forty members in our choir who had reserved permanent seating at the front, on one side of the pulpit, permanent, that is, until altar service time, when they each picked up their folding chair and moved and stood it against the wall to make some space at the front to pray.

Early church choir

Folding chairs were placed at the end of each pew and in front of the front row, all the way to the pulpit. My husband could reach out and touch those sitting

in those chairs. At the end of the service, these people also had to "pick up their chair and walk" to make room for people to come to the altar and pray.

My husband was getting so discouraged because it seemed we could not find a larger place to worship. We needed a bigger church. We had grown as far as we could.

One time, right before a church service, my husband observed from his little office window, which looked out over the parking lot, cars that would pull into the lot, drive out, and drive away because they couldn't find a parking place.

Packed parking lot

The two dumpy little house units next door to the church were for sale. He went and inquired about them. They wanted $50,000 for them, which were sitting on less than an acre of land. He was so discouraged. This was the only time, before or after, that he felt like leaving Raleigh. He thought maybe God was finished with him because his hands were tied. We needed a miracle.

On Sundays, we began holding services at Christy's school (Garner Elementary School Auditorium). It would seat a whole lot more than our church building. We moved our sound system and our organ every Sunday. We had a revival in that place.

The Tom Phillips clan came during that time. One Sunday night, his family (about ten of them) was lined up across the front, and several of them received the Holy Ghost. Tom and Minnie Phillips have been faithful members ever since.

We would have youth classes in a motel room close to the church. The beds and furniture would have to be moved, and chairs would have to be set up. We were doing what we could to expand.

Our pastor, Brother Wayne McClain, came and preached during this time. After one particular service, Brother McClain said, "I feel that in the near future, this church is going to need $50,000, and Apostolic Temple is going to give the first $1,000. My husband jumped up and said, "I claim five acres of land for this."

Our church began to raise money with great enthusiasm. Children were giving their birthday dollars; people were giving their tax refunds. If they found money on the ground, they would give it. We all pledged that if any unexpected cash came in from anywhere, it would be put into the building fund. It is astounding how much money came in and all the places it came from.

One Sunday night, after an exciting service in our 'packed out' little building, my husband got all excited, as he was wont to do on many occasions. He jumped up and began to exclaim and project, "Church, we are going to have a big, major barbecue chicken dinner sale. We are going to sell one thousand tickets. We can deliver plate lunches to businesses at lunchtime and have folks come to the church to eat. We can make several thousand dollars in just one day."

On the way home that night, he anxiously exclaimed, "Patsy, how in the world are we going to do this?" Well, we *did* it. I organized it, and we sold about a thousand plates. We delivered many, and a large number came to the church to eat. That day, we made several thousand dollars, just as he had proclaimed.

My husband has always been a dreamer! He dreams it (big), and others make that dream a reality. We all have our place. I am not so much a dreamer, but I am an organizer. We work well together. Isn't God amazing in how He knows just how and who to put together? That's why it's so important to pray for God to put you in the right place and at the right time to meet Mr. or Mrs. *Right.*

It wasn't long before the rainbow on the back wall of our little auditorium, depicting our progress, was all filled in because we had raised $50,000!

Wayne had gone to preach for Brother Tommy Craft in Jackson, Mississippi. After church, Brother Darrell Johns, who was working in Brother Craft's church at the time and who was also hosting my husband, asked him, "Would you like to meet Sister Frazier?"

"Sure."

Wayne had heard of Sister Frazier, a blind woman in Brother Craft's church, who was known for her tremendous prayer life, her walk with God, and the times she had a "Word from God" for many individuals.

They found Sister Frazier. Brother Johns walked up to her and said, "Sister Frazier, this is Brother Huntley."

She grabbed Wayne's hand and started shaking, reeling, and rocking around, speaking in tongues, and said, "You have had a long-time prayer that you have been praying, and you have been discouraged and don't know why God has not answered. Thus sayeth the Lord, in a few days, you will get your answer."

Wayne came home, and three days later, he got a telephone call.

Brother Stoney Chance was a land planner, and someone was developing acreage on Lake Wheeler Road into residential lots. Brother Chance asked the developer/owner, "If I can get the number of houses you want on this piece of land and have five acres left on the front along Lake Wheeler Road, will you sell those five acres to the church?"

The developer said, "Yes." I don't think he thought Brother Chance could actually do it. But he did!

That day, when my husband answered the phone, Brother Chance was on the other end of the line.

"Would you like to purchase some land on Lake Wheeler Road, just 3.6 miles from downtown Raleigh and the steps of the State Capitol Building?"

"Yes, yes, yes! How many acres?"

"How many did you want?"

"Five."

"That's how many there are, five!"

"How much money?"

"What did you want to pay?"

"Fifty thousand dollars."

"That's how much it is, fifty thousand dollars."

Praise the Lord. That is how my God works! Years later, my husband kicked himself over and over again when we became landlocked on those measly five acres. He said, "Why didn't I ask for twenty or thirty acres? That would have been just as easy for the Lord." But of course, five was a stretch beyond anything we could imagine at that time!

We kept raising money, purchased the land, and went to work clearing it. Meanwhile, we began trying to get a loan from Central Carolina Bank. They gave us the runaround for several months. We kept raising money and kept working.

On Mother's Day, 1984, all our church people left 105 Yeargan Loop Road after Sunday service and drove to 2312 Lake Wheeler Road for a "groundbreaking" service.

Ground-breaking service for the new church on Lake Wheeler Road

Brother Turner and some of the men had marked off the exact place where the foundation would be placed, and our people made a huge circle or square around the perimeter. We all joined hands and prayed, and Pastor Huntley turned over the first shovel of dirt. *We were on our way!*

The Turners had been wanting a baby, to no avail. But God had a plan. Jim Turner was an architect, and we needed one. Remember, the "coin is in the fish's mouth." So, Brother Turner drew plans at *no charge* to the church. It was at least $50,000 worth of work!

Brother and Sister Turner had also been trying to adopt an infant, but this, too, seemed to be an impossibility. There were some stipulations that a parent could not be but a certain number of years older than the child to be adopted. They could easily adopt an older child, but not a baby.

But God! As we began the process of building the church, after he had donated his architectural services, God intervened, and they were able to adopt an infant boy. They named him Christopher.

They had only had him about one week when Frances discovered that she was, astonishingly, expecting. Nine months later, Joel came bounding into their world. So, they had two boys who were under one year old. Irish twins.

About three years later, Frances got sick and thought she had a tumor, but she didn't. She was expecting their third child, a girl, Courtney, who was born into their happy family.

Our good Lord will not be indebted to anyone. He pays outstanding dividends, above and beyond what any of us can deserve. They wanted a *baby*; God gave them a *family*, a quiver full of children.

Brother Huntley visited the bank many times, and one day, finally, we were approved. The bank officials told us that they were so slow in giving us the loan because they could not believe how much money our church was generating per person. They said they had never seen it like this and just couldn't believe it. The banker said, "Congratulations on acquiring this loan. When do you want to start?"

"They are pouring the foundation right now as we speak!"

The banker was undoubtedly taken aback. "What would you have done if you had not gotten this loan?"

"We would have made it somehow. God would have provided. We would have just paid as we went."

There has never been a more exciting time in the history of our church. Dennis Landtroop (my brother, M.C. Landtroop's son) and my husband worked so hard mixing mortar and hauling cinder blocks and bricks. Sometimes, when my sweet husband would come home at night, he could hardly straighten his fingers because he had carried so many heavy cinder blocks. He was not used to this hard manual labor. But, you know, everybody was working hard, and everyone just did what had to be done to get the job done.

Charles and Diane Duncan started coming to the church on Loop Road, and they had been doing so for several years. He was a big part of the men of the church who came after work many evenings and worked on the building. In fact, he was working on a scaffold about twenty feet up in the air, on the platform area, when he fell. He landed just about on the spot where the pulpit was going to be located. All the men gathered around and prayed, and he suffered no injuries. Praise the good Lord! We did not need for him to be badly hurt or possibly die on the very spot where life would be extended to the lost. During this time of working, the Duncans received the Holy Ghost. They have been faithful members ever since.

Mother's Day 1984

Something a bit funny happened one day. I came and looked around, as I was wont to do on just about a daily basis. By this time, the side walls were in place, and the brick mason was putting in a weight-bearing wall in part of the building at the front. Naturally, I am a curious person. I had been studying the plans in great detail. I understood the plans, or at least I *thought* I did. So, in my most polite voice, I asked the mason (whose name has been omitted to protect the guilty), "Isn't this wall you have started building going across a hallway?" He had it built about four feet high by this time.

He said, "I am the brick mason; why don't you go on about your business of being the pastor's wife?"

I didn't say anything else; I just went and found Brother Jim Turner, the architect, and told him what I thought. He looked at the plans and said, "You are exactly right." I'm sorry, but it did give me probably a little too much pleasure when Jim went and told him he had to tear out that wall and move it out of the hallway.

Christy was thirteen or fourteen years old during the construction, so she also spent a lot of time there. She actually learned to drive the little Toyota Corolla in the parking lot. She could jerk the car around all she needed to as she learned to shift gears. She is glad she learned to drive in that little car, as it comes in handy once in a while, knowing how to drive a stick shift.

In the summer of 1985, Dedie Beckham (Cooley, now) came and spent the summer between school years at Jackson College of Ministries, helping us with music and teaching Christy piano. Before Dedie, Christy had sort of played the piano like me, as I had taught her chords, but now she was so much better and, indeed, through the years, has become a very accomplished pianist—my favorite, of course! Many thanks to Dedie for sowing seeds into her life at a pivotal time and encouraging her to go forward in God's plan for her life.

The move-in was that same summer, 1985. We had our dedication in September, and Dedie was so kind as to make the trip back to Raleigh from Jackson College of Ministries to help with the music for the much-anticipated dedication of our new church facility. Our theme was "Preserving the Original Flames of Pentecost." We had three nights of exciting services: "Celebration, Appreciation, and Dedication."

Invitation to our dedication services, 1985

The top of the building of the The First United Pentecostal Church

After we moved in, my husband said he wanted the church to have a time of "reprieve" from raising money. Everyone had worked so hard, and we had raised around $250,000. We had also borrowed $250,000. So, we didn't have any money-raising programs for a couple of years. However, in 1989, after just under four years in our building, we proclaimed "The Year of the Miracle" and worked to pay off our mortgage. That was a happy day.

It took about sixteen months to complete our lovely 26,000-square-foot church. Later, we would complete 15,000 square feet of upstairs Sunday school and office space, and then, around 1996–1997, we finished our JIM Building, which served as our gym.

When we moved to Raleigh in 1978, Interstate 40 was not completed. When we went to Fayetteville, we had to drive the back roads to get to Interstate 95 and then on to Fayetteville, Lumberton, or those cities in the area to the south. Leaving our house on 401 King Arthur Trail, we would turn left on Raynor Road and make another left onto White Oak Road, which led to North Carolina State Highway 50.

On White Oak Road was a beautiful home. Coach house brown, cedar siding, sitting on 3.25 acres, built in (guess when?) 1978, the year we moved to Raleigh. This house literally jumped out at me every time we passed by. I would exclaim and proclaim, "I love that house!" I never, in my wildest imagination, ever entertained the thought that I would ever live there. It was above and beyond *our pay scale!* But you know, God is at work *for us* when we have *no clue.* (*"desires of our heart, request of our lips."*) I am always reading and quoting important words from an important Book!

I had seen a "for sale" sign in front of the house. One day, as we drove by, we saw people there. We decided to pull in and see if we could look. And, of course, "I loved the house." It was the owner's father showing the house. He told us that the asking price was $250,000, but they had lowered it to $225,000. Again, it was way beyond anything we could afford.

One day, the Godairs were visiting us in Raleigh, and I took my friend, Mickey Godair, to *"see this house that I loved."*

We drove down the long driveway, turned into the backyard, got out of the car, and started walking across the lawn to look in the windows. As we walked across the yard, I began to cry, and I said, "Sister Godair, *I feel like I have come home!"*

We stepped inside the screened-in back porch, and Sister Godair said, "Patsy, let's just pray about this." And so she said, "God, you know if this is Patsy's house or not. If it is, and it's Your will, just work everything out so she gets it."

So, I kept hounding my husband to go and talk to the owner, because by this time, it was no longer being sold by the real estate people, but was for sale by the owner. He kept saying we couldn't afford it and anything else he could to discourage me. But one day, he came home and said, "Get in the car."

"Where are we going?"

"It doesn't matter; just get in the car; we are going somewhere."

We got in the car and ended up at the owner's place of business in Cary, North Carolina. My husband thought he was just going to shut me up and get me off his back.

We went in and had a long talk, telling him how much we loved the house and would love to buy it, but we didn't have much money. It's not exactly the usual way to tell a person you want to buy their house! At the end of the interview, the man said, "Can you get a loan?"

We said, "Yes."

He said, "It's costing me quite a bit of money each month for insurance because the house is empty. When can you move in?"

"Now!"

So, we moved in and lived there for several months rent-free while we procured our mortgage loan.

Frances Wilder, Central Carolina Bank's branch manager, told us, "You should have an income three times as much as you have in order to afford this house, but I see a way around it; we're going to get you this loan." And she did!

We were so excited about this beautiful 3,000-square-foot house that God gave us for just $170,000, which was the price when we actually bought it.

We moved from one home that was just over 1,000 square feet to one that was 3,000 square feet. After a while, the *inside* of the house felt like *home, but the outside was always* overwhelmingly lovely to us, and we just felt like there was no way that this home should be *ours!* We would often comment to each other as we drove up the long driveway, "Someday, the owner of this house is gonna come back, retrieve this home, and throw us out!"

We moved in December 1986. January 1987 was our first real heartache.

Dennis Landtroop, our son, by adoption (not by reality, but by heart), was leaving Raleigh to begin evangelizing and to get married. He had come to us, lived with us for some time, and been his Uncle Wayne's shadow for seven years. So much so that once, late at night, we received a phone call from an unknown woman. We had already retired for the evening, and my husband answered the phone. I heard him say, "Just a moment," and he handed me the phone. He said, "It's for you."

"Who is it?"

"I don't know. She just asked for you."

I took the phone and said, "Hello."

"Hello, you don't know me, but I am calling to tell you that I am having an affair with your husband."

"What? You are a liar."

I probably shouldn't have said it just like that, but it made me angry. I *knew* better.

I said, "You are a liar because, if you are, you are also having an affair with my nephew, Dennis Landtroop, because he goes every single place that my husband goes and follows him day and night. So, if you are having an affair with my husband, they are both in on it, and your affair is with both of them!" It was just a prank caller who probably didn't know us at all.

Dennis taught many home Bible studies. At the time of this writing, some of those very people continue to be a part of the Temple of Pentecost.

Wayne had a radio broadcast, and when he had to be away, Dennis could fill in for him, but nobody was ever the wiser.

I remember his last evening in Raleigh so well. Uncle Wayne had already gone to bed, and Dennis and I were still up. I was very nostalgic, and yes, just

Dennis and Christine Landtroop

sad to see him go. He was the son I never had. Although I was not old enough to be his mother, he always seemed younger than he was. He was like a son and remains so to this day. He and his precious wife, Christine Fritzenschaft Landtroop, are genuinely like our own children.

At the beginning of the year, in January 1987, my husband had a "come-to-Jesus" meeting with our church family. He said that every Easter, half the church stays, while the other half goes to see Mama or some other relative. The following year, the other half stays home, while the other half leaves and goes off to visit. I am asking each of you, dear church people, to make this year the year we all stay home and have all our

relatives come to visit us. If we all pull together this year and work together, we can have a thousand people.

We all did it. I don't know of one saint who left for Easter weekend that year. We had 1,012 and were beside ourselves with excitement.

Our choir singing on "Round-up Sunday"

Our second greatest heartache came in September 1990. Christy had just graduated from the Durham church's ACE Christian school the previous year, in 1989. She was able to graduate one year early and wanted to attend Jackson College of Ministries. I didn't want her to leave home until the regular time that she was supposed to graduate from high school, so she enrolled in a one-year business course at our local Wake Technical College. They offered a one-year business course that resulted in a degree. We didn't realize it, but it was actually a one-year course, which is twelve months. She graduated on a Sunday afternoon with that business course and left the next day for Jackson, Mississippi, and Jackson College of Ministries.

All her "stuff" was loaded into her car: a little 1985 four-cylinder, stick-shift, silver-grey Ford Mustang. We had gotten it for her sixteenth birthday. She always said, "One of these days, this little Mustang is gonna grow up."

My husband had always told me, "If anything ever happens to me, be sure that Christy gets that Mustang." But he decided that we weren't going to wait for anything. We wanted to buy it so we could enjoy giving it to her, *both of us!* So, twenty-four years later, in 2012, we had a 2010 blue Mustang convertible waiting for her on her fortieth birthday. Her little Mustang had indeed grown up!

But that morning, in the fall of 1990, the last thing to be brought down was an armload of her hanging clothes. On the way down the stairs, the scent of her perfume wafted up into her Daddy's face from her clothes. Suddenly, he began to cry. Christy was leaving. Hopefully, not for good, we prayed.

We left the house and stopped just up the road to fill up on gasoline. As my husband handed the clerk the payment, tears streamed down his cheeks.

We cried about half the way to Jackson, eight hundred miles from the house. Coming home from there and leaving my baby was so very hard. Every mile, the weight on my chest got heavier and heavier. It felt like a literal weight pressing on me.

Bible college was so good for Christy. She flourished, and her singing and piano playing went to a whole new level. She was part of the Lanny Wolfe Trio and traveled to the Philippines, as well as to many places in the United States.

Christy Renee Huntley Becomes Mrs. Bryan Starr Ballestero

It was the best of days; it was the worst of days! It was December 4, 1992. Christy and I had been hurrying and scurrying all over town for six months. There had been this to choose, that to pick out, and the other to discard. We had chosen red, green, hot pink, and purple satin with black velvet. Sister Joyce McClain and the extraordinary ladies from Apostolic Temple had been working on making beautiful corsages, boutonnieres, bouquets, and table centerpieces, but most importantly, Christy's bridal bouquet.

It was December, so, of course, there were Christmas decorations. The table centerpieces were sleighs filled with Christmas balls. The platform had two giant wreaths on either side of the baptistry, numerous evergreen trees decked with twinkling lights, and quilt-batting snow on the floor. It was breathtakingly gorgeous.

Beautiful Christy came down the aisle on her daddy's arm, stopped at the front, and then proceeded with Bryan to the platform. Both sets of parents followed them and stood beside them on either side as they repeated those most sacred vows that bind two lives together. Forever.

Christy and Bryan Ballestero with Brother and Sister Huntley and both sets of grandparents

Wayne and I reached the milestone of twenty-five years of marital "bliss" in 1994. Brother Bobby and Sister Elaine Edwards were also married in the same year as Wayne and me in 1969, so we got together and decided to take a trip to Israel to celebrate.

Brother Ron Wall and Brother Charlie Mahaney were our tour guides. This was when we really got to know Brother Mahaney and his lovely wife, Nita. We would become close over the years, and our lives would surely mingle with theirs. Charlie would preach for us on numerous occasions in Raleigh.

Going to the Holy Land was a life-changing experience. We were riding on the tour bus, entering the city of Jerusalem for the first time, well after dark, one night. The Israeli tour guide set the mood by playing a song over the intercom: a boys' choir singing, their high tones uniquely touching my heartstrings.

Jerusalem, my happy home,
When shall I come to thee?
When shall my sorrows have an end?
Your joys, when shall I see?

*Jerusalem, Jerusalem,
God grant that I may see
Your endless joy and the same
Partaker ever be!*

Joseph Bromehead, 1795

  I was absolutely not prepared for the myriad of emotions that would overwhelm me as tears poured down my cheeks. I truly felt like I was coming home to a place I had never seen and had never felt an affinity to until this very moment. I thought, "This is my homeland. I am not a Jew, but I am a spiritual Jew. I have been added to this family as a child of God and also as the Bride of Christ, and this is Jesus' homeland. Therefore, in a sense, it's mine, too."

  On a particular day, we were to go to the upper room to hold a service, if you will, to re-enact the day of Pentecost. When we got there, for some reason, the door was padlocked, and we couldn't get in. We tried another door on the back side, but to no avail. We decided to go to the front and try again. Someone just pulled on the padlock, and voila, it opened, and in we went. We just knew that we were supposed to have that service. My husband had been asked to preach that day. The room had open windows and a little staircase that ran up the wall to a small balcony overlooking the room where he stood to preach. While we stood in the small room, with no chairs, and sang some songs, we all noticed that there were doves perched on those open window sills, cooing and fluttering around. But, when my husband began to preach (you guessed it, Acts the second chapter), and when he got to the part where the Holy Ghose fell, those doves flew right into the room, up to that little crow's nest, and flew around my husband's head a couple of times and then just flew out the window. It seemed to be a sign and a witness that we really didn't need, but it was exciting. Although I know the Holy Ghost is *not a dove,* it is likened to a dove in the Bible.

I'd like to share a story with you at this time. Once, we were preaching for Brother and Sister Doyle Spears in Jayess, Mississippi. (Yes, the same one who preached at the youth camp when Wayne received the Holy Ghost at the age of thirteen.)

This little country church was located on a crossroads corner. On one corner stood the church building; diagonally across from it was the parsonage. Straight across from the church was a little cemetery belonging to the church. After a Sunday morning service, while walking to the parsonage, I strolled through the graveyard, reading names on tombstones, as is my custom. For some reason, I love doing that. I was standing there, and a shiver ran over me, and I thought. "These are the saints of this church through the years. They are buried here together, waiting for the second coming of the Lord. And, as they worshipped together in life, when Jesus comes, they will rise *together in the rapture* to meet the Lord in the air."

As I write this, I again get chills, thinking about that glorious day, just as I did *that* morning, standing in that little cemetery. I wanted this for our saints in Raleigh.

So, in 1995, when I got home, I started looking. It just so happened that Montlawn Memorial Park in Raleigh was getting ready to expand and open up some new areas for burials. I went in and spoke with them, and they offered us some tremendous introductory prices on burial plots. We got them for $400 each. We sold over one hundred plots. We now have our church cemetery within the cemetery. Now, we saints will also be able to rise "together" to meet Him in the clouds, and so shall we ever be with the Lord!

When my Mother passed away in 2004, Lenda and I, and Steven and Lisa Davidson were by her side. She brought my sister and me *into the world*, and we were able to hand her over to the angel of the Lord to *escort her out* and into the loving arms of our dear Savior, who loves her more than we. She wanted to be buried with the church saints. North Carolina was now home; she was transplanted from Texas and was planted in this North Carolina sod to await the rapture when the *"dead in Christ shall rise first."*

Now, when *my* time comes, I will be laid to rest right beside her. I, too, have become a transplanted native. I told everyone that I was born in Texas, but I got to North Carolina just as soon as I could.

One day, I was riding down the road and listening to a recording of the Bible. He began to read 1 Kings 13:31, and I began to cry. I know I took the verse out of context, but it said exactly what I wanted to say on my tombstone.

"...When I am dead, then bury me...wherein the man of God is buried; lay my bones beside his bones:"
(1 Kings 13:31)

It is now engraved on a beautiful, four-foot, red marble bench in Montlawn Cemetery, Raleigh, North Carolina, right next to the plot where I will be laid to rest. I will be buried right next to *my* man of God, the most important man and person in my life, Wayne Huntley. Our bones will be laid to rest in death as we have always been in life, side by side, to await the rapture; that is, unless we are still alive, and if so, we will be caught up together to meet Him in the air!

I thought about what to use for Wayne's epitaph and for it to be chiseled on that beautiful red marble bench. The most important significance of his life is the call of God to preach the Gospel and his anointed ministry. So, I felt some selected verses in Luke, chapter 4, summed it up just right.

"The Spirit of the Lord is upon me, Because he hath anointed me to preach the gospel...for his word was with power."
(Luke 4:18, 32)

On the other side of the bench, facing the road for all to see, is the Gospel message of Acts 2:38, telling the world even after we are gone on to our reward.

"Then Peter said unto them, Repent, and be baptized every one of you in the name of Jesus Christ for the remission of sins, and ye shall receive the gift of the Holy Ghost."

(Acts 2:38)

Wayne and Patsy's grave marker

God has undoubtedly helped him to do and be that. We thank God for the many, many people who have said that one of his messages has been their *nail in a sure place:* their *Rhema* (which is an exact word for a precise time)*: is the* *direction that changed their lives, saved their spiritual walk, or gave them encouragement and direction for their ministry or church.* He is definitely *my* favorite preacher, and many, many, many have said that very thing to us personally and publicly when they were introducing him to preach or when they have come to preach for the Temple of Pentecost! This is not something either of us takes for granted, and we know this special anointing is not a *given*. I pray fervently and often that God would help us imperfect, fleshly human beings that we are, never to do or say or be anything that would cause the Spirit of God to be grieved or the anointing to be lifted from his ministry. It is truly divine and a God thing that can be taken away at any time if we do not hold it in high esteem and treasure it.

There was a time when it seemed that very thing had indeed happened, and I guess that's another reason we are so careful with this highly revered gift.

For some time, my husband had not felt the anointing like he was accustomed to. When he preached, it just seemed to go out a couple of feet and fall flat. He had no flow of the Spirit, no overshadowing of the Holy Ghost as he ministered. He was getting very, very unnerved by this and was afraid that the anointing had left him for good. No matter how much he prayed and fasted, the heavens seemed like brass, and he couldn't get an answer from God on this matter.

We were scheduled to preach at the Michigan Camp Meeting, and he told me, "I feel like calling them and telling them that I cannot come. I don't feel like I have a message, nor can I deliver one; I just feel so empty and have nothing to offer."

This was Saturday night, and on Monday, we were to begin that camp. At the prayer meeting that night, I earnestly prayed for him. I said, "Lord, this is something I cannot help him with except to pray. I don't know what to do or what to say to encourage him. I only know one person who can help him. Please,

please, help our pastor, Brother Wayne McClain, to call him and give him a word of encouragement."

The next evening, right before Sunday night service, the church telephone rang.

"Hello, this is Brother Huntley."

"This is Brother McClain. How are you doing, Brother Huntley?"

"I'm fine, Brother McClain; how are you?"

"You are fine, are you?"

"Well, you are doing the talking, so you tell me."

"Ok. You have been going through something. You cannot feel the anointing like usual. You feel empty and can't seem to get a hold of the Lord. It is an attack of the enemy, so don't worry. Your anointing is coming back, and it's going to be greater than ever. God is going to use you in greater dimensions than you have seen."

Brother Huntley and Brother McClain

When he hung up the phone, I said, "That was Brother McClain, right?"

Wayne said, "Yes. Did you call him and tell him to call me?"

"No, I didn't call him. I prayed to God, and God spoke to him, and he called you!"

On Monday, we went to Michigan camp. The first night my husband was preaching, nothing happened; he had the same problem. He couldn't feel anything; he felt empty. He felt no anointing until about halfway through the message. I saw it when the anointing dumped on him. Oh, happy day! He looked at me, as he often does while he is preaching, and gave me the thumbs up. Praise the Lord. God had answered our prayers. Oh yes, our God is a present help!

Speaking of him watching me while he is preaching. Many people have commented about this over the years. I think he accrued this *habit* while we were evangelizing. He told me he knew there was at least one friendly face of someone who was always on HIS side in the audience. So, he watched me as sort of his *preaching barometer*. I began to be able to *help* him as he was preaching; for instance, if his tie was crooked, his pocket was hanging out from when he removed his hanky, or anything else I needed to tell him. I have always had a *one-track mind*. I can usually do one thing pretty well, but don't ask me to do two things at once! For him, it seems, he has sixteen tracks. He is a nosy person, I say. He says he is just interested. When we are in a restaurant, he knows every conversation between all the people seated around us.

Once, my husband was having a meeting and a meal with our then General Superintendent of the UPCI, Brother Kenneth Haney. During the conversation about revival and outreach, of which Brother Haney was committed and quite the advocate, my husband just mentioned that the motto of the UPCI was:

*"The whole Gospel,
to the whole world,"*

But he would like to see it changed to include one more line:

*"The whole Gospel,
to the whole world,
by the whole church!"*

Brother Haney got very excited about it and said he liked that idea. Eventually, it was done, and that is now our motto!

From 1996 to 1997, we built our gym. We wanted to have an original name. (My husband and I are always mavericks when it comes to things like this. Everybody calls their gyms 'the Life Center' or something uninteresting like that. Hahaha!) We decided to open it up for suggestions. Sister Janice Schreck had the winning suggestion. We had gone with her to the service where she was *excommunicated* from the Church of Christ when she first became a tongue talker and was baptized in the name of Jesus. That was quite an experience!

But she said that Brother Jim Turner had donated his time and much money to the construction of both our auditorium and the gym. Therefore, her suggestion was to call it the JIM Building, which would be an acronym for "Jesus In Ministries Building." We liked it, so that's what it became. It's different and very fitting and honors a very deserving man who has been such an intricate part of our church through the years!

Grandbuddy and Gramommy-1997

The years 1995–1997 were undoubtedly the most trying and difficult times of our lives, for reasons that I will not go into on this written page. It's over and done with, and God is the judge of everything we are and have ever done and all that we have been. We just want our God to be happy with us and the way we have led our lives. We have sincerely tried to be Christians in everything. He alone knows our hearts. But he does! I would be remiss if I did not mention our precious, supporting friends, Mark and Karla Christian, for being our shoulder to cry on, our ear to listen to, and our encouragement during these days. We are forever indebted and grateful for their friendship then, which continues to this day!

God knew this would be a difficult time in our lives, so he prepared something so special that it would completely cover up and eradicate any feelings except utter joy!

August 19, 1997, began very early in the morning, well before daylight. We got a call from our daughter and son-in-love that they were on the way to Rex Hospital in Raleigh. Our precious first grandchild was about to be born. We didn't know if it was a boy or a girl. The proud parents wanted it to be a surprise for them and the rest of us as well.

We arrived at the birthing center and went to the waiting room to 'wait.' Dr. Stewart Carr, a personal friend and part of the Temple of Pentecost, was the attending physician.

When the time drew near, Wayne and I were in the delivery room. He was behind the curtain at the door, and I was at the head of the bed, with Daddy Bryan on the other side. There is very little excitement that can compare with witnessing the birth of your grandchildren, especially the first one!

When the baby came into the world, he was perfect: the most beautiful baby you've ever seen. *"No brag, just facts!"* We were so excited that the first human hand to touch our baby boy was a Holy Ghost-filled doctor.

When Dr. Stewart Carr handed our baby to Daddy Bryan, and Bryan held that precious bundle of sweetness in his own hands for the first time, he looked over at Wayne (Grandbuddy), who by now was standing next to me, and said, "Dad, his name is *Huntley*!" My husband did not know that they were going to name the baby *Huntley* if it was a boy, so he was taken totally off guard. Of course, he began to cry. Now, he would have someone to carry his name into the future.

To *top it all off* (pun intended), Huntley was born with red hair and hazel, blue-green eyes. We were all so shocked. I really don't know why we were so shocked. We were just not expecting that our baby would be privileged to be born with beautiful, dark auburn red hair. Everyone asked then, and still does, "Where does that red hair come from?" Well, neither side of the family can take credit alone for red hair. It is a recessive gene and must come from both sides. However, my second-oldest brother, Ken, had the same color of red as a youngster, so I will quickly take credit for the lovely color of auburn. Huntley has always projected the aura of his mother. Even as a child, when I would hug him, I felt like I was hugging her. It's still like that today.

We had no idea that God, along with the help of Bryan and Christy, would bring us four more grandchildren to love. We are forever grateful that God allowed Bryan and Christy to co-create "with" Him five precious grandchildren. And we thank God that they were also born healthy and perfect.

Twenty-two months after Huntley's birth on August 19, 1997, Christyana Content would join her big brother on June 17, 1999, in the Ballestero household and bring such joy that only a girl can produce. She, too, was born with beautiful auburn red hair. What a privilege to have two grandchildren with this gift. Her eyes, like her hair, are the color of copper. She has always had a prayer life and can fall into travail at a moment's notice. What in the world would we do if 'Ana' had not graced our lives?

We had to wait for a few years before Christian Bryan made his entrance into our world. The good Lord (along with the help of Mommy Christy and the good doctor) had to work out a few complications before we could have the blessing of more grandkids. But almost eight years later, on March 1, 2007, our blue-eyed, blonde baby boy came marching on the scene. Even though he was about three weeks early and his little body was thin, he let us know that he had arrived safely. He loves people and easily meets and makes friends. He has always been such a loving and sweet boy. He is most like his mother in terms of looks. He looks like his mother 'spit him out.'

Again, we had to wait for our next special boy to come. Almost four years passed, and then, guess what? February 17, 2011, along came our baby boy with black hair and dark chocolate chip brown eyes, Caison Judah. To me, he favors the Ballestero side of the family more than any of the other children. They all have something of both parents, but "Cai" seems to be, at this time of writing, the most like them. He is sensitive to the Spirit and knows how to pray and worship like an adult. He is an awesome Bible quizzer and, at one time, was listed as the number one quizzer in the nation for his age and category.

Caison's birth is the only one that I did not have the privilege to be present in the delivery room. This is a hurt in my heart that can't be healed and does not go away with time (so far). I loved being present at each of my grandchildren's entrances into the world. To hear them cry for the first time is truly amazing. I had been diagnosed with severe eye issues and was in Arizona, seeing a specialist. I was in the process of a procedure when he decided that he just could not wait any longer to join his family "in the world." Daddy Bryan was so kind to have his cell phone on speaker so I could hear him cry his first cry. I'm sure that Caison was the first and only baby born in that homeopathic ophthalmologist's office. (Even if it was only on the phone!) I was hoping Caison would wait for my return home, but alas, no!

Then, it was April 9, 2013. Genston Hebron Carl came roaring onto the scene. He has brown hair and another shade of brown eyes. He has long, thick eyelashes and is the man who is always in charge if you let him. He is a definite leader and always has an opinion (like Gramommy) and a plan of action. He is very loving and affectionate and is always sensitive to the feelings of others. He is always thankful and appreciative of anything that is done for him. He keeps us all jumping and laughing and is always a barrel of fun. How boring all our lives would be if God had not chosen to give us "Gent."

I must pause this writing to express my heartfelt thanks to my "best in the world" son-in-law. He had allowed me the privileged honor of being present in the delivery room when four of our five grandchildren were born. It would not really matter if my daughter wanted me to be involved in the delivery process if Bryan was not comfortable and okay with it. So, Bryan, thank you from the bottom of my heart for allowing me this great honor.

One common thread in all of our grandkids' entrances to life was the very first place on earth that they would visit … the church! The Temple of Pentecost! First of all, we wanted to thank God for their mother's health and their safe and healthy birth. We would lay them on the altar, signifying that they would always stay near the altar. Church would always be the center of their lives, and everything else would revolve around this fact. God, His house, His people, His ways, and His desires were always to come first. So, on their way home from the hospital, the church was their very first place to go.

As they grew older, Grandbuddy started a tradition with them that came to include many other children of the TOP during our Saturday night prayer meetings; as he prayed on the platform, they would come up to him, one by one, and he would pray over them. The prayer had many parts at different times, but the last line, especially, would always be included.

"Lord, help them to love You, Your ways,
and Your church all the days of their lives.
Don't let the spirits of this world get into their heart's desires.
May they always serve You, and You only, forever.
Don't ever let them pursue anything
or want to serve anyone but You.
Keep them in body, soul, mind, and spirit.
Protect them from predators of the body, mind, and spirit.
Give them gifts, talents, expertise, and abilities
that will 'horrify hell' and 'honor heaven.'
In Jesus' Name!"

We have lived long enough to see this, at least *in part,* come to pass. Our grands love and serve the Lord diligently and are very talented; for this, we praise our God.

Huntley posted something cute on some of his social media. He had been asked the question on several occasions, so he decided to answer socially.

"My name is 'Huntley'.
Yes, as in 'Wayne Huntley,' he is my Grandfather.
No, my name is not 'Huntley Huntley';
My name is Huntley Ballestero.
Christy Huntley Ballestero is my mother.
Bryan Ballestero is my father."

Huntley Starr graduated from Indiana Bible College in 2020. Yes, the year of COVID-19, so we weren't sure if there would be an actual graduation ceremony or not. It was canceled from the standard time of May/June and was held in the fall, but IBC pulled it off professionally. He was the guitarist for the school group "Praise" and traveled across the country, representing IBC. In his last year, he decided not to try out for or be involved in any of the music programs but to put his time and effort into his major, *Biblical Studies.* We were very proud of him for doing this.

The Bible (Bridal) colleges of the UPCI are indeed the perfect places to meet your spouse. Wayne and I met at Texas Bible College. Christy and Bryan met at Jackson College of Ministries. Christyana met Jordan Blake at Indiana Bible College, and Huntley also met Abigail Haworth at Indiana Bible College. What better place than a college where young people are preparing to use their lives for the Gospel?

When Christyana got ready to go to Indiana Bible College in 2018, I purchased her a very lovely, soft leather journal to be used for her college years. She had been journaling since she was a little girl, and I wanted her to have a special one for this important time in her life. On the inside cover, I wrote a message to her. These scriptures are written in my study Bible. The Lord first spoke these to my heart for our daughter, Christy. Now, I pronounce them over our grandchildren.

"And give unto ~~Solomon, my son,~~
(Christyana, my granddaughter),
a perfect heart, to keep thy commandments,
thy testimonies, and thy statutes..."

(1 Chronicles 29:19)

"This is our prayer for you, sweet Ana girl...there are many voices all around you, but we pray that you will have the strength and willpower to listen to the voice of God for YOUR life. No matter what anyone else does or says, you will pray and find the will of God for your own personal convictions. I don't know exactly what God requires of us, but His will is what matters. Pray...seek Him...listen to Him, and no matter what anyone else is doing, be strong enough to stand...alone if necessary...and do what He whispers in your heart!"

Christyana Content graduated in 2021 from IBC as Valedictorian. She worked very hard for this award, and we were so proud. She served as a member

Christyana, around three years old, playing the piano.

Christyana playing at her senior recital at Indiana Bible College.

of "Chosen," and in her senior year, she was in the group "Praise." She wrote the song "Worthy," which was recorded on the 2021 Live album as the title song. What an anointed composition. (*Gifts, talents, expertise, and abilities that horrify hell and honor heaven.*) She introduced her song on the recording, and it was so anointed. Afterward, one of the instructors (the name has been omitted to protect the guilty) said to us, "We won't tell the guys, but Christyana is the best preacher in the school this year!"

She met Jordan Blake, her love, and they were married with much fanfare on October 23, 2021.

One of my greatest privileges was when Christyana and Christy invited me to accompany them (along with Abigail Haworth and Cyrilla Landtroop) on the trip to the bridal shop to find that perfect dress. It was amazing that the very first dress she looked at was the one she purchased. That's precisely what her mother did about twenty-nine years earlier. She chose the first one she had looked at.

A month or so before her wedding day, I took out one of my keepsakes, an earthly prized possession, and brought it to Christyana.

As mentioned in Chapter 6: "Evangelist and Mrs. Wayne Huntley," my husband had purchased an Elgin watch for me for Christmas when Christy was only eight months old, so it was forty-nine years old. As traveling evangelists, we were not very set financially. We lived from week to week, depending on the place where we happened to be ministering that week. But he was so sweet and wanted me to have a nice, pretty watch. So, to Zales Jewelers in Waco, Texas, we went and came out with a beauty. We purchased it on "time," and time is what it took to get it paid for. Seven dollars a month. After adding the interest, we have no idea how much we actually spent or how many months it took for the watch to finally be mine. Too much, I'm sure!

When you get older and have grandchildren, something happens to your heart. There are things you hold dear and things that, even though they may not be expensive, are worth a lot to you. So, you begin to give those things away to the people you want to keep your keepsakes after you are gone. You hope they will take them out once in a while and look at them, remembering you with warmth, fondness, and love.

I brought *my watch* (that was still keeping time when I could remember to wind it), which was beautiful, petite, and elegant, and said to her, "The old saying about brides is, '*Something old, something new, something borrowed, something blue.*' Well, I would like for you to wear this watch on your wedding day, as the 'something old,' because this watch is forty-nine years old, and it was your Gramommy's. I'm giving it to you, whether or

not you wear it at your wedding, but it would make me so happy if you would do so."

Thankfully, she loved the watch and did wear it on her wedding day, October 23, 2021. It made her Gramommy's heart so very happy.

So now, it is important not only to me but also to her. Should the Lord tarry, and now that God has blessed her with her very own daughter, Clara Content Blake, maybe one day, she will pass it on to her on her wedding day.

The day Ana married was another one of those days (and we have had many during our lifetime) on which we had mixed feelings–sad and happy at the same time. We are not quite sure how this happens, but it does indeed!

We were happy because she met and married a wonderful man with an incredible family, but sad because her sweet face would not be in our world on a

210

Gentson, Christian, Christyana, Huntley, and Caison

daily basis. But off she went, marching boldly into the will of God for the rest of her life. For this, we *must* be happy!

Huntley and Abigail dated for several years before tying the knot on their personal "Balle-story" on October 14, 2022, one year after Christyana and Jordan married.

It was the most beautiful setting for a wedding that I have personally been a part of. The venue was located in Ocala, Florida, at Protea Weddings and Events. It's an actual working horse farm, accessible by driving down a long, winding road lined on both sides with beautiful, old oak trees whose branches intermingle overhead, with Spanish moss dripping from their branches.

The actual spot of their vow exchange was in a grassy field beneath a 150–200-year-old tree. It had a huge branch that extended horizontally over their

Huntley and Abigail's wedding

heads. The tree was absolutely gorgeous, but not any more stunning than the sweet couple standing beneath it.

Huntley, like his mother decades ago when she brought us Bryan, brought us a jewel when he added Abigail to our family and our church. She is very talented and fits in so well with all of us.

If being grandparents has taught us anything at all, it's that *love flows down*. It's like a river. You don't really realize it until your children become parents, and one day you wake up and realize that you have dropped significantly in importance. When children are little and young, you are everything to them.

Lots of little children declare to their parents, "I'm not ever going to get married. I want to live with you forever." Of course, that all changes when they become teens, and even before. They begin the process of leaving home.

What do I mean?

Ask yourself this question, and answer in your mind: Who do you love more, or who is higher on your priority list–your parents or your children? Of course, it's your children. That's not wrong! That's the way it's supposed to be.

It's another one of those life lessons that you cannot learn until you experience it. It's inevitable; it's just the way life is, and if you embrace it and accept it, life will be better for you.

You are always going to love your children more than they love you, and it's that way across the board. Parents always love their children more than children love their parents.

"Love Flows Down.
Remember, you love your kids,
More than you love your parents!"

If you understand this with both your heart and mind, you will save yourself a lot of heartache. As parents, we *want* to be involved with our kids. We birthed them, raised them, fed, clothed, and took care of them all their lives until they met, fell in love, got married, and started their own families. Then, we *must* give them the freedom to live their lives and raise their own families. We have been involved with them in everything they do, and all of a sudden, it's as if you know nothing about their day-to-day lives, which seems unfair. However, it is just the process of life.

Once, I got the app 360, which helps families to know where other family members are located at any given time. It's great for parents to be able to monitor and keep track of their minor children. My husband and I really like it. I sent my daughter an invitation to join our family group. It's not that we wanted to be nosy, but we genuinely are interested in their lives, and it seems that the longer time goes, the further we get from being involved in their lives on a day-to-day basis. Parents feel disconnected, displaced, and uninvolved. But it's back to the matter of "love flows down," or children want to have their own identity. There comes a time when they no longer want to just *be the kids*, but they feel they are now *the adults*. Parents feel *their children will always be their babies,* no matter how old they get. But we *have to let them go!* Anyway, I never heard anything from her about the "360" invite, and I never asked her about it because I knew that adult children do not always want their parents to know every move they make.

If I ever feel unloved or left out of their lives, I always run this little scenario in my mind. *How would "I" have felt if the roles were switched and this was "my mother and me" instead of "my child and me?"* I know that I didn't always want my mother to know everything about my life. It's that parent-child thing of pulling away or cutting the apron strings, wanting to be the "adult." I can't really explain it; it's just a feeling. When I do that, I would understand. We, as *parents,* don't really like it, but that's the facts as they exist! They are not *trying* to exclude you from their lives; they are just busy with their own. Don't let your feelings get hurt; don't retaliate. When they *do extend* invitations and plan things with you to be involved, don't pout and think, "*I thought you'd never ask."* No, be thankful and gracious, and take them up on the invitation! When they do have a minute and call or text you, don't say, "I thought you'd never call," or "It's *about time!"*

> *Don't be the kind of parent that makes*
> *your children dread to call or visit,*
> *because you are never satisfied with what time,*
> *and attention they give you.*

You know, and I know that I'm not saying that children shouldn't take care of aging parents. Wayne and I have personally demonstrated that adult children should see that their parents are taken care of in later life. My mother lived with us for a little while and then in our backyard, in her own little house, for twenty-five years.

Wayne's father passed away in 2000. God spared him repeatedly throughout his lifetime. Once, after several years in Raleigh, when our church had grown and Wayne's ministry had begun to flourish, he and his dad had an unusual heart-to-heart talk. His dad told him. "You know, I had it once (referring to the call of God and a ministry), but I lost it. It is evident that God gave it to you; His anointing is on your life, and you now have what I also should have had." During the time of his departure from this life, when he was actually near death, Wayne was able to have another heart-to-heart talk. With tears flowing, he told him that he forgave him for all the anger, fear, sadness, and heartache he had caused him during his childhood and teenage years. Not so much that his father had actually asked him to forgive him, but that Wayne needed to forgive him for his personal benefit.

After his death, Mama Frances also had her trailer moved to our backyard for the last ten years of her life so that Wayne and I could see that her needs were met. Most grown children have to do this, either sooner or later. Hopefully, (for parents and children alike), it will be later.

Chapter Eight

Senior Pastor and Mrs. Wayne Huntley

Temple of Pentecost
2312 Lake Wheeler Road,
Raleigh, North Carolina
2003–2015

In 2003, we held an election at the First United Pentecostal Church to elect Bryan and Christy Ballestero as co-pastors. In 1993, as newlyweds, Bryan and Christy became youth pastors. In 1998, they became assistant pastors. Now, in 2003, it was time for them to step up and become co-pastors with my husband. Brother Huntley would be the senior pastor, and Brother Ballestero would be the pastor. Bryan would remain pastor until January 2015.

It was always part of the plan that in January 2015, after my husband turned sixty-five in December 2014, Brother Ballestero, at age forty-six, would actually take over the pastorate, becoming senior pastor, and my husband would become bishop. My husband said that "bishop" was just another name for "old man," and as Dwayne Shubert coined the name for me, I would become "your bishopness."

So, in January 2015, this, indeed, happened as planned. Brother Ballestero had patiently and faithfully served Brother Huntley and the TOP. He never seemed to get antsy and nervous about getting his time. He had never promoted himself and had waited, having confidence that Brother Huntley would do as he had said. My husband is a man of his word, so when January 2015 rolled around, big plans to pass the torch went into action. (More about this in Chapter Nine: "Bishop Wayne Huntley, and Your Bishopness, Patsy Huntley.")

It seems that January is always the month of new beginnings and big-time happenings for the Huntleys and our church family.

We arrived in Raleigh, North Carolina, on January 8, 1978, and had our first service with fifteen people in attendance.

On January 8, 2005, Wayne Huntley suffered a heart attack that scared all of us terribly.

It was on a Saturday. We were having the funeral of J. C. Britt, the father of one of our long-time members, Brother Rudy Britt. After the funeral, the church family prepared a nice meal for the family and those involved. We were in the JIM Building, finishing our meal. My hubby was not feeling well, and at one time during the meal got very nauseated. Christy was sitting across from her daddy and saw the look on his face. She said, "Dad, what's wrong?"

He said, "Oh, nothing, just a little tired." (He always wanted to protect his little girl and not scare her.)

The burial was to be about an hour away from Raleigh. Bryan uncharacteristically told Wayne, "Dad, I'm gonna ride with you to the burial." He told us later that the Lord had nudged him to go with him. On the way, my husband started getting sick and weak and was flexing his left hand over and over. Bryan noticed this and kept watching him. After a while, Wayne told Bryan that he would have to drive because he felt himself losing consciousness. When they pulled over for Bryan to drive, Wayne had to hold on to the hood of the truck in order to get around to the passenger side.

Bryan said, "I'm going to take you to the hospital."

Of course, my husband said, "No, just take me home, and I'll be okay."

They called me to let me know because Wayne knew that I would realize something was really wrong with him for coming home and not going to the burial. Brother Rudy Britt, a licensed minister himself, actually had to do the committal at the cemetery because my husband did not make it.

I asked Wayne to call Dr. Stewart Carr, the doctor in our church, and tell him how he was feeling. Whatever he said Wayne should do, that's what he should do.

Brother Carr asked him a few questions and then said, "I do not want to scare you, pastor, but you have symptoms of a heart attack, and Brother Ballestero should drive you straight to the hospital emergency room."

My husband hardly remembers the thirty-minute drive to Rex Hospital in Raleigh. When they arrived, the hospital staff took him right in, hooked him up to an EKG, and immediately told him, "Sir, you are having a heart attack right now!"

To which my husband responded, "That's just what I needed to hear."

Christy was about to enter the emergency room cubicle where we were. He had one tear dripping down his cheek. His arms were immobilized, preventing him from bending them due to the numerous tubes and lines. He, always the strong "Daddy," and not wanting to scare his little girl by seeing him cry, said, "Patsy, wipe that tear away. I don't want Christy to see it!"

One of Raleigh's top heart doctors, Dr. Depak Passi, happened to be in the hospital at that moment. (We know God orchestrated it all.) They took him right in and performed a heart cauterization, discovering that he had one artery 98% blocked, one 80%, and another 70%. They were able to insert two stents into the one 98% blocked. He had to come back to the hospital three weeks later and have two more inserted. He was told to do nothing until the second stents were put in to keep from having another heart attack while we waited for his body to heal a little bit from this attack and the stents. They also discovered that he had previously had another mild heart attack. Looking back, there were a couple of times when he felt that he knew when that attack could have happened.

The hospital staff told us, "Whoever brought him to the hospital today probably saved his life." Thank you, Bryan Starr, for listening to the Lord that day when you *thought* you were going to drive him to a burial committal, but indeed, you gave us many more years with our loved one by driving Dad to the hospital emergency room.

This happened on Saturday, January 8, 2005. The next day, Sunday night, January 9, Wayne and I were sitting in the hospital room, and Wayne looked over at me and said, "Patsy, I'm scared."

Unbeknownst to us, as the church service was beginning that night at the TOP, one of our ushers approached Christy and handed her a piece of paper, saying, "Give this to your dad." She didn't have time to look at it at that moment, so she shoved the paper into her Bible, which was lying on the keyboard beside her. She forgot it till she came to the hospital after church.

As we were conversing, she said, "Oh yes, Dad. Brother Wilson told me to give you this paper."

She proceeded to open her Bible and get the paper. The paper reads Isaiah 41:10. The next thing is to find the scripture in the Bible and read it. To her amazement, her Bible was opened in the correct place. She had just randomly shoved the note into her Bible *in the exact spot of Isaiah 41:10!*

"Fear thou not; for I am with thee:
Be not dismayed; for I am thy God:
I will strengthen thee; yea, I will help thee;
yea, I will uphold thee with the right hand of my righteousness."

Neither she nor Brother Wilson knew what Wayne had said to me in the hospital, but Jesus *did*. What a consolation to know that Jesus was holding him in His hand and had told him to fear not. Just about twelve days before this heart event, the Lord gave Christy this song: "I'm Not Gonna Worry."

I'm Not Gonna Worry

"I'm not gonna worry, I give God the glory
I'm not gonna reason or doubt; try to figure it out,
Wonder what it's all about.
I'm not gonna question, Why?
I'll lift my hands and magnify.
I'm not gonna worry, no, I'll give all the glory to God."

I.
"There is only one God; He makes no mistakes.
He is always right on time; He is never late.
So, when worry comes around, I won't let it stay.
I throw my hands in the air and whisper a prayer
And this is what I say."

II.
"I know there are times life takes us by surprise.
When the pressure is great, And troubles arise
So, when worry tries to come, You don't let it stay
And be anxious for nothing, 'cause God's up to something,
The answer's on the way."

"I'm not going to contemplate; I'll trust in God. He's never late.
I'm not gonna worry, no, I'll give all the glory to God."

He was letting us know that HE had it all in control, and we were not to worry or fear. Remember:

> *"The 'man' of God is indestructible*
> *Until God is through with him."*

These days, we want to make sure he stays very usable to the Lord, so that God will indeed continue to use him and, therefore, keep him around.

That same year, in 2005, Brother Johnny Atkinson's mother passed away. He was one of our trustees and also one of the original voting families who voted us in as pastor in 1977. After her funeral, my husband and I were leaving their house, where we had greeted all the family. As we were getting into our car, we were talking about the fact that now Johnny and Linda Atkinson would be the sole caregivers of Johnny's brother, Donald, age fifty-one, who had been born with cerebral palsy, could not talk, walk, or feed himself, and was not supposed to have lived past around twenty years old. (He lived to the ripe old age of sixty-two!)

As we stepped into the car, something came over me, and I said, "I am going to pray; I believe Donald is going to receive the Holy Ghost!"

I'll never forget the day that it happened! Donald never spoke or could say words; he just always made that very distinguishable sort of hollering sound. But on that Sunday morning, when he was filled with the Holy Ghost, he was moving his mouth and tongue as if he were talking, and such a beautiful aura came over his countenance. That was a happy, happy day.

He loved attending church. He would wave his pillow around and around when the Spirit would get on him. Truly a miracle of God's great grace! He was baptized in the Atkinsons' big bathtub, and there were more in attendance at his baptism than were present at our first Sunday service in Raleigh back in 1978!

In 2008, we remodeled the exterior of our existing building. Our family had taken a trip to Lancaster County, Pennsylvania, to the *Sight & Sound Theatre* and enjoyed one of their Christian, biblical productions. My husband was so moved and impressed with their fabulous building that later on, we actually took a busload of our church family, which included Brother Jim Turner, our church architect, to look at and to be impressed with this building that spoke so strongly to my husband's spirit.

When we redesigned the exterior, we based it on the look of *Sight & Sound*. Of course, it is on a much smaller scale, but it is beautiful just the same. At this time, we changed the name of the church from *First United Pentecostal Church* to the *Temple of Pentecost,* which resulted in the acronym TOP.

This change was brought to our attention by Bryan, our pastor and son-in-law. (My husband was still senior pastor, and Bryan was pastor.) Yes, we had finally made it to the TOP as a church body!

Our family had been hunting in Tillery, North Carolina, in Halifax County, for about twelve years when, in 2012, we lost the lease on our little cabin and the place where we parked our individual trailers and motorhomes. We began searching for a place to buy near our hunting lease, if possible.

We discovered that an old, dilapidated double-wide trailer was sitting on a couple of acres right next to our lease. We looked at the aerial view and got so excited. It appeared to be exactly what we wanted. The next time we were in the country, we drove to the location. As we arrived at the property, we felt this heavy feeling. It wasn't the light and free feeling we needed to have. It was almost a sense of depression. After we left, both of us said, "No, that's just not it." The Holy Ghost has always led us in these situations. We both felt and knew that God was leading us away from this location.

Charles Tillery, the landowner of the hunting property, told us that he had a small, approximately twenty-acre farm located right on Gravel Pit Road that he wanted to sell to us. This was actually the same road, just a mile from the cabin we lost. We thought, "Yeah, right. No way we can afford that."

He took us, and we were amazed at the property. About five acres was a crop field. On the left were about five acres of trees, five acres of trees across the back, and five acres of trees and a swamp on the right side. There was also a creek running all around the property. We *both* knew immediately that *this was it!* He said the asking price was fifty thousand. We told him if the land would perk (good soil with adequate drainage), he should consider it sold.

We told Bryan and Christy, "If you don't like this, you'd better speak now or forever hold your peace. We are getting ready to spend your inheritance. The rest is history. In 2013, we purchased the land and moved in a modular log cabin home. It had been sitting in Rocky Mount on a sales lot as a model for five years and had not sold, so we got it for half price. The Lord had it and was just waiting for us to acquire the land to place it on.

The Huntley and Ballestero family

Wayne named our place "Non-Typical Family Farm." It's "non-typical" because we are non-typical people. There are typical deer and non-typical deer. The antlers of a typical deer are symmetrical. On non-typical deer, they aren't. There are typical hunting clubs, which usually consist of men drinking and cursing with no wives or children present. Then ours is a non-typical hunting club because we have our clean, wholesome men who bring their wives and children.

Our entire family on four-wheelers

My first time to drive a tractor.

My Browning rifle, engraved with my name.

Many preachers, their wives, and children have come with us there for a reprieve from their labor in the *field of the Lord*. Plus, many, both young and old, have also harvested their first deer or turkey. My husband gets so excited to bring friends to our place and to act as an "official guide" for these excursions.

Not only that, but this location is where we found Izzy, or I should say that Izzy found us!

One morning, just a few short weeks from when we moved in, I looked out the door and saw a puppy running through our yard. A little later, my husband opened the front door, and our grandchild number four, Caison Judah (age two at the time), was sitting on the porch, an oversized cowboy hat perched on his head, and that same pit bull mix puppy (red nosed pit) was being cuddled on his lap. This scene was to be repeated many, many times in the future by all our grandchildren. Thus began a love affair that would run very deep for years to come (but, of course, not long enough). My husband quickly got his phone camera and snapped a picture.

Caison and Izzy

We later framed a poster size of this significant event, the initial introduction of Izzy to our family, and it hangs proudly at our home in Raleigh, on the wall by Izzy's inside crate. She has since become my constant companion and my bodyguard when my husband is away. She really takes her job of protecting what is hers seriously, and as a few specific people have discovered, she doesn't always *play well with others*. But, *her people*, and most everyone else, she is very loving after you get acquainted with her, on her terms!

The year 2013 was also a red-letter year for another reason. Wayne was re-elected as North Carolina District Superintendent. He had said that the Lord would have to call him on the phone, and then he would trace the call before retaking this position. (From 1995 to 1997, he was North Carolina District Superintendent amid much confusion, tears, and hardship.)

But that was then; this was now!

God spoke to him in several ways, confirming to him that this was what he was supposed to do.

Wayne praying over North Carolina counties

God began working on Wayne in 2012. This year, the district conference was held in the fair city of Raleigh at the Temple of Pentecost.

He had been burdened by the fact that we had sixty counties, out of one hundred, that had no church or Apostolic witness. It seemed every time he turned around, something else was whispering: *North Carolina. North Carolina. North Carolina!*

Brother Anthony Mangun was our conference speaker this year, and one night, after he had preached, my husband fell on the altar, burdened for our great state. Brother Roy Barnhill, one of Wayne's best friends and buddies since their young teenage days, said he saw it when the burden settled on Wayne and knew it was happening. So, Wayne determined that our church, Temple of Pentecost, would take it upon ourselves to open as many churches as possible. But as you know, there is power in numbers. If one can send one thousand to flight and two can send ten thousand, how much better it would be if we could have many churches involved?

My oldest brother, Garth, was with us at our hunting lease in Tillery, North Carolina, and one morning, he called and said, "I need to come to your motor home. I need to talk to you". He began by saying, "I am no one to be telling you what to do, but the Lord has burdened me to tell you that you are to be the next North Carolina District Superintendent."

Wayne's brother, Gerald, who has never been one to advise Wayne on such matters as this, said, "Wayne, you have got to allow your name to stay in the vote."

During the summer of 2012, he preached at a camp in the Texaco District, just outside Amarillo, Texas. As he was walking from the evangelist's quarters there on the grounds to the tabernacle for the evening service, Evangelist Preston Plemmons came hurrying up to my husband. He said, "I've got to talk to you." (I was acquainted with Brother Plemmons from my hometown of Waco. He had been a wonderful friend to my sweet mother, and she loved him dearly). He proclaimed, "I have driven several hours to get here to give you this message that the Lord told me to tell you. I don't know what it means, but here it is. *'The coming elevation is from God!'*"

"So, who have you been talking to in North Carolina?"

"No one. I know nothing about what this means."

Well, this was like God calling Wayne *on the phone*. He did indeed have his number.

So, at the beginning of 2013, at our annual North Carolina District Conference, held this particular year in Winston-Salem, North Carolina, Wayne, for the second time in his ministerial life, was indeed elected to the position of North Carolina District Superintendent. This time would be completely different from the first time in 1995. Thank you, Jesus!

My husband had such a deep love and respect for the people of his precious Tar Heel State and a desire for there to be an Apostolic witness in each county. God began to give Wayne signs and intensify his burden to start churches and encourage other churches to do the same.

Brother David Sanders, who is in our church, gave him a vintage, antique North Carolina map. While we were setting up our Non-Typical Family Farm Cabin, we found a rock almost exactly the shape of North Carolina.

The rock in the shape of North Carolina

Once, when my husband came off a plane at the Charlotte, North Carolina, airport, he noticed a man standing, leaning against a column. He was dressed nicely and looked very neat. You do notice people like this, as most travelers dress so sloppily and unkempt these days. As Wayne walked past, they made eye contact and acknowledged each other. The man said, "Sir, I have never done this, but do you believe in divine appointment?"

My husband said, "Yes, of course."

"Well, the Lord told me to tell you that you have been making plans that are small steps that are gonna lead to big steps of great significance."

Wayne began to promote: *"Every pastor, a bishop, every church, a mother."*

He encouraged pastors and churches to sponsor crusades, start churches, or establish preaching points so that a county would at least have a preaching point that would hopefully one day become a full-fledged, autonomous church!

In 2018, North Carolina had ten crusades in ten different counties, all running simultaneously on the same date and time. The following year, we had ten more. The third year, we had five.

In this first year, excitement was running high! The Temple of Pentecost's crusade was held in Tarboro, North Carolina, at Clark Park. If memory serves me right, we had about 150 people receive the Holy Ghost in Taboro alone and 500 for the whole state during the ten crusades.

Brother Jack Cunningham was the crusade evangelist for Taboro, along with Brother Gordon Mallory, Brother Doug Klinedinst, Brother David Smith, Brother Kenny Marshburn, Brother Nick Mahaney, Brother Greg Godwin, Brother Tim Green, Brother James Starks, and his son, in the other nine cities.

October 18, 2014, when my husband and I (along with Brother and Sister James Carney and Brother and Sister Larry Hoyt, who had flown up to be a part of this exciting first Carolina Crusade) drove up on the grounds where the Tarboro, North Carolina crusade was to be held, it looked like the North Carolina State Fair traffic. In this little town of Tarboro, with a population of around 10,000 souls, cars were everywhere. We had to park a block away, and people — individuals, groups, and families — with their kids and dogs in tow were all walking toward the area where the crusade was to be held. Of course, we had done much advertising and had a carnival atmosphere with blow-up jump houses and slides for the kids, games, many fabulous giveaways, and, of course, "food!"

"Food." Yes, we had food, but surely not enough prepared for this crowd. On this particular day, at this location, we were not launching *one* church but *two*. One was English-speaking, and the other was "Spanish" speaking. The hard-working Spanish ladies had volunteered to make Mexican food. They had prepared enough for two hundred plates.

During the afternoon, a mighty miracle happened. These ladies in the serving line said that as the food in the big pots kept getting lower and lower, they finally became afraid to look down into the pot. They just kept putting their big spoons down, and somehow, when they brought them back up, they were always full of beans and rice to be served to the next person. The men said that when they would take an empty ice chest that had held the barbecue chicken back to the holding place, the next time they would come for chicken, there was always another one full. After the fact, they told us that they had served over seven hundred plates of food, all with just enough for two hundred dinners. They knew the number because they knew how many disposable plates they had purchased and how many were left after the fact.

Yes, God did it again. This was indeed the modern-day miracle of the *loaves and fishes,* except in this case, it was *beans and rice* and barbecue chicken. We had the privilege of being part of the number that got to *eat*.

Chapter Nine

Bishop Wayne Huntley and Your Bishopness, Patsy Huntley

As in other Januarys, 2015 was no different. Something of great significance happened. It marked a momentous change in the lives of Wayne and Patsy Huntley, as well as Bryan and Christy Ballestero, along with the Temple of Pentecost family.

We, Huntleys and Ballesteros, worked very hard for many years, in fact, to make this transition from us as senior pastor to bishop and the Ballesteros from pastor to senior pastor as smooth as possible for the Temple People. We didn't want them to feel a jerk in the transition, but a smooth changing of the gears, or the changing of the guard, if you will. For an extended amount of time, Wayne and I had been decreasing our being at the forefront and had been pushing the Ballesteros to the front. It's what we wanted: for us to decrease and them to increase. This particular date in time was the actual change. We would no longer be the lead pastor. We would bow graciously to our new pastor, who now has the final say on everything. Yes, even the money. My hubby has always said,

*"If they are not in charge of the money,
they are not really 'in charge,' or the pastor."*

As the second man, Bryan Ballestero was a tough act for my husband to follow because, in this position, he was perfect. He was always so *supportive* and never once questioned my husband on anything, although he had been voted to be a pastor by ninety-eight percent of the church. My husband, being the senior pastor, would not have done every single thing as Pastor Ballestero would, but if he ever disagreed, he never voiced it to anyone. We did try, and to this day, we stand with and for our senior pastor, Bryan Ballestero, and try to help him and hold him up in prayer and support to the TOP family. How could we do less now than he did for twenty-two years when he was the second man?

Below are my remarks to Christy on the night of the passing of the mantle.

Christy, when you were around two years old, we asked you, "What does daddy do?"

You said, "Daddy pweach and pway."

"What does Mommy do?"

"Mommy pway waag-an".

"Yes, and what does Christy do?"

"Sisty pway Piani!"

From that time until this most memorable day, that's all you have ever wanted to do...play piano and sing in church, lead in worship, work for God, be a good witness for the Lord, and represent these Temple People well.

Nothing is going to change. You are still going to play piano, sing, lead worship, work for God, be a good witness to those you meet, and represent this TOP family well. Only now, because you have been faithful in the past, the recognition and respect that you have EARNED will be yours.

I couldn't be more thankful, and yes, a little bit proud.

Days like today are why your Daddy and I wanted you to be born! That's why we raised you in the church and taught you to pray and worship, but most of all, we tried to transmit the love we have for our precious Savior to you.

Today shows. Thank God, we must have done something right.

Yes, we did something right because you were led by the Holy Ghost when you brought Bryan Starr Ballestero into our home, our hearts, and our church!

He has been nothing but a blessing in every way.

We have given, and are giving to him, everything in our lives that's important and good, everything for which we have loved, lived, and labored.

First of all, on Dec 4, 1992, we gave him you.

And now, secondly, today, January 11, 2015, thirty-seven short years from its humble beginning, we give these wonderful saints at the Temple of Pentecost into his safekeeping.

Dad and I are not one bit worried. You and your sweet children have been in HIS strong, protective hands since the day you married and Huntley, the first child, came along.

And now, we rest in the confidence that Pastor Bryan Ballestero is capable, that he loves US ALL, and will only do what is best for us, after carefully praying and seeking God.

We believe that God has brought you both to the Kingdom for such a time as this,

Congratulations are in order because today your faithfulness is being rewarded!

My husband tried to make comments, but he was only able to make a few before breaking down in tears. Here is the gist of what he tried to say.

Christy Renee Huntley and the Temple of Pentecost are the two things that represent my whole life's work and my entire heart. Bryan, in 1992, when Christy came down the aisle in her beautiful white wedding gown, and I put her hand into yours, I gave you half of my heart. Today, January 11, 2015, in this transition service, I give you the rest of my heart as I place the Temple of Pentecost into your hands. I have nothing else. I have given everything, not just my past but also my future, into your capable, reliable hands. Thank you for being the kind of man and Christian that I can do this with all confidence.

The Huntleys and Ballesteros in the transition service

After this transition service, not much seemed to change, as we had been in the "process" for several, several years. We had to decrease, and they had to increase, and that was done slowly. When we actually got to the date of the 'changing of the guard,' so to speak, "we" felt it more than the TOP did.

When you are used to carrying the weight on your shoulders, and it's suddenly lifted, it is like a change that you must get used to. Bryan told us that before he became senior pastor, he slept pretty well, but since the transition, he has not.

When Christy went to Bible school, and our nest became empty, we still caught ourselves thinking, "Where is Christy? Is she in for the night? How will she ride home from church?" and so on.

It takes a while for the change to mentally sink in so that we no longer have to worry about day-to-day pastoring. After the initial shock, it's actually liberating.

Now, we would not go back to pastoring because we don't feel we have the mental or physical strength. But even if we did have all we needed to keep pastoring, it was the right thing at the right time.

*"You don't have the younger man take charge,
when the Older man is finished:
but rather, the older man relinquishes,
when the Younger man is ready.*

Pastor Ballestero is such a wise man. He received incredible training during his great upbringing from his remarkable parents, Martyn (Marty) Joseph and Marcia June (Starr) Ballestero. How thankful Wayne and I were that Bryan was raised in such a spiritual, conservative, Christian, Apostolic, and loving environment. It made our transition so much easier. My older brother, Garth Landtroop, said when he retired from pastoring, he went from "Telling people what to do *to being told what to do!"* I guess that's an excellent way to put it, and it sums it up pretty well.

How incredible that when you get older and more tired physically, you can put your "baby" into the capable hands of someone who will care for the flock, and as Christy said about her songs when she made a recording, "Not dress your baby in funny clothes!" Meaning not to change the way they look or sound!

Oh, sure, I had a few issues and battles to fight when I transitioned from being a senior pastor's wife to a bishop's wife, mostly in my mind.

There are a lot of different feelings. *It was the best of days; it was the worst of days.* (I've mentioned this a few times in this book, but it's true in every case.) It's what you wanted to happen, but it's what your heart tried to hold on to in order to keep things as they were. I felt so good because I knew this was the right thing; all at the same time, I felt so unnecessary, or, for some reason, in some ways, unimportant now. It is scary and frightening to know you are on the way out and not in. Your very reason for existing is basically over, not beginning.

Life is finishing and not happening. Your motivating factor, your reason for existing, seems gone. Your life is no longer on your terms, but it's theirs. They must appear, and you must disappear. They must increase, and you must decrease.

No person made me feel unimportant or less needed; quite the contrary. It's just that sometimes, I didn't really know where I fit. I wanted things to move forward and new people to do things, but when they did them in my place, my heart would hurt and ache in a way I didn't know it could or would. I knew that time and things were passing me by. I was moving *out* of what I love, but I was moving someone *in* whom I loved and wanted them to be there. I wanted it to happen, but then, when it did, for some odd reason, my heart kind of hurt. Why? Why? I don't really know. I guess more than anything, it was just knowing I was not only moving out of the place I had held for years, but also the way my flesh was fighting against getting older, realizing that we are not on the way up but on the way out of even life itself!

Princess Alice of Battenberg said, "There came a moment, around seventy, that it dawned on me. I was no longer a participant but rather a spectator, and it was just a matter of waiting and not getting in the way." I guess this sums up how you sometimes feel.

So, when all these feelings kept surfacing, I just had to push them aside and do as Dr. Laura Schlesinger used to always say at the end of her radio program when she advised people on their problems: *"Now, go do the right thing!"*

> *Sometimes, you just have to*
> *"Go and do the right thing,"*
> *so that the "right thing"*
> *can come out of all the things*
> *that you've been doing your whole life.*

My husband was preaching in some state for some preacher somewhere, a while after we had the transition service, and as I had said, we had privately struggled with our feelings, not that we didn't *want* to transition. Just flesh that fights against getting old and the thought of being 'finished.' But while he was out of town, riding in someone's car, he noticed a sign in front of some random church. It changed our lives. We have made it the theme of our latter years.

"Don't 'CRY' because it's 'OVER,'
'SMILE,' because it 'HAPPENED!'"

Dr. Spock

We have been smiling ever since! We have tried to incorporate two things into our lives–coaching and cheerleading. We have vast knowledge that we can help advise (when we are asked) so that our years of experience are put to good use. Then, it is our job to cheer on and encourage the younger pastors and leaders.

We genuinely don't want to *be* pastors anymore. We just want it done. We know it will be done differently than we would have done it. We must allow them to pastor their way in the same way we were able to do it our way!

Different is not wrong; it's just different!

Once, during prayer before church, when my husband was still senior pastor and Bryan was the pastor, my husband noticed that the lights were somewhat dim in the sanctuary.

He called for an usher and said, "Why are the lights so low? It's dark in here."

"Well, Pastor Ballestero said he wanted the lights low during prayer, and when the church service begins, bring the lights up."

"You know, that's a good idea. I don't know why I didn't think of that. Let's leave them low before church."

He could have said, "I am still the senior pastor around here, and I like light. Get those lights up."

That was true; he was still senior pastor, but would that have helped to bring the Ballesteros into their place as senior pastors, or would it have undermined their authority?

As long as the church is growing, moving onward and upward, souls are being won, the Temple People's needs are being met, and the church remains Apostolic, this is all that matters. Praise the Lord, the church is still on the move, and we are thankful every day for Pastor and Sister Ballestero and their commitment to Apostolic doctrine and lifestyle.

The years get better and better for us. Because we actually let the Ballesteros be the senior pastor, and not just in name, we are allowed the privilege to remain in Raleigh, at the TOP, with the people we really love. We don't have the day-to-day burden of the church, but we still get to be a part of this wonderful group of people called the TOP family. Pastor Ballestero calls on my husband to preach fairly consistently (when he is not out of town preaching somewhere else), and I am still on the rotation to direct the choir and sing with the worship leaders (which I love). We have the best of both worlds. Why would we not embrace it, appreciate it, and simply just live it and love it?

June 16, 2016, was quite an ordinary day. But are there really any ordinary days? When I woke up that morning, I had no idea of the turmoil I would be in when I lay my head to rest that night after midnight, not in my bed but at our daughter's house and in her bed, which she and Bryan so graciously insisted we sleep.

Gentson Hebron Carl, our youngest grandchild, at the age of three, spent the night with me on Monday, June 15, while my husband was away.

When we woke up Tuesday morning, June 16th, Gent and I went out on the deck. I watered the flowers, puttered around, and prepared the pool area for a birthday party our granddaughter, Christyana, was hosting that evening for her girlfriends for her seventeenth birthday, which was on June 17.

Gent had gone home earlier that day, and my husband had returned home. It was around 6:30 p.m., and we had just sat down on the couch to catch up. My husband took off his shoes, which he never does, and I was barefoot, as is usual for me while at home. (or anywhere, actually, that I can shed my shoes).

Suddenly, we heard a pretty loud pop. We both exclaimed, "Did you hear that?" I thought it was the door of our screened-in back porch, which would slam when the wind would blow if we had forgotten to latch it or if someone would come to the back door and let it slam behind them. I got up to see.

I opened the back door and said, "I don't see anyone." So, I stepped out onto the porch and noticed dark gray smoke swirling and curling around the bottom of a side door of the porch leading to the pool area. I went out and opened the side door, looked, and saw flames licking between all the horizontal cedar siding boards that were around the glass electrical meter box on the back of the house. The flames were about head high and about four feet wide. I ran back into the house, screaming to my husband that our home was on fire. He ran outside, and I went to the house phone to call 911.

The phone was already inoperable as the house phone line came directly through the electrical box, which had exploded. That was the pop we had heard. I grabbed my cell phone from the couch where I had been sitting and ran outside. In just a matter of a minute, the flames went from head-high to roof-high.

My husband was trying to get the water hose from the adjacent deck. Thankfully, he was unable to turn on the water, as our outdoor supply comes from a well that is powered by an electrical pump, which was also inoperable because of the electrical fire.

Later, a fireman told him that he could have been electrocuted if he had held the hose and sprayed water on the electric fire. (Because water is a conductor of electricity, it would have followed the water flow up to his hand.) God is good, and He was looking out for us.

If the meter had exploded at 6:30 a.m. instead of 6:30 p.m. (just 12 hours earlier), I would have been alone in the house with my three-year-old grandson sleeping. If I had heard the pop and been awakened, I would have needed to get both myself and a sleeping baby out of a window as the fire started in a place where we would have had to go through the flames to get out. That is, *if* I had woken up! God was surely looking out for us!

After I called 911, my husband and I stood in the yard, barefoot, with only the clothes on our backs, and watched thirty years of memories go up in flames, but no person was hurt, and we still had each other. God was still good!

One of our remarkable men, who had been raised as a young boy in our church, had been a fireman. Brent Barnhill (known as Slick at the firehouse) had suffered years with a disease in his body that had finally taken his life. The doctors could not really put a name on it (other than Crohn's disease). He fought long, hard, and bravely. Because of him, the fire station employees were familiar with the TOP and us. The fire chief was actually working his last day before retiring. As the firetruck came rumbling down the street, he commented to his fellow firefighters, "I hope that's not Pastor Huntley's house."

But, alas, it *was*. He told my husband, "I'm sorry it's *your house,* but a fireman retiring could not go out any better than fighting a big fire on his last day of work."

We felt helpless as we stood around in the backyard and watched as the flames engulfed our beautiful home. The firemen told us that it was a stubborn fire. There was just enough wind that every time they almost got it calmed down a bit, the wind would blow new life into it. All they could do was try to control it.

One of the firemen came around the back of the house from the front, carrying our daughter's beautiful 24" x 30" bridal portrait. He said, "We are not supposed to bring 'stuff' out of the house, but I just couldn't leave this portrait to be ruined by fire, smoke, and water." We were so very thankful.

I have never seen so many fire trucks. There must have been ten or more. They had used so much water that they finally blocked the entire busy street in front of our house by putting a large inflatable container, looking a lot like a big above-ground swimming pool. It covered both lanes of the street. They would bring up a firetruck full of water and empty it into the pool, which had fire hoses hooked up to it. They would then spray it on the house. They continually sprayed water using two to four sprayers–two on the front and two on the back–for five hours before they could extinguish the fire.

There were so many firemen from so many different stations. From our vantage point in the backyard, we would see four or five firemen sporting the uniform with the emblems of their community come and work the fire hoses, suit up with the oxygen tanks, and enter the house. We could see them on the third floor, walking around. In a bit, we would hear their tanks begin to beep, notifying them their oxygen level was low and that they had to come out and let someone else go in.

Then, these firemen from one community would leave for a break, and another community of firemen would take their place.

I had an extensive book collection on that third floor; occasionally, we would see pages from some book come fluttering down.

Word got out in the United Pentecostal Church International. My husband had called his dear friend, Brother Mark Foster, and his sweet wife, Paulla, while the fire was burning. We called a few people we didn't want to find out about it from someone other than us.

Mark immediately began to call other friends of ours, and the calls started to come in–prayers, encouraging words, and offers of help of all kinds. There is truly nothing like this United Pentecostal Church!

Brother Anthony Mangun called and said, "Wayne, this situation is going to be 'Leah' in your life. You are going to meet Leah through all of this. The end result of this tragedy will wind up being a great blessing."

(In the Bible, Leah turned out to be the greatest blessing in Jacob's life because she produced more sons. Leah, the less desirable, was the one that Jacob requested to be buried beside instead of Rachel, the beautiful.)

He said, "God is gonna give you a message out of this, and you will preach it at Because of the Times, 2017."

Wayne wasn't particularly inspired at that moment. He thought to himself, "I'm not feeling very spiritual right now or searching for a message. I'm watching my house burn!"

The Red Cross always comes out to offer help in times like these. They took my husband, me, Bryan, and Christy into their work truck to glean information. It was quite a large truck with built-in seating around the sides. They began to ask questions as to what we would need. My husband told them, "You know, we do appreciate you making this offer, but please save the Red Cross dollars for people who are in greater need than we are. We have a large network of family, friends, and church family who will help us."

Patsy, Wayne, and Leah

They gave us a small check for necessary things for now. As we stood up to depart, the young woman who was directing the interview said, "Tonight was my very first time to interview a family during a situation like this, as I am a new employee. So, before you leave, let me introduce myself. I am Leah!"

What?

From beginning to end, we felt God directing and speaking to us in very specific terms. He had us in the palm of His hand. *"The steps of a good man are ordered of the Lord."* We may not have been able to see the end of the road at this particular time, but God definitely had a plan which He unfolded in His time.

Brother Owen Egger, a member of the TOP who had twenty years of experience as an insurance adjuster, would become such an integral part of this amazing process. He came up to my husband as the fire was raging and said,

"Pastor, if you let me, I will get you every penny the insurance company owes you and more. Just don't sign anything without my approval." He knew the ins and outs of insurance policies and was also a building contractor. We cannot fathom going through this incredible journey without him at the helm! Thank you, "Owens" (a special private joke), for making the construction of an elegant 4,600-square-foot farmhouse seem easy. I couldn't have done it without you! And thank you for getting *every penny* the insurance company owed us!

At one point, while we watched our home literally go up in smoke, I began to think about my study Bible. It was a Royal Bible, one my husband had given me in 1974, and it bore this inscription written to me by my one and only sweetheart.

> *My vagueness of vocabulary would not allow me*
> *to express myself aptly words of love and appreciation.*
> *This book speaks of supreme love.*
> *I find my love for you within its covers.*
> *As a flame to a candle, the sun to morning,*
> *and breath to a body,*
> *so have you become the smile on my face,*
> *the joy of my heart, and the song of my soul.*
> *I'll love you always,*
>
> *Wayne*

We all have one special Bible, which is "the Bible," in our lives. I loved this Bible, and I prayed that it would be okay. And thank the Lord, it was!

It was in a case, inside a carrying bag with my home Bible study lessons. Thank God it survived without any damage.

Waking up Wednesday morning, June 17, 2016, was probably the most unusual day of my life.

My whole world had become strange to me. I woke up in an unfamiliar bed, in an unfamiliar room. (Thank you, Christy and Bryan, for giving up your bed and room so we could be as comfortable as possible on this most uncomfortable night.) I was thankful, but it was strange to me.

I had a new toothbrush and a comb for my hair that I didn't really like. I had worn a nightgown that didn't fit me correctly.

I had no shoes except some flip-flops that my niece, Denise, had so graciously given to me, and my husband was wearing bedroom shoes that she had also *dug up* for him. We had no clothes or underwear, except for what we were wearing and a few things that some precious Temple People had kindly gotten together for us. But it was strange stuff and didn't seem to be mine.

I didn't even have my purse! What? I always have my purse wherever I go! But, alas, it had been on the kitchen table of my burning house, and as I would find later in the morning, it was black with smoke, edges curled with heat, completely wet, and totally demolished.

It was the most feeling of helplessness that I have ever known, and I felt as if I were floundering around with no anchor. I just lay there and cried, my mind going one hundred miles an hour, asking my husband, "What in the world are we gonna do?"

All my church clothes were gone! For a few days, I was devastated. You know, for a Pentecostal woman, to lose all her clothes is just plain terrible. We can't just go and buy something. We usually have to search for things we need–certain clothes that are modest and godly. I had been collecting them for years. What in the world was I going to do? By Saturday night, after prayer, just four days later, I had received two packages from two different wonderful ladies who sell "Pentecostal" clothes – Sister Renee Willbanks and Sister Nila Ballestero Marxer. These women saved my life! I publicly thank them. Blessings to both of them today.

During this whole ordeal, *this* first morning, as we were still lying in bed, trying to get enough strength to face this most horrific day, was one of only about three times that I actually broke down and cried.

The first time was while my husband and I were standing in the backyard, with only the clothes on our backs, both barefoot, holding each other, waiting for the fire trucks to arrive. I was crying then.

I was crying, "now."

Then, when we went into the burned-out house for the first time on Wednesday, June 17, the morning after the fire, and saw the grandfather clock that my husband had purchased for me on our twentieth wedding anniversary, with the brass plate attached that read; "Celebrating 20 years of marvelous marriage, Wayne and Patsy," I realized that all that was left of my beautiful clock was part of the giant brass pendulum lying on the floor. For the third time, I burst out crying.

While we were observing this terrible scene, water dripping all around us from the unusual amounts of water sprayed the night before, and looking at a house that was completely black from smoke and fire, and standing in the middle of that room that looked like someone had taken a giant paint sprayer and from floor to ceiling sprayed black paint on *every surface,* to the point that you could not recognize the furniture, or tables, or other items; our dear friends, Alex and Mary Lee walked in.

Alex and Mary have been our long, long-time friends. In fact, my husband conducted his very first funeral after becoming pastor of First United Pentecostal Church with Bryan-Lee Funeral Home in Garner (which is their impeccable place of business). It was his first, but surely not the last, with these dear people. Many, many funerals and many years later, we have become "fast friends" and have formed a lasting bond.

There was something funny that happened when Wayne had his heart attack in 2004; Alex and Mary heard about it, called us, and left us a message on our answering machine. Here is the gist of that message!

Alex: "I'm so sorry to hear about your heart attack. I hope all goes well for you, and *should you <u>need</u> us, don't hesitate to call."*

Mary, in the background: *"No, don't say if you need us; call. We hope they won't need us!"*

We were glad that we didn't NEED them or their business (Bryan-Lee Funeral Home) and that Wayne survived and has thrived since that scary day.

Yes, standing in that horrible, blackened, sickening, burned-out home, the saying that I had said many, many times before and certainly knew to be true now came to mind in full force.

> *"<u>Things</u> do not make you happy.*
> *They make you more comfortable,*
> *But they do not make you happy."*

I knew all the "things" that we possessed were *gone!* But now I know firsthand that things do not make you happy. More comfortable, yes! Happy, no! I could still be happy with nothing. I still had my husband, my children, my family, and my church family. I was happy.

"I have learned, in whatsoever state I am, therewith to be content."
(Philippians 4:11)

Looking all around at this burned-out shell of a house, I realized that I had to build a house! I need to explain that I didn't *want* to build a house! I didn't want *another* house. If the fire had not come for six more months, until December 2016, that would have marked thirty years of living in this home. It was my safe place, my comfort place, when my husband was traveling away, preaching.

I remember saying to my husband on several occasions, not long before the fire, "Have I told you that I love my home? I feel so good here, so safe, and I love it."

Just one week before the fire, Gerald and Susan Huntley, Wayne's brother and sister-in-law, were staying in our home during our NC3E Conference. This is our North Carolina District Conference (Encouraging, Equipping, and Empowering) and camp meeting. Gerald and I were talking one evening before church, and he said to me. "Patsy, do you ever think about selling this house and building or buying another one?"

You have to realize that I was not the person who looked at houses. I didn't read real estate books. I didn't muse over floor plans and dream of a new home. I felt I was in my dream home; I was 100% satisfied and happy with my home. But *it* was gone, along with all my earthly possessions, in just one short summer evening!

A special event occurred just as we were about to demolish the house and remove everything from the property site. We had been throwing trash in a massive pile on the garage floor for several months. It was an astronomical pile of stuff that we had collected to discard. This was the last day. Demolition would begin in approximately an hour. This morning, the giant crane would begin to knock down what remained of our home, and dump trucks were standing by to be filled with debris and hauled away.

I walked into the house for the last time and prayed. I said, "God, if there is something I need to find, perhaps it's in a cupboard, or maybe some ceiling Sheetrock has fallen on something important that I have forgotten to check on. Please help me think about it now. Please don't let me forget it now, and in a month or so, or a year or so, have an "Oh, no!" moment when I remember it, and then it will be too late. Please help me think about it now, or please never let me think of it again."

I walked out of the burned ruins and into the garage, to where this pile of trash was that I told you about. Just know that this pile had been growing in size for several months, and we had been adding to it daily.

Standing beside this pile, I was taking some hardware (drawer pulls) from the drawers of one of my bedroom dressers, thinking I might use them someday. I was holding the drawer, using a screwdriver, when it slipped and flew out of my hand. I began to search this pile of trash with my eyes, looking for where the screwdriver had fallen. At first, I couldn't find it, but as I looked, my eyes fell on a piece of cloth that gave my heart a lurch. I recognized that cloth. I knew it, but what was it from? Oh, it's my little quilt top that my grandmother had hand-pieced, and I used it for a blanket with my dolls! Then, to my surprise, I noticed "my dolls from my childhood" lying together on that black and white quilt top, all seven of them, on top of that trash pile!

My dolls

What in the world? Where did they come from? There is no way that those dolls had been there all the time. I had not seen my dolls for two months, and suddenly, there they were! I don't know how they got there, but God had answered my prayer and preserved something special for me.

If it's important to you,
It's important to God!

We had no idea that God wanted to bless us with a new home that would be much more conducive to our needs as we grew older.

But that day, Gerald asked me, "Do you ever think about a new or different house?" I answered, rather indignantly.

I said, "No! I don't want another house. I love my house and plan to go up in the rapture or die right from this house."

But God had other plans for us. At first, I thought, "I'll just rebuild my same house. I like it, and I have no other house in mind." But the more I thought about it, the more I knew that because we were both nearing the "decade of the seventies," we did not need a three-story house!

But I had no clue where to start. Christy to the rescue! She called me one day and said, "Mom, I was looking at house styles, and I believe the style that suits you best is *Elegant Farmhouse.*"

When those words flashed through my mind–*Elegant Farmhouse*–I had a mental picture of precisely the style of house I wanted. She knew me so well. I like fancy with touches of galvanized things, Edison lights, a club-footed bathtub, a farmhouse kitchen sink, and a replica of an old kitchen stove! Yes! Yes! Yes! So, I began to look for those kinds of houses.

I had decided on a barn-shaped house with three sections, all of which were mostly on one floor. Again, Christy came to the rescue. She sent me a picture of a home worth millions that had a barn-shaped roof for part of it. So, I incorporated that shape into the front. I drew the floor plan haphazardly on a paper napkin. I knew how I wanted the rooms to flow.

We devised a plan with the help of Jim Turner and Daniel Beavers. Whew! We were on our way.

We were so thankful that the TOP had a little missionary evangelist house on the church grounds called "The White House." We had started calling it "The Guest House," but because it was white, the Temple People just started calling it "The White House," and that name stuck. That just had a nice ring to it, anyway.

We could live there for the eleven months our *Elegant Farmhouse* was being built.

When the studs for the walls had been put in place, Caleb and Brittany Douglas, pastor of our Impact Student Ministries and licensed UPCI minister, came out one Wednesday night during class time, bringing the whole class, and wrote on the inside of the outer walls. They composed some interesting and sweet notes and scriptures, and now, I can be assured that our walls are filled with love from our sweet Temple teens! This is what Brittany and Caleb Douglas wrote.

"May your walls know joy,
and every room hold laughter,
and every window be open to many blessings…
We are so thrilled for you guys!
Wishing you both years of peace and happiness in your new home!"

Caleb and Brittany's Blessing

What an exciting day it was when, in the month of May 2017, just eleven short months from tragedy, we moved triumphantly into our new home, which was exactly as I had envisioned, except much better. To make it even better, we did not have one personal dollar in the building of the house or the furnishings of this lovely 4,600-square-foot home. Hallelujah! Won't He do it?

Our house is undoubtedly "custom-made." We can see beautiful horses from the windows of our "Texas Room" (an actual apartment above our two-car garage). From our balcony on the second floor, out the back of our house– Wayne's favorite place– we could see "cows" (that is, until they decided to build a housing development behind us and remove all the cows). We have a "Foster" guest suite painted in our friend Mark's favorite color, teal! Our great room has a balcony ledge. The ceiling is twenty-three feet high, with my husband's latest and best deer mounts—a 200-class and two whole-body mounts. He has an Axis buck and a full-body mount of a long-beard turkey, plus others. These are set among trees and greenery and look as if they could be Cabela's decorations. My favorite place is outside, beside our above-ground pool, with a deck and privacy fence all around, with my hanging baskets of petunias and big pots of zinnias. This is truly my happy place to sit in the evening and watch nightfall come.

I thoroughly enjoyed overseeing the building of this "house that insurance built." I was never overwhelmed by anything. Each week, Brother Egger would say, "Sister Huntley, this week you need to decide what kind of flooring you want in each room, or choose all your paint colors, or select all your plumbing fixtures," or whatever was the pressing need of the day. So, I did not have the whole building on my shoulders; only what was needed this week, or today! Thank you, Brother Egger! You are the best!

The front view of our new house

The back view

September 2018 found me very distressed. Wayne was going to Madagascar for ten days. We had never been separated that long in forty-nine years, and I did not like it!

I decided that while he was gone, I would take our new 2018 36-foot Laredo travel trailer to Myrtle Beach. My hubby didn't care much for the beach, anyway, which would give me something enjoyable to do while he was away.

I had some of my family come and join me on different days. The vacation started with Barbie Landtroop, my nephew DeWayne's wife. Then it was Loretta Simpson, my niece, and it ended with Christy and the three youngest boys, Christian, Caison, and Gentson. We planned our days, and I was driving home on the two weekends. We all did wind up having a grand time. But one weekend, I was having a big-time pity party as I drove home with my sweet companion, Izzy, my Red Nose Bully. I was telling God just how lonesome I was, how far away Wayne was from me, and how much I felt like I was sacrificing, which was a new emotion for me. Usually, things never seem like a sacrifice when the will of the Lord is being accomplished.

The Lord spoke to me so strongly. It was not an audible voice, but it was just as powerful as if it had been, and was indeed loud and clear!

The Lord said, "At least he _is_ coming home and not gone _forever._" I was pricked into the deepest part of my soul. My heart had grieved for some of my special friends whose companions had passed away, and they were never coming home _in this life._ I repented right then and there, with many tears rolling down my cheeks as I drove down the highway. I began to count my blessings in earnest. It's so easy to get our minds and spirits on the wrong emotions when we have so much to be genuinely thankful for.

I didn't grieve anymore. Every time I would get lonesome, my heart would sing out, "But at least he _is_ coming home!" I must admit, though, that when he made it home from that very long journey, I held him tighter and a little longer than usual.

2018 Madagascar UPCI General Conference

This particular year (2018), our family had more than one personal trial. We seem to have been spared from many heartaches, but we are all flesh, and it does rain on the just and the unjust. Just because we are the children of the Lord does not exempt us from the pain and suffering that affected the whole human race when Adam and Eve sinned in the garden.

So, when our whole heart, the apple of our eyes, our one and only darling daughter, was diagnosed with breast cancer, we were devastated beyond words and thoughts. My husband went into panic mode. We have always tried to live our lives so that we can call on Jesus and feel that we have a *straight line* to the throne! But this was different. This was our "Christy." This was our future. All our eggs were in this one basket. We couldn't even conceive of our life without her. And, of course, our negative human brains always chase those evil thoughts to the end. This was a roller coaster ride of ups and downs, but thank God, He came through.

God gave us signs by many infallible proofs that He was in total control and was working for all our best interests.

The actual day that Christy and Bryan came to our house, on their way home from the doctor with that overwhelming news, God sent our first encouraging sign.

Unbeknownst of the situation or just what was transpiring *right then,* even as the Ballesteros were in our driveway, leaving after they had delivered this most lamentable news, my husband received a text from Brother Josh Herring with a message of a marvelous healing of cancer! God said, "I am an on-time God. Before you need Me, I am here with encouragement and inspiration."

My husband went like a madman with prayer and fasting. God, this just cannot be. We must have an answer; Christy has to be healed. We *believe,* we *trust;* it is *so* by Your *power.*

One morning, Brother George Guy called with a word from the Lord. He saw us standing, looking into a huge storm of black clouds. Brother Guy said, "Lord, why are you taking Brother and Sister Huntley through that terrible storm?"

The Lord said, "I am not taking them *through* that storm; I am just showing them what I have saved them *from.*"

We did not know if she would have to have chemo, radiation, surgery, or just what the diagnosis would deem necessary. Of course, the medical field really wanted her to do "all of the above." One doctor told her, "You will lose all your beautiful hair!" This was a personal despair and apprehension for me. Not that she was any dearer to God than anyone else, and absolutely not to judge anyone else's situation, but I could not wrap my brain around her losing all her beautiful "glory" that went well below her waist. December 3, 2018, right after our "Ladies' Morning Prayer Call," God quickened this prayer to my heart, and I began to pray it with all the fervor and faith I could muster.

My Prayer for Christy

Dec 3, 2018, 7:04 a.m.

Dear Lord,

You said that we have not because we ask not
Lord, I am asking!!! Therefore, I believe I shall receive!

I cannot perceive that it would be Your will for Christy to lose her glory. Somehow, I have to believe that it is Your will for "Her glory to not depart."

It's a personal covenant that we have with You. It's a generational covenant. My own mother began this covenant with You as a very young mother and Christian. She passed it to me, and I have made this covenant my own, and my hair has never been cut. I passed this covenant to Christy when she was in our care. Her hair was never cut, and she carried this on into her adulthood. Christy passed this covenant to Christyana, and her hair has never been cut. It's our glory, and we have covenanted with You. It shall remain this way. "The glory shall not depart!!"

You said in Your Word that You are able to keep that which we have committed to You!!!

We have kept it; now it's in Your hands for keeping. It's out of our personal control, but it's not out of Your control.

Thank You for keeping her glory, because we have committed it unto You for safekeeping!!!

You said that if we drink any deadly thing, it shall not hurt you. I know these treatments are poison and do hurt a person. But we are not like everyone else. We are Your children. We are Your Bride!

Dear Lord, Jesus,

I <u>plead</u> the <u>blood</u>. I call on Your great name today,
I <u>invoke</u> the sweet <u>name</u> of <u>Jesus</u>.
I <u>believe</u> what is written in Your <u>Word</u>.
We have the privilege as adopted children to receive every promise in Your great Word.
The stripes that You took on Your back for our healing give us the privilege of receiving healing!

Therefore, I declare,

1. *You are going to keep that which we have committed to You.*

2. *This deadly thing (treatment) shall not hurt; only do the good that it is supposed to. (No sickness or hair loss, only the good of killing cancer cells)*

3. *The glory shall not depart but stay intact as a memorial of God's miracle power.*

My sweet Lord, I claim it, I declare it,
I lay hold on it; I believe it. I shall receive it; it is so.
But if not,

I Peter 1:24, 25— "For all flesh is as grass, and all the glory of man as the flower of grass. The grass withereth and the flower thereof falleth away: But the word of the Lord endureth forever. And this is the word, which by the Gospel is preached unto you."

We do not tell God *how* to answer, for He is sovereign and does as He pleases. I thank God that she did not lose her glory and that she did not have to undergo chemotherapy. She did have radiation, and the Lord helped her through that. Maybe I should not have prayed that, should she have had Chemo, she would not lose her hair. But as I said, *"Ye have not because ye ask not."* So, I asked, and He did answer, and God's way is always best!

Chapter Ten

The Golden Years

Seventy Plus Years!
Our Golden Wedding Anniversary!

The year was 2019!!! Fifty years??? How in the world did so much time go by? So quickly, it seemed.

An old saying is, *"Time flies when you are having fun!"* We must be having a "blast" because the years have flown by like lightning!

We were celebrating fifty years of marvelous marriage. As I write this, my eyes fill with tears, just thinking about our lives and all God has done for us, and how much love there is "still" between us. I had to stop and thank God for His many, manifold blessings. I could never have imagined "this many blessings." (My sweet Red Nose Pit Bull dog, Izzy, my friend, heard me crying and talking to the Lord and came into the room to check on me.)

The TOP pulled out "all the stops" and threw a celebration fit for a king (and queen). I didn't know anything they were doing. It was all a surprise. I only told Christy and Sister Tamera Holloman, who was pulling it all together, that I wanted pink Flamingos somewhere in all the decorations. Sister Tamera looked at me, sort of sideways, and said, *"Pink flamingos?"*

I said, "Yes, pink flamingos." She didn't understand just what pink flamingos meant to me. Through the years, pink flamingos have been completely uncouth and totally classless. However, in recent times, they have become trendy. Everything goes in a big circle.

I told her the story of our "luxury" bridal suite (not!) in the Flamingo Inn in Waco, Texas, in 1969. Then she understood. The flamingos used for decoration were beautiful and were everything I thought they would be.

The JIM Building was decorated like a fairytale wedding. When Wayne and I walked in the door, it looked lovely, and romantic music played on a tiny replica of an old-fashioned Victrola. I could not help but start to cry. I can't even begin to describe all the love and hard work that had gone into our "Golden Wedding Celebration." It was beauty beyond description.

The delectable food, prepared by our dear friends, Brother Shane and Sister DeAnna Britt, along with their helpers, looked magnificent, tasted delicious, and was displayed with class.

My sweetheart surprised me with a beautiful 4' x 5' painting of the two of us. The painting showed a boy (Wayne's face) with a fishing pole in his hand, sitting on a rock jutting out of the ocean. The fishing line had caught a mermaid (me!). The caption on the painting read *The Catch of a Lifetime.* Is that not the sweetest thing in the world and so very romantic?

The Catch of a Lifetime

Wayne and Patsy Huntley, 1971

My husband had seen a similar picture during his travels at a hotel or restaurant. He came home and told Brother Eric McRay, our resident artist at the TOP, a renowned Professional Visual Artist and Art Educator. My husband commissioned Brother McRay to paint it for him. He agreed, and it turned out so very lovely. It has a place of honor in our bedroom at home, where I gaze at it every day and feel so very loved.

Our anniversary gift from Christy, Bryan, and the family was a photo shoot. We wanted our immediate family to be part of this momentous occasion, and Heather Follmer did an excellent and professional job. Most of the photographs from our 50th Anniversary featured in this book were taken by her.

Now, my 2018 Black Toyota Avalon sports a custom license plate on the front bumper, made and given to us by our sweet, forever friends, Mark and Paulla Foster.

It simply reads:

"Just married! (50 years ago!)"

My husband asked me what I wanted for our fiftieth anniversary. After much thought, I told him I would like to enjoy just one month of his time. As I have said on other occasions, we do not *need* time away from each other, but we have had a lot, mainly because of his traveling and preaching. We thank God for every one of his many invitations that he has had through the years. It is a distinct honor and the blessing of God, but every fulfilled invitation is hours, days, and nights spent away from each other. I have been lonely many times, and I guess this is just *my cross* to bear. I have not always borne it gracefully, so I probably need to repent. However, his traveling has kept my husband sane, encouraged, and excited about preaching and life in general.

He tried to set aside the whole month of July 2019 in honor of fifty years of togetherness, in spirit if not always together physically.

It seemed everything that could prevent this from happening did happen. There were TOP deaths, family surgeries, a North Carolina Junior Youth camp that he, as District Superintendent, needed to attend, and numerous other incidentals that just got in the way. We did our best, but when the month ended, we found we had not spent the quality time, just being together, that I had envisioned and anticipated.

Oh, well, that's life in the fast lane.

But then, the year 2020 came, and along with that, COVID-19. The whole world changed. Some people so very special to us had contracted this most dreaded sickness and, sadly, were overtaken by it. We could no longer have church services as usual. We had no services, online services, outside services, and services with no people present except those involved. We made do. Everybody around the country (and even the world) was in the same situation. We got through it. We didn't like it, but we made it. We were so thankful when we could begin to have regular services again. But COVID-19 was not all bad for us on a personal level.

I told you that Wayne and I did not get to have our anniversary month together as I had hoped and planned in 2019. COVID shut down everything at the beginning of 2020, stopping all travel and special services, so Wayne Huntley stayed home! One morning, our good friend, Brother Bobby Edwards, called. When Wayne answered the phone, Brother Edwards said,

"Wayne, I have a word from God for you."

"Are you serious?"

"I have never been more serious."

"OK, I'm listening."

With much projection in his voice and great emphasis, he loudly exclaimed, "Stay home."

"Ok, I will."

So, he did. We had a blissful year of togetherness. I loved it. He psyched himself out, put his mind and travel energy on hold, and enjoyed the year. He was, however, ready for 2021 and had the year all planned out. This summer, he was at seven camp meetings or district conferences (not counting our own). He would either preach or conduct business meetings as the Executive Presbyter for the UPCI or both in Texas, Kentucky, Maine, Wisconsin, Pennsylvania, South Central Texas, and Idaho.

It was such a busy summer, but he was back on the road and oh-so-happy.

If possible, 2022 came and began a busier time than 2021. I didn't think that was possible, but it was true. This year proved to be the busiest of his ministry. I think he felt he was "chasing the clock." He turned 72 in December 2021, so he was filling every available slot possible. We enjoyed good health but knew we were only one sickness away from being sidelined. We are not promised tomorrow. None of us are, including the young, but we older ones are especially vulnerable.

An old saying is, "Hindsight is always 20/20." It is a shame sometimes that we cannot see our future. When we are young and looking forward, we cannot know all that God will do for us, the things He will keep us from, and the things He will work out for us—all the things that will make us profitable for His Kingdom. It's only when we have grown older and have our lives behind us that we *know*.

It is too bad that we cannot know *as we live our lives*. But that would take faith and trust out of the equation. I have told many people during our long tenure as pastor that:

"God doesn't give you a road map
of where the rest of your life is gonna take you…
He only whispers in your ear what your next step is to be,
and that is when He is ready for you to take that step."

Now that we are nearing the end of this journey, *"this wonderful life, serving the Lord,"* we must take heart and learn from our *past* experiences that God will take care of us in the future.

He did not bring us this far to fail us now. Just as He has been with us all through this wonderful life, He will never leave or forsake us now, but He will go all the way with us, even to the end of the world.

Once, when we were much younger and preaching at Ohio Camp Meeting, Wayne was exhausted after a service one night and was kneeling to pray there on the platform and catch his breath. An older Christian gentleman, Brother Norman Paslay, came over and knelt beside Wayne, slipped his arm around him, and whispered remarkable prophecies into his spirit, encouraging him that God would continue to *"use"* Wayne in His service in extraordinary ways. Wayne felt Brother Paslay get up and heard the wooden floors creak as he started walking away; then he heard him stop, turn around, and come back. He got back on his knees and said, "Oh yes, and the Lord would have me to tell you He loves you. He doesn't just want to *use* you; He *loves* you."

We all know that God loves us, but to have this knowledge spoken to you, specifically in a prophetic way, was almost an out-of-body experience. This prophecy has been a source of encouragement many times.

In 2023, God again spoke His words of love to Wayne at the "Sons of the Gospel" conference sponsored by Brother Terry Ballard and his church in McComb, Mississippi. One of the conference evangelists, D. C. Corson, awkwardly walked up to Wayne and timidly told him, "I have a word from the Lord for you." I'm not sure why the Lord wants me to tell you, but He said to tell you, 'I love you.'"

It was humbling to have our great King tell him emphatically, not once but twice, "I love you."

In times of discouragement, our own sinful flesh and the enemy of our soul always want us to think that God will not come through *this time!*

Yes, God has definitely done it for you many times in the past, and I'm sure He will in the future, but this time, *in the present*, He will not!

The words in another one of our daughter's songs fit this place in the script.

He Will Not Fail

Song written by our one and only daughter,
Christy Renee Huntley Ballestero

Verse 1
"Surely, this will be the trial that He won't come through
After countless innumerable times, He's been faithful and true… so true.
Surely, this will be the night that I'll face alone.
But what's that I see? It's the light, and it's the breaking of dawn.

Verse 2
Surely this will be the hill that I'll climb all alone
After countless innumerable mercies and grace, He has shown.

Surely this will be the mile that I'll walk alone
But He's at the finish line waiting, and I'm almost home…

Chorus

He will not fail me. He will not fail me.
He is bound to His word, and His word stands alone
It will not pass away
For the flowers may fade, all wither away
But the promise of God it's here to stay
He will not fail me… He will not fail."

When my sweet Mother was nearing the end of her earthly journey, she always seemed to be just a little apprehensive about dying. I was praying for her and asking God to give her peace. I felt the Lord gently remind me and speak the words of an old song to my heart for her and me.

Mother and daughter – Patsy and Christy

"I won't have to cross Jordan alone
Jesus died all my sins to atone
When the darkness I see, He'll be waiting for me
I won't have to cross Jordan alone."
Daniel O'Donnell

Sister Thetus Tenney said to us one day. "Our 70s have been great, our 80s, not so much."

So, we, being in our 70s at the time of this writing, are trying to make the most of our 70s, knowing that the 80s are coming, and we will have another decade of "slowing down." We will be fine as long as things don't come to a screeching halt! God has got this and us.

To Sum It All Up

How privileged we have been. God has allowed Wayne to preach many messages that God gave him. Back when we were still evangelizing, and Wayne was beginning his ministry full-time, he would take a blanket to the church, spread it on the floor, and get down and pray this prayer: "God, anybody can 'read' the Bible, but I want 'You' to tell me what 'You' are trying to say. Please give me an understanding and revelation of Your Word."

I cannot tell you how many times, from then until now, it has happened just like this.

He wakes up early, usually before daylight, and something is rolling around in his spirit, heart, and mind. Many times, it is something he has never thought of before. It is a revelation of the Word from God. It is Divine, just something God dropped into his heart. Most often, it was not something he read or heard but *God supernaturally speaking to him.* This is why I feel that his messages have had and continue to have such an impact and meet individual needs.

Quite a few years ago, Brother Tom Trimble asked my husband, "How did you become the master of alliteration?"

"The master of *what?*"

"Alliteration."

"What's that?"

"The occurrence of the same letter or sound at the beginning of adjacent or closely connected words."

"Well, I didn't know that's what I was doing. I just heard years ago, when I was a young preacher, that if you wanted to show importance to something, you would emphasize it with three words that describe it. So, somehow, I just started to string words together using the same letter or the same sound at the beginning."

This is now known as the "Wayne Huntley" preaching style, "alliteration!"

Below is his ministry as defined by him, showing an example of how his mind works in alliteration.

> *"As a young man, in my early ministry, I desired to be*
> ***"informational."***
> *As I progressed a few years, I desired to be*
> ***"inspirational."***
> *In my seasoned ministry, I want to be*
> ***"transformational,"***
> *(to make a difference and help change*
> *other people's lives, attitudes, and thoughts)."*
>
> Wayne Huntley

As a full-time evangelist of the UPCI, the very first camp meeting at which he was privileged to preach was in 1976, at the age of twenty-six, in the state he loves above all others, North Carolina, at Camp Dixie in Fayetteville, North Carolina. How fitting that this first launching of his camp meeting ministry should be here, at home!

Since then, I could not begin to name all the states in which he has preached at youth camps and camp meetings. They are too numerous to list, but there are only about five states where he has not, primarily in the extreme northeast. This is an honor beyond comprehension. My husband has said many times, "There are hundreds of preachers in the UPCI, good ones, and many never heard outside their place of labor. I don't understand why I have had the honor of having so many invitations."

All we can say is that it's a God thing and not something we orchestrated, for we absolutely could not have done this, even if we had tried. We most assuredly did not realize the full extent of this privilege. Many ministers keep excellent records of the times and places they have been the "Vessel of Opportunity," but we did not. As we were living our lives, we *knew* that the way God was blessing us and the doors He was opening was truly overwhelming; however, we could not completely comprehend the extent of those open doors! It was only when I began to research this book that we were made aware of the overwhelming blessings of opportunity that my husband has been given.

Over a thirty-year span of time, he has been privileged to preach "Because of the Times" twenty-five times. From the first message in 1987, when he was only thirty-seven years old, "Preach Them Out of Hell," to the last one in 2019, at age sixty-nine, "Stretch For the Supernatural," and all those in between, God spoke so explicitly.

These are some of the most memorable:

***1987*, "Preach Them Out of Hell"**

***1990*, "The Second Dimension of Spiritual Deliverance":** When we first receive the Holy Ghost, we are alive, but holiness delivers us in the second dimension of deliverance when we get the grave clothes of the world removed by the preached Word. (Lazarus was alive when Jesus said, "Lazarus, come forth," but someone had to remove his grave clothes. Then he was truly free.)

***1998*, "The Margin of the Miraculous":** What you need is always beyond what we can do. We must have His help.

***2000*, "When Your Ship Comes In, Don't Be at the Bus Station.":** When what you have prayed and believed for so long begins to happen, make sure you are in a place to receive what God is sending.

***2001*, "You Can't Fake It, You Have to Faith It"**

2006*, "There Is No Substitute for Sons": Having people come to your church from some other Apostolic church is not the same as winning your own sons.

2008*, "Hath Israel No Sons?": Does Israel (the church) have sons to carry on this Gospel? That night, he brought up our current three grandchildren and had them running across the platform, hitting a target of things (like soul-winning, holiness, etc.) he wanted them to accomplish in their lives. This was when he told of the prayers he had prayed for them at our Saturday night prayer meetings. (See Chapter 7: "Pastor and Mrs. Wayne Huntley" for this prayer.)

Brother Huntley, Christyana, Brother C.M. Becton holding Christian, and Huntley Starr

2010*, "The Conception of a Wild Man": The temptation to try to produce in the flesh the things that can only be appropriately provided by the Spirit.

2013*, "The Most Serious Sickness of the Soul": (Discouragement).

2014*, "The Last Giant Before Canaan": The last hurdle before we receive what we need and want from the Lord is a king-size bed, the spirit of complacency.

Many have approached him and told him how his messages have changed their lives and ministries. We understand and appreciate this great privilege, for it was from this platform that his ministry was most certainly elevated beyond his wildest dreams. For this, we give God glory and thank Brother Anthony Mangun and the Pentecostals of Alexandria, Louisiana, for this great honor.

From 1983 to 1995, I was honored to work in the Ladies Auxiliary Department, now known as the Ladies Ministry. For the first seven years, I served as the secretary of the North Carolina District's Ladies' Auxiliary. Over the last five years, I was the president. I acquired a greater burden and understanding because of my involvement in this great department.

My husband preached at the Mid-America Revival Conference, the East Coast Conference, the Power Conference, the Impact Conference, the Landmark Conference, Touch the Future, and the R3 (Renew, Refresh, Refocus). Those came to my mind, and there may be others.

In August 1981, at the age of thirty-one, he preached "The Curse of Meroz" at the second North American Youth Congress in Shreveport, Louisiana. He said that we "all" must do our part for the Kingdom of God; if not, we are cursed.

Nashville, Tennessee, August 6, 2009, at the age of fifty-nine, Wayne preached at the NAYC to approximately twenty thousand, mostly young people. His message was titled "The Temptation of This Time," which is that, as humans, we are tempted just to be common, to be normal, to be average, to go along so you can get along, to be, to please, and to compromise for the sake of camaraderie and companionship. It is to be reduced to the lowest level of acceptance rather than to rise to the highest level of challenge and reach the potential God intended.

He was privileged to teach at the Global Missions School of Mission in 2016. How far-reaching and significant this seminar is in saving souls around the world. He was honored to participate in such an integral event of the UPCI.

School of Missions

If my research is correct, he has preached at general conferences fifteen times. That is way beyond the privilege that any one person should ever have.

His first time was in <u>1983</u> in Louisville, Kentucky, to approximately twenty thousand people, when he was just thirty-three. **"Not Discerning the Lord's Body":** Which is failing to appropriately evaluate the significance of the church in the world today.

Brother Rex Johnson preached the night before, and Brother Nathanial Urshan, the then General Superintendent of the UPCI, preached the night after.

<u>–1993,</u> Louisville, Kentucky, "**What Have You Packed in My Lunchbox, Mommy?**" At age forty-three, he preached the Sunday School Service. This particular day, he had a high fever and returned to bed after preaching that service. But God gave him strength, and we have heard many people comment on this message through the years.

–1996, San Antonio, Texas, Youth Service: **"Abraham's Last Trial."** This has been one of my favorite messages, and it has changed how I worship in my own life. The trial of Abraham was that God wanted to know if he loved Jehovah as much as the heathens loved their gods. In that day, they would offer their children on an altar of sacrifice. When Abraham proved that he was willing to do that, then God said, "Now I know." In Acts 19, it is recorded that for two hours, the heathen people cried out to the goddess, Diana, "Great is Diana of the Ephesians." For *two hours*! Some of us cannot hold our hands up in worship for more than twenty seconds! God looks at the people who worship false gods, and He wonders, "When will my people worship Me like the heathen worship their gods?" (Sports, money, sex–anything that comes between them and the one true God is a false, idolatrous god.)

–1999, Global Missions, Nashville, Tennessee: **"Giving, a Matter of Life and Death,"** where, at the time, the highest offering for a mission's service was taken.

> *"People don't give because they have,*
> *They have because they give!"*

–2008, Greensboro, North Carolina, Sunday School Department: **"Why Some Pentecostal Kids Will Not Be Saved."** Parents, it's not enough to live for God; how we live for God makes all the difference. Deuteronomy, chapter 28, states all of the *blessings* that will come on you and overtake you IF you will hearken diligently unto the voice of the Lord and DO all His commandments. In verse 15, the Bible begins to reiterate all the curses that will come on you IF you do not. Verse 32 states one of those curses, *"Thy sons and thy daughters shall be given unto another people, and thine eyes shall look, and fail with longing for them all the day long..."* (Use a spiritual application for this verse.) Then we come to verse 47, where the Bible gives us the reason why our children *are given to other people* and leave and do not stay in the church. *"Because thou servest* *not the Lord thy God with <u>joyfulness</u>, and with <u>gladness of heart</u>, for the abundance of all things;"* Yes, how we serve the Lord does make a difference; we must do it with joyfulness and gladness of heart, because;

>*"You can teach what you Know,*
>*But you reproduce what you Are."*

<u>–2018</u>, Louisville, Kentucky, Children's Ministry Service (former Sunday School); **"The High Cost of Carrying Glory"** The price that people have paid who have watched their children and grandchildren go "off" into the ministry and "into" the will of God, to work for the King, and have been left at home to mourn. Not as some mourn because you are happy they are in the "Gospel work" (As the older generation said it), but mourning, nonetheless, because we are human, and when you love, you miss their presence in your life. When they are absent, your heart hurts, even though your head says, "You go on into the will of God, and we will just wait until we see you again, either *here* or *there!*" (At home or in heaven.) Not much has ever been said about this group of people, but these people pay the highest price for "*Glory to be carried* to a world that needs salvation."

<u>–2019</u>, at the North American Missions service, at age sixty-nine, in Indianapolis, Indiana, he preached **"The Treasure is in the Field."** Oh, what a mighty move of the Spirit. We were on target to have at least

one crusade per state on one specific day in the year 2020, duplicating what was done in the counties of North Carolina. Sad to say, this was stolen from us by that dreaded, horrible intruder, COVID-19. Most everything for 2020 was canceled because of this unwanted epidemic.

Around the time of COVID, Wayne started the Superintendent's call each Sunday at 8:30 a.m. This call was for the North Carolina District ministers (Plus anyone nationwide who desired to participate). It is primarily to encourage each other and pray together. At the end of the call, which only lasts about fifteen minutes, he gives a little sermon in a nutshell. Those in attendance go away each Sunday morning with a message that can be used in their church.

Humbly, I say this is an actual shortlist; he has preached many more. You might think that he must have a "big head" after being able to preach all those times and places.

When we married in 1969, Brother Duane Kramer and his brother, Louis, who was from South Carolina at the time, came to our wedding. (It was an honor for them to be there, as they were the only actual "old" friends that Wayne had in attendance.) All the rest were new friends he had met when he came with me to Waco to meet *my* family and friends. None of Wayne's family were able to be present.

Fifty years later, in 2019, at this particular general conference in Indianapolis, Indiana, after Wayne preached *"The Treasure is in the Field,"* Brother Duane Kramer stopped us in the hall. He said, "Wayne always has a message to fit the occasion. If it's a children's service, it's a message for children. If it's missions, it's a missionary sermon, and he always does it with excellence. You, probably in private, have to pop his head like a balloon."

I said, "No, he does that for himself; I don't have to do it." (However, I would if I needed to … smile.)

As much or more than anyone else, Wayne is always a bit surprised and excited by the anointing and power of the Word. He knows it's not him; it's God. That is why he never listens to a recording of himself preaching. I do, but he doesn't. He says, "This anointing is divine, and it seems almost sacrilegious to me to listen to *my* voice speak what God said. God did it; it wasn't me, and I never want to think it was!"

This is one of the many things I love and appreciate about this man–his humility.

I am his biggest "fan" and his "lifetime coach." I help him improve his presentation, how he looks, and how he appears and comes across. I am always on the lookout to correct any annoying habits that preachers occasionally pick up, and I *always* have his best interest at heart. I *never* tell him in public or correct anything in front of others. I would never want to come across as bossy, embarrass him, or want him to appear hen-pecked. But I do want him to always be at his best! He knows this and has always accepted my constructive criticism!

I feel one of the reasons that more ministers are not used to their full potential is that they don't give God the glory, and God said He would not share His glory with another. Many start with a bang ministerially and fizzle to a bust because of this. There is no end to what God will do with the person who truly gives Him the glory and knows that the magnificent things happening come from God above, not our human ability!

*"God will do nothing,
With an arrogant and egotistical person."*

If we are to be used by God to our full personal potential, we have to conclude that we cannot just be like everybody else, not only sinners but even good Christians. There are consecrations and dedications that we must make, as well as a lifestyle that is to be lived according to the will of God. There are things that others may do that we cannot do. There are places that others may go, but we cannot go. There are things that others may *be that, if we are to be utterly pleasing to God* and are genuinely *used* by God, we <u>*cannot be.*</u> It is not necessarily sin or things that are wrong; it is just sacrifices we gladly make to be used by God.

We have given the writing "Others May, You Cannot" (by G. D. Watson) to our grandchildren and the youth of our church, encouraging them to willingly give of themselves to God and realize that it's an honor to be asked by God to live a set-apart life.

<u>Others May, You Cannot</u>

G. D. Watson

If God has called you to be really like Christ in all your spirit,
He will draw you into a life of crucifixion
and humility and put on you such demands of obedience,
that He will not allow you to follow other Christians,
and in many ways, He will seem to let other good people
do things which He will not let you do.

Others can brag on themselves, and their work,
on their success, on their writings,
but the Holy Spirit will not allow you to do any such
thing, and if you begin it, He will lead you into
some deep mortification that will make you
despise yourself and all your good works.

The Lord will let others be honored and put forward,
and keep you hidden away in obscurity because He wants to
produce some choice fragrant fruit
for His glory, which can be produced only in the shade.

Others will be allowed to succeed in making money,
But it is likely God will keep you poor because
He wants you to have something far better
than gold, and that is a helpless dependence on Him;
that He may have the privilege of supplying your needs day by day–out of an unseen treasury.

*God will let others be great, but He will keep you small.
He will let others do a great work for him and get credit for it,
but He will make you work and toil on without
knowing how much you are doing;
and then to make your work still more precious,
He will let others get the credit for the work you
have done, and this will make your reward
ten times greater when He comes.*

*The Holy Spirit will put strict watch over you,
with a jealous love and will rebuke you for little
words and feelings, or for wasting your time,
which other Christians never seem distressed over.*

*So, make up your mind that God is an infinite Sovereign,
and He has a right to do what He pleases with
His own, and He will not explain to you
a thousand things which may puzzle your
reason in His dealings with you.
He will wrap you up in a jealous love,
and let other people say and do many things
that you cannot do or say.*

*Settle it forever that you are to deal directly with
the Holy Spirit, and that He is to have the privilege
of tying your tongue, or chaining your hand, or
closing your eyes in ways that others are not dealt with.*

*Now, when you are so possessed with the Living
God that you are, in your secret heart, pleased
and delighted over this particular personal, private,
jealous guardianship and management of the
Holy Spirit over your life, you will have found the
vestibule of heaven.*

Brother Bryan Ballestero, Huntley, and Brother Wayne Huntley

In January 2021, Huntley Starr, age twenty-three, our number one grandson, went before the North Carolina District Board and was approved to be licensed with the UPCI. Then, in April 2023, our granddaughter, Christyana (also at the age of twenty-three), met the Illinois District Board and received her approval for the General License of the UPCI. We were so Holy Ghost proud that our grandchildren were beginning to start their journey as ministers of this great Gospel of Jesus Christ. We couldn't be more proud and thankful. This is our greatest joy for them.

Below is a letter written to Huntley. My husband doesn't remember writing it, but it is fantastic advice for all our grandchildren and any young and aspiring minister.

Christyana Ballestero Blake

Dear Huntley,

I rejoice in hearing that you have a passion and love for the Word of God, the Spirit of God, and the work of God.

The single, superior prerequisite to be used by God is passion. Tradition and heritage are priceless, the ability is advantageous, the potential is noteworthy, but only passion can activate in our lives that which is handed down or lies dormant.

The theme of my personal ministry has always been, "If you make God's business your business, God will make your business His business." The ministry should never be viewed as a pastime or part-time, but a high, holy vocation deserving and demanding nothing less than my best!

As you prepare yourself for God's ultimate will in your life, give attention to this: to know God, to love people, and to serve both.

The key to having influence with people is not to be an <u>interesting</u> person but rather to be an <u>interested</u> person.

There is no substitute for the divine favor of God.

Remember this: at the end of your life, there will be only four things with you, so give attention to them.

1. *God*
2. *Family*
3. *Friends*
4. *Yourself*

Your goal in life should be to walk with <u>God</u>.
Stay close to your <u>family</u>.
Learn the value of having and being a <u>friend</u>.
Be somebody <u>you</u> like.
May God's anointing rest heavy upon your life.

Wayne Huntley,

Your loving, proud Grandbuddy

One January, my husband taught the *Temple of Pentecost* family an eye-opening lesson. Later, I wrote a periodical with this information. Below is that writing.

"A Personal Spiritual Inventory for the Beginning of the Year"

The years on the calendar of life fly by with amazing speed. Why, it seems it was just *a few years ago* that I was graduating from high school and starting on my personal journey. Only *last year*, I was a young preacher's wife with so much ahead of me. Then, could it be more than *a few short months* ago that our sweet daughter, Christy, was born, and we pressed our noses against the hospital nursery window, and our hearts were so warmed by her perfectness and beauty? But then, was it only *last month* that she came down the aisle to the "Bridal March"? Then, another page turned on this journey called life as we joined that most precious privileged group and became grandparents to the five most special people in the world. *Last week* (was it?), we came to Raleigh, North Carolina, with such enthusiasm. *Yesterday*, we were already stepping down as senior pastor of the Temple of Pentecost, and our son-in-law and daughter, Bryan and Christy Ballestero, were stepping up into that position of honor, but *today*, I feel a real need to do a check on my spiritual condition. The years can slip by so swiftly, sometimes almost as rapidly as the narrative above, and we must be careful that it doesn't go by so fast and furiously that we do not maintain our walk with God and move forward and onward and upward in the will of God.

These ten questions are for your self-examination. They are a type of spiritual gauge that will help us see where we stand.

They are questions to *ask oneself as* one year ends and a new year begins. Many New Year's resolutions are started in January. But, this time, let's look *back at the old year* and see how well we have progressed since last January. This is not the time for slacking or turning around in our walk with God, but we must take ourselves by our bootstraps and run across the finish line of life. To put it in the words of an old song:

"Search me, O God, and know my heart today.
Try me, O Savior, know my thoughts, I pray.
See if there be some wicked way in me.
Cleanse me from every sin, and set me free."

Edwin Orr

"Examine yourselves, whether ye be in the faith; prove your own selves…"

(II Corinthians 13:5)

1. Am I closer to God in my spiritual walk at the end of this year, or have I drifted away?
2. Has my participation in church events and ministries increased or decreased?
3. Am I praying more or less since the beginning of the year?
4. Have I been more faithful or less faithful in my finances to God's cause?
5. How many souls did I win to the Lord this year through home Bible study or other methods of evangelism?
6. Has my faithful attendance to church services increased or decreased?
7. Has my commitment to holiness and separation from the world in activities, apparel, and conversation changed or remained the same?
8. Has my knowledge of the Bible and love for Jesus increased?
9. Do I feel more or less connected to my church family?
10. Are my dreams of the past greater than my vision of the future?

EXAMINE YOURSELVES TO SEE WHETHER YE BE IN THE FAITH!

Chapter Eleven

Conclusion

Standing at the end of life, at the top of the mountain, we are making our preparations to start that slippery slope down to the place we cross old Jordan. Looking back at the road that brought us "here" to this place in time made us realize just how much God has blessed, directed, and led us. The road has twisted and turned, straightened out, and become wide at times; then, at some places, it would be so narrow that we could hardly make it forward, and there was barely any place for footing. Then, it would be smooth sailing without a care in the world. Some days were so dark that we could scarcely see our hands in front of our faces. Then the sun, in all of its glory, would appear and make life grand again. It takes all kinds of days to make up "a life's journey." It takes rain to make things grow just as much as sunshine; thus is life. We learned that even when it was raining and dark clouds were all we could see, the sun was shining all the time. We just had to have faith that the clouds would roll away and the sun would again appear in our sight.

This is part of the story of "our lives." It is the view from this end of the road. It is our journey to the TOP and beyond, our ultimate goal, Heaven!

So, dear friends, on *your* journey home, take note of two people who know. Don't lose hope; you have *an expected end*. Don't forget in your day-to-day battles that God will see you through. The good always outweighs the bad. In any situation, you can always find God there, leading and guiding. And the times that you honestly can't see Him or seem to find Him, take heart and trust the process, because in the end, you will always look back and realize God had His hand on you.

Once, Wayne took Huntley, our oldest grandson, to the Dixie Deer Classic at the State Fairgrounds in Raleigh. This is a man's world, filled with hunting and fishing supplies and new gadgets. The place was loaded with people, shoulder to shoulder. He and Grandbuddy were walking along, and somehow, Huntley got ahead and slightly separated from him. Huntley was only around five years old, and *everybody* was taller than him, so when he looked around, all he could see were men's camo or jean-clad legs and belt buckles. All of a sudden, my husband saw him look around and say, "Grandbuddy."

Looking around, now with a little more thought and with just a tinge of anxiety and questioning, said again, "Grandbuddy?"

Now, he is getting really scared and frantically says, "Grandbuddy!"

About this time, Grandbuddy reached him and said, "Here I am, Huntley!"

"Grandbuddy, I couldn't find you. I couldn't see you!"

"That's okay, Huntley. You really didn't need to worry or be afraid because I had my eyes on you, and I could see you all the time. You were never in real trouble. You were never out of my view."

What a consolation! We are always in His view, always in His care, always in His heart. He knows us by name, and the very hairs on our heads are not just counted but numbered, and He knows which hair is number 777.

Our lives have been so fulfilling. We are at that point in life where, for the most part, we are actually looking back on our lives. We don't have dreams that need to become a reality. God has made all our dreams come true on so many more levels than we could ever have imagined, and on an even grander scale than we thought possible. We have lived a fairy tale life.

How awesome it is, at this place and time of our journey, that we look back and know what God will do *for* you, *with* you, and *through* you, if you are humble and give God the glory for all things.

Our journey to the TOP and beyond has the ambiguous meaning of:

a.) Temple of Pentecost, and,

b.) *Heaven.* Heaven is the ultimate TOP, the whole reason for this astounding journey, which we have almost completed. I would love for us to go arm in arm, sweeping through the pearly gates together, as we have been in life, or to rise together to meet Him, our Lord and Savior, in the air. And so shall we ever be with the Lord. Then, we will have truly made it to the TOP.

We have no regrets, except that we could never do enough for our Lord and Savior, Jesus Christ, for what He has done for us. As Paul the Apostle said, *"I am a debtor."* He has given and given and given to us, and we will leave this world owing Him for His continued blessings and goodness.

From where we are right now, things look pretty good. I'm glad God let me walk this life with Wayne Huntley, my only sweetheart and love, for over fifty years. I have loved every minute of our life together. God indeed gave me the very best. I have always known that we have an exceptional bond and connection that many married couples do not have. I have always appreciated and been thankful for it. It's an unusual relationship, a special love that we share, and I think the words of this song, sung by Ray Price and written by Larry Bastion/Craig Morris, say it just right!

This Thing of Ours

Just look at you lying there
You should see the way the morning dances in your hair
I'm tempted just to wake you just to see you smile
And hold you gently to me for a little while.

Like an old guitar growing sweet with age
Like that book, you can't put down until you've turned the page
It's knowing that you're always there to fill my glass
You and me together, we've made the first time last.

This thing of ours, this love we share
The comfort knowing when I turn, I'll find you there
By my side for the long, long ride
This thing of ours.

When it's done and the credits roll
Let it be said together that we stole the show
We'll save the last "I love you" for the curtain call
Let it be said there is a happy ending after all.

This thing of ours, this love we share
The comfort knowing when I turn, I'll find you there
By my side for the long, long ride
This thing of ours.

He has opened the windows of heaven to us, and we can say without reservations that for Wayne and Patsy Huntley, it has been **A Wonderful Life, living for the Lord _together_!**

The End

Epilogue

Words from Family, Friends, and the Field

A Tribute to My Pastor, by Brian Angel

(Written for our 25th Pastoral Anniversary–2003)

I must admit today that my time is too short, and my words are too limited to adequately and accurately express how I feel toward this man and his wife! I will, however, say without hesitation or reserve that no one person has had the impact and influence on my personal character, calling, and career as this man. Without exception, I have aspired and attempted to emulate his example, duplicate his desires, and preserve his passions in my own life. My speech, my strategies, and (prayerfully) my spirit all bear the markings of this man's handprints on the making of my ministry.

Thomas Carlyle said it this way: "Show me the man you honor, and I will know what kind of a man you are, for it shows me what your ideal of manhood is, and what kind of a man you long to become."

The following is my interpretation—

My exposure to the Apostolic atmosphere and Pentecostal preaching started early on.

My unsolicited, unprompted, and often unappreciated attraction and attention to its excitement, energy, and fire was initiated and instigated by one man, Wayne Huntley.

From the moment I walked into 105 Yeargan Loop Road as a six-year-old kid, I knew I wanted to be like the tall man who stood before me with a handkerchief in his pocket and reading glasses not yet needed.

I wanted to preach like him, to pray like him, to pastor like him. My intentions today remain the same.

I can still recall and recite the messages I heard as a child, such as "Living in a Haunted House" and "Somewhere in the Blacksmith's Shop!" I was inspired by "Make God's Business, Your Business, and God Will Make Your Business, His Business."

I was intoxicated with "A Drink From Joel's Place." I was challenged by "Don't Lose Your Head." I was convicted by "Don't Forget your Appointment." I was changed by "How Far Is It From Heaven to Hell," "Sounds That Satan Cannot Stand to Hear," and "You Can Be Your Own God, but You Can't Be Your Own Savior." "When Your Ship Comes In, Don't Be At The Bus Station" kept me grounded. "The Holy What, The Holy Who, The Holy When, and The Holy Why" kept me guessing.

The list is endless!

And I might add that the toughest and timeliest messages didn't always come from 'him'; Sister Huntley had a unique way of getting her point across as only she could, and I imagine she still can. Sitting on the front row as a teen boy, I can still recall the organ wailing and the church weeping to "Where Will You Spend Eternity? You Never Mentioned Jesus To Me" and my personal favorite, "Take Me Home Last."

It was in Raleigh that I received an affinity for signs and a burden for souls. It was Sunday night revival services where the Holy Ghost would correct the confusion and forge the future of a teenage boy!

In 1983, you baptized my father; In 1999, you buried your friend!

I am a recipient of riches; I am a product of Pentecost at its finest. My healthiest memories and happiest moments usually included the Huntleys and Raleigh's First United Pentecostal Church, The Place Where Good Things Always Happen. And yes, I know it's a different day and a new name, yet 2312 Lake Wheeler Road will always be my home, heritage, and heart.

How do you repay that? You don't. You can't. You just say thanks. Thank you to the Huntleys for twenty-five years of leadership direction, influence, and impact.

Caison Judah Ballestero
Grandchild number four

I truly am so privileged and thankful to be able to say that Wayne and Patsy Huntley are my grandparents. They always set an example of how your love for God and the things of God should look like. They always make me feel so loved and safe when I am in their presence. I have been so blessed by their ministry, and it has impacted my life deeply.

Some of the most precious memories of my life were spent with them. I will never forget going hunting and fishing with Grandbuddy, whether we were deer hunting, turkey hunting, or fishing. I would always have a blast. While being able to kill a deer was so exciting, spending time with him was always the best part of it. Spending the night at Grandbuddy and Gramommy's house was always so fun and exciting. Staying up at night, eating Gramommy's breakfast and Grandbuddy's steak, and swimming in their pool on a hot summer day are some of the greatest moments of my life.

They are always there for you, supporting you and making you feel like the most important person in the world. I love you, Gramommy and Grandbuddy, so much, and I pray that I can have the same love for the Kingdom of God that you both have.

Christian Bryan Ballestero
(Grandchild number three)

My thanks and gratitude cannot be expressed in words to have the honor and privilege of calling Ronald Wayne Huntley and Patsy Sue Huntley my grandparents. Their unparalleled tenderness and love for me have been a prodigious factor in who I am today. Not only do they sacrifice their time and efforts for my sake, but they also sacrifice their own wants and desires to satisfy mine. I am forever indebted to your incomparable influence and your constant example of what a Pentecostal should look like. You are always watching out for me and are always there in times of desperation and need. No matter how much I try, I will never be able to express or repay the love I have been shown in the seventeen years of this wonderful life. My walk with God is constantly being strengthened because of the wonderful leadership of my grandparents. They are the most selfless, compassionate, kind, loving, reassuring, sweet, amiable, and most of all, holy and submitted to the wonderful truth of Pentecost.

I love you both unremittingly. I am the person I am today because of the superb and incomparable example you have set for me. You have aided my walk with God tremendously, and that, of all things, is the most important thing to me. As I pursue my calling for God, their teachings are a constant guide to whom I want to be like.

I love you, Gramommy and Grandbuddy. Thank you for being a perfect example of who I want to be in my walk with God.

Love,

Christian

Huntley Starr Ballestero
Grandson (Our first)

Vince Lombardi, a historic American football coach, has been quoted as saying, "Winning is not a once-in-a-while thing; you can't win once in a while. You don't do things right once in a while; you do them right all the time. Winning is a habit." You will find no better example of a winning team than Wayne and Patsy Huntley. They have made a habit of winning in every major aspect of life, pursuing excellence in God, family, and ministry. Through a lifetime of ministry, they have earned many prestigious titles and accolades in the Kingdom of God, but their dedication and love for the family have made the biggest impact on my life.

Grandbuddy and Gramommy have always been present in the lives of their kids and grandkids, no matter how busy they were or how inconvenient. They have simply always been there. And that is what makes them winners to us.

LeDon Barnhill
Pastor of The Pentecostals of Lumberton
Lumberton, North Carolina
District Secretary, North Carolina District of the UPCI

Since the early '80s, the Huntleys have been a part of my life and ministry. Some of the earliest memories I have of Bishop Huntley and the impact he's had on my life were sitting around a campfire at his home, along with several other PK (preacher's kids) boys.

The day was filled with playing ball, swimming, fishing, and other activities, but the highlights were the evening devotions that Bishop Huntley shared with us.

It was during these moments that we heard of the joys of ministry, the excitement it brought to his own life, and the reward it would bring to ours. He taught us that God-called ministry was more fulfilling than that of being a king.

From his teenage years to adulthood, he's always had a timely word or humorous story that would have you smile and uplift your spirit.

At the passing of my father on November 26, 2020, at 1:20 a.m., I was at a crossroads that I had never faced. My father had been my shepherd for forty-three years, and now I found myself without a pastor. Although the natural man was devastated and hurting, the spiritual man was without a covering.

Of the many things that Roy Barnhill instilled into me, he constantly stated, "Son, if a man doesn't have a pastor, do not lend an ear, for his words are useless."

By 2:30 a.m. of that same morning, I called Bishop Huntley and said, "I need to ask a question I've never asked before. Will you be my pastor?"

Thank you, Bishop, for my covering. Thank you for your example, encouragement, prayer, and support. I am honored to serve with you in ministry!

Roy Barnhill 1951- 2020
Bishop of the Pentecostals of Lumberton
Lumberton, North Carolina
District Secretary, North Carolina District of the UPCI
(Submitted by his wife, Deborah Barnhill.)

To my confidant and best friend, Wayne Huntley,

Our friendship first developed at the North Carolina Youth Camp in the 1960s. After we finished high school, we geographically took different paths; however, our spiritual paths came full circle. Following Bible college, we returned to our North Carolina roots, assuming pastorate roles in small home missions churches (1978 and 1980). Our lives were instantly intertwined through ministerial work, and I was honored to serve as the District Secretary as you served as the District Superintendent.

From the fields of Texas to the coastal plains of North Carolina, we shared a plethora of hunting and fishing adventures and memories. The greatest memory of all was sharing our visions and dreams.

Our friendship was built on trust, rooted in wisdom, and sustained by loyalty. Thank you for sharing your life and love with me and my family; we are better because of it.

My confidant, brother, friend, mentor, and hunting buddy, I will see you again just inside the Eastern Gate!

Thomas Batts (Tommy)
Raleigh, North Carolina

Thanks for this opportunity. Once I got through all the tears, I finally could get a few words down, although it was hard to pick and choose. The memories are so good, and there are so many.

"Even Losers Win Sometimes; I have a right to know!" These are just a few words from a song Sister Huntley sang several years ago that forever impacted my life. The echoes of that memorable moment continually resonate in my heart, soul, and spirit.

"The Spirits of Just Men Made Perfect" is my all-time favorite message by Brother Huntley. This message stuck deeply into my heart, moved me to tears, and now drives me to live it out today. The spirit of men like Brother Huntley and others must live on through us.

Brother Huntley taught me how to clean my first deer and, on several occasions, has told me, "I love you like a son." These words I shall never forget.

Kimberly Batts
Raleigh, North Carolina

I was thirteen when I walked into a small church on Loop Road. Little did I know how my life would change. Brother Huntley preached, "God Is Not Ashamed To Be Called Their God."

Since then, they have been my pastor and wife. They have been an example to me in so many ways. They are my heroes. They corrected me with love, and I never doubted they wanted what was best for me. Their faithfulness to the call of God to Raleigh is evident in generations of families that now know the Truth, mine included.

Christyana Ballestero Blake
(Granddaughter)

There are few adequate words to describe how blessed I have been to grow up under the shadow of Wayne and Patsy Huntley's ministry. The greatest privilege was not growing up on Wayne Huntley's preaching, even though I consider that a tremendous blessing. Nor was it the instruction by this couple in training for Apostolic ministry, although it shaped my life in many ways. The greatest blessing was simply to call them "Grandbuddy and Gramommy."

As a young child, I got the opportunity to know what they were like behind closed doors. I saw that their character was the same in public as in private. I heard the wisdom that was not always included in a sermon. I witnessed passion and prayers not expressed to the eyes and ears of others; my respect for them was all the more enlarged. I cannot thank them enough for all that they instilled in me, not just through instruction but through action.

One of my greatest treasures is the time spent with them. Whether it was sitting in a deer stand eating honey buns, going to Disney World, relaxing on their back porch, or swimming in their pool in the heat of summer. All my moments with them were something I wanted to remember. One of my favorite moments was my wedding day. I remember thinking how blessed I was that my Grandbuddy could perform the ceremony, and my Gramommy helped make certain the alterations on my dress were done perfectly. They always made sure that my needs were taken care of, as well as some of my wants. They're grandparents; they can't help it!

The most precious thing they have given me was not an expensive item; it is a love for the things of God. They always made God the priority and passed on their love for Truth and prayer. I'll never forget a specific time that I walked into the church on a weekday afternoon and heard my Grandbuddy praying for me. All I could do was sit and listen, feeling the presence of God. He had prayed over me hundreds of times during Saturday night prayer meetings, but this time, he had no idea that I was there, and it touched me. A lot of people have been blessed by the prayers of my Grandbuddy, but I know that just as many have been blessed by my Gramommy's prayers. They don't have to be exquisite or masterful prayers; in fact, most times, they are simple but powerful. I know that she touches the throne room of heaven.

I consider them both to be my mentors as well as some of my biggest supporters. I would not be the person that I am today without their prayers and devotion to the Lord. They are my heroes, and I pray that one day, I can be the same godly witness for my children and grandchildren.

Gerald Blake, Evangelist
Raleigh, North Carolina

1979 was the start of the greatest blessing my family has ever been privileged to be a part of. Because of the TOP in Raleigh, the ministry of Pastor Wayne and Patsy Huntley, and their investment in my family, today, thirty-plus family members have been added to the church. Many are still in the church, serving God, and some are in heaven. There are pastors, evangelists, missionaries, and singers. Whatever I am for God is a direct result of Brother and Sister Huntley and their sacrifice of love for my family and me.

Susan Blake

In 1983, my two boys (Joe and Jeff Cecil) and I moved to Raleigh and became a part of the TOP. I have experienced many blessings in forty years under the leadership of Pastor Wayne and Patsy Huntley. After giving birth to my third child, Marcus Blake, and being close to death, I could hear Sister Huntley's precious voice calling my name, and it brought me back from that deep place where I was. God was not finished with my life. My involvement in ministry in the Kingdom of God includes pastoring and evangelizing with my husband, Gerald. I am forever thankful. Thank you both for loving, trusting, believing, and caring for me and my family.

Shane and DeAnna Britt
Pastor, Hartselle, Alabama

To try to put into words what the Huntleys mean to my wife and me would simply be impossible. Messages like "The Treasure is in the Field" and "Hath Israel No Sons?" have impacted our lives for the better, and we have been forever changed! However, our fondest memories have been sitting in your home talking, catering banquets, fishing, and hunting. These moments have left an indelible mark on our lives, and we are so blessed to have been connected.

Thanks for sharing your life with us. We love you!

David and Ashley Cadd, Raleigh
Missionaries to Madagascar and the Democratic Republic of Congo
Arthur, Winston, and Rosalie

One very distinct memory that has always stuck with me is the night I talked to the Huntleys about going to Bible college. I can remember the nervousness and the conversation that followed. He asked point-blank what my intentions were and why I wanted to go to Bible college. I told him I felt a call to missions and wanted to go to Texas Bible College for their missions program. He looked back and said, "That is one of the things I cannot teach you in Raleigh. You can go!"

Walking out of the church that night, I turned and looked back at Pastor Huntley right before I stepped out the door. The snapshot in my memory is of Pastor Huntley with a thumbs-up and smile, giving one last encouragement as I was heading home.

I'm thankful to have a pastor who invests in the dreams, burdens, and callings of the young. This decision changed my life and led me to where I am today!

Jeff and Heidi Cecil (Raleigh)
Missionaries to the Gambia

The Huntleys loved us from day one.

My single mother, Susan Cecil Blake, along with her two small boys, Joe and Jeff, needed love, healing, strength, and renewal. I thank God every day that we moved to Raleigh. We weren't family, just ordinary church saints, but I have childhood memories of being in the Huntley's home often. The best was when the Huntleys hosted church leadership meetings at their home, and they let us kids swim in the pool while the adults handled business.

The Huntleys love us.

For some reason, I was allowed in Pastor Huntley's church office to use his shoe buffer machine. I can still see the forest mural on the wall behind his desk. This was way before my teenage and young adult years, when I actually received invitations into "the office."

The Huntleys love us.

One of God's greatest blessings in my life is the Huntleys. I thank God every day for their love, integrity, and perfect example. Heidi and I are now on our own journey, striving to fulfill our God-given purpose. Every time I take a glance in the rearview mirror, I see the Huntleys and the Ballesteros with their hands on the truck, pushing us and cheering us on. Dear Bishop Wayne and Patsy Huntley, Heidi and I thank you, and

We love you.

Stan Cook
Evangelist

It's been my privilege to know Bishop and Sister Huntley for many years now, and I consider them close friends. He's one of the most passionate, anointed, articulate preachers I've ever heard. Yet, he makes everyone feel comfortable. I always enjoy just being around him and his magnetic personality and smile. He's so down to earth. That's why I've always said he doesn't just preach good; he's a good preacher. She is the ultimate lady of God who speaks the truth in love and proudly stands by her man. One of my favorite memories is when we were together at a camp meeting and sat in the hotel lobby eating tomato sandwiches! What fun! They are givers, some of the most generous people I know. They are fierce lovers of Truth and souls. What a couple! My life has been enriched just to know these great people of God! They are "TOPS!"

Jack Cunningham
Pastor of Bible World Church, Chesapeake, Virginia
District Superintendent of the Virginia District UPCI

Honoring a Pillar of Apostolic Faith: Wayne Huntley

Throughout the Apostolic world, few names resonate as profoundly as that of Wayne Huntley. A man whose life and ministry are a testament to unwavering faith and relentless dedication, Wayne Huntley has left an indelible mark on countless lives and churches. His contributions to the faith are vast and varied, making him a towering figure in Apostolic circles.

Wayne Huntley's reputation precedes him. His is a household name, synonymous with preaching, church planting, soul winning, church growth, and revival. His presence is a familiar one at general conferences, district conferences, camp meetings, and an array of national and international events. His voice has echoed through the halls of countless churches and auditoriums, bringing with it messages of hope, conviction, and divine promise.

Bishop Wayne Huntley's preaching is characterized by his profound love for the Word of God. He is a "Word preacher" whose sermons are deeply rooted in scripture. His messages are not just inspiring but are a call to action, urging believers to embrace the promises of God with unshakable faith. Bishop Huntley believes that God is true to His Word and that He will fulfill every promise made. This unwavering faith is evident in every sermon he delivers, making him a "faith preacher" in the truest sense.

Furthermore, Bishop Wayne Huntley's commitment to righteousness is uncompromising. He stands firm on the truth of the Apostolic Doctrine, preaching it with a fervor that is both inspiring and challenging. His sermons magnify God and uphold the principles of Truth and righteousness, urging believers to live lives that are pleasing to God. He is known for his no-compromise stance—a rarity in any age where convictions often waver.

The impact of Wayne Huntley's ministry is immeasurable. Hundreds of thousands have been touched by his anointed preaching. His messages are meticulously prepared and delivered with a skill that only years of dedication can hone. Those who have the privilege of hearing him preach often find their faith strengthened, their commitment deepened, and their vision for their spiritual journey lifted. Bishop Huntley has the unique ability to make believers feel that God will indeed do exactly what He has promised.

On a personal note, Wayne Huntley is not just a minister but a cherished friend. His loyalty and support have been unwavering, standing by his friends and colleagues through thick and thin. His integrity is beyond reproach, and his walk with God is one that I trust implicitly. In a world where true friendships are rare, Wayne Huntley's friendship is a treasure.

In conclusion, Wayne Huntley is more than a minister; he is a beacon of faith, a pillar of the Apostolic church, and a true man of God. His legacy is one of unwavering faith, profound wisdom, and steadfast commitment to the Word of God. It is an honor to know him, to learn from him, and to witness the powerful impact of his ministry.

He is, without a doubt, the finest Christian man I have ever had the privilege to know.

Steven Davidson
(Nephew)

Dear Sweet Aunt Patsy and Uncle Wayne,

I could write so many things. From the first time I saw you and Uncle Wayne at Granny's house in Waco, with that loaded down car towing that ole travel trailer (and how much that inspired me), or how I would sit in the kitchen of the old church in Garner, North Carolina, on Yeargan Loop Road, listening to Uncle Wayne pray (and how much that touched and helped me ever since), to all the times Aunt Patsy would, without judgment, step in and help everyone in our family (and, I guess, anyone else's too). I Love You So Much!

Uncle Wayne and you have been such a great inspiration and influence to my family. I wouldn't know where to start or what to even say, but I do thank you for all those anointed sermons, and I still love to hear my Aunt Patsy sing.

Granny Landtroop may have brought us to the church, but Wayne and Patsy kept us at the altar.

Thank you for your faithfulness, leadership, and unconditional love for all of us. We wouldn't be here without you.

Johnny Dean, Bishop
Bentonville, Arkansas

Our earliest memories of the Huntleys go back to Texas Bible College in Houston around 1970. They included us in services at Champion Paper Mill in Pasadena. Working men had lunch while listening to singing and preaching, as young men and women developed their evangelistic skills. They became examples of successful ministry for many young couples. Though distance has kept us separated during the years since, we still enjoyed visits to their church, home, and hunting "lodge."

Our interests provided wonderful fellowship, laughter, and memories between our families. He still holds the place as one of our favorites when it comes time to be encouraged by the Word.

Having the Huntleys in our home or church was and is always "special."

Debbie Dean

Wow! What an amazing friend to have in your life. We've been friends now for fifty years and will always cherish the times we've had together!

I will never forget the invitation to come minister in Raleigh while our children were small. You took them to the beach, an outdoor drama, fishing, and swimming. What a time they had, and the memories that were made.

Huntleys are the kind of friends you just pick up where you left off from the last visit. We love you dearly and thank you for being our friends! Patsy, let's go flea marketing!

James and Carolyn Douglas
Trustee, Temple of Pentecost
Raleigh, North Carolina

We never imagined what a blessing awaited us at the TOP! Our lives were forever changed by the spirit of excellence Sister Huntley demonstrated in leading the music ministry and Christian education, to the preaching of Brother Huntley, challenging us through messages like "Abraham's Last Trial" or "What Have You Packed in my Lunchbox, Mommy?" Through their Christian example, consistent prayers, and faithfulness to God, they exemplified the heart of true shepherds.

Thank you for standing with us in the good and challenging times! Only eternity will reveal the true blessings from our personal journey to the TOP.

Gene and Iva Easterling
Pastor, Christian Faith Outreach
Ashland, Kentucky

When we think of Brother and Sister Huntley, these words immediately come to mind: genuine, real Christians, and an inspiration of how it is supposed to be done! Brother Huntley has always been our favorite preacher. His feeling for the heartbeat of God and his anointed burden for the field have always inspired and motivated us to reach the lost. As young pastors, Brother Huntley's messages, like "The Treasure Is In The Field," "The Dream Is The Thing," and "Serious About Saving Our City," helped us believe that we could have Apostolic Revival in Ashland, Kentucky! And we have!

Bobby and Elaine Edwards
Vidor, Texas

Wayne Huntley is the voice of Pentecost!! Any good word you could think of would describe Wayne. He is our best friend, loyal, and the best preacher. He loves God and loves to preach more than anyone I know.

I met Wayne at Texas Bible College over fifty years ago. It was an instant friendship and has lasted all these years. He has always been there for us through the good and the bad. He is trustworthy personified. When he married Patsy, it stayed the same; we all became best friends.

We were a small part of them going to Raleigh, and we are so glad we were. When anyone mentions Wayne Huntley, I say, "There is only one."

We have enjoyed these many years of friendship and look forward to many more.

Wayne and Patsy, we love you dearly.

Patsy, Wayne, Elaine and Bobby Edwards, and Cathy and David Fauss

David L. Fauss
Bishop, Greater Bethel Tabernacle, Houston, Texas

I first met Wayne and Patsy Huntley in 1970 at Texas Bible College. They influenced me immediately. I was not the only one. However, Wayne

Huntley soon became everyone's preacher. His voice is now known around the world. He is a gift to the body of Christ.

Cathy and I treasure the times we have spent together with Wayne and Patsy. Not only have we had fun and laughter, but recently, when we needed direction, they shared their experiences similar to what we were going through. Their counsel was invaluable. Their story will also change your life!

Jill Fierge
Executive Assistant to the General Secretary
UPCI World Headquarters

As a former pastor's wife, now divorced for a few years, my confidence in my identity and place in ministry was quite shaken. But after a few years of healing, I obeyed the voice of God and pursued my UPCI ministerial credentials. Brother Huntley took the time to congratulate, encourage, and challenge me. It meant so much that this giant of the faith believed in my calling and ability to minister. His act of kindness further confirmed that God still had a place for me in His Kingdom. Brother Huntley's sermons have long blessed me, but he preached his most profound one to me that day.

Mark and Paulla Foster
Bishop/Evangelists
The Pentecostals of the Twin Cities
West Monroe, Louisiana

Oh, the treasure of memories and blessings of our friendship. Too many to just choose one!

How God used you to get us to North Carolina! The services in which we have worshipped together across the continent. The fun times and trips. There are so many "Memory Bank Moments"—from days spent at the farm to time spent in the Foster Room at your house, and great hunts across the

country (and Canada). We've laughed, rejoiced, wept, prayed, enjoyed highs, and experienced lows together.

Your friendship remains the same through it all. We cherish you both, and you have greatly influenced and impacted our lives!

Talmadge and Rebecca French
Apostolic Tabernacle, Pastor
Jonesboro, Georgia

We are deeply grateful for the friendship of the Huntleys! 2010 was a year of transition for our family. Talmadge was finishing his doctoral thesis at the University of Birmingham in England. We needed a home base for our family as Talmadge traveled. It was a difficult season, but the Huntleys and the Temple of Pentecost opened their arms to us, and a friendship was born that we cherish greatly! They have made an incredible impact on our entire family. It's wonderful to have friends who are "heroes of the faith" for our sons and their families.

Scott Graham
General Secretary-Treasurer
United Pentecostal Church International

A young preacher watched with wide-eyed wonder and "hero worship" as Brother Huntley skillfully and passionately preached from an obviously deep well. I cannot remember the actual content of the sermon. What I do remember is lying on my face, promising God that I would pray, study, and prepare to preach the best I could. After the service, I spoke with Brother Huntley and told him how he inspired me to serve God better. He kindly affirmed my desire. I've never forgotten it. He is a young preacher's friend. Now, he is the friend of a no-longer-so-young preacher.

Bishop Jerry and Barbara Green
Porter Apostolic Church
Porter, Texas

Dear Brother and Sister Huntley. I would just like to say thank you for being the great example that you have been throughout the years. What a wonderful testimony you both have been of love, faithfulness, endurance, service, giving, and so much more to so many. Our world would be so much better off if it had more people like you in it. I count myself to be especially blessed, not just to know you but to know you as longtime and forever true friends.

Much love.

L J Harry
United Pentecostal Church, Inc.

Brother Huntley,

Your message from the 2008 General Conference has never left me. "Why Some Pentecostal Kids Will Not Be Saved" causes me to pray that I will serve God with joyfulness and gladness of heart, so my family will see the joy that comes from living for Jesus. You are such a blessing to our world and ME!

Deuteronomy 28:32, 41, 47

Jeremy Hart
Evangelist

Preachers have always been my heroes, but none any more than the preacher I met as a three-year-old child at the Oklahoma Youth Convention in December 1993.

I heard Rev. Wayne Huntley preach the first night and met him in the elevator the second night.

Instantly, he became my favorite preacher. His message that evening became my favorite message, "Tell Hell, I Ain't Coming." For the duration of my childhood, I had one message to preach—"Tell Hell I Ain't Coming." I still have that copy of the cassette tape!

It became a part of who I was, along with the continued influence of one of the greatest preachers of our time.

Patrick and Rhonda Harvey
Pastor, Pentecostals of McDonough
McDonough, Georgia

I've been impacted by Brother Huntley's ministry since I was fourteen. Through the years, that impact has grown, and the Huntleys have become cherished friends to my wife and me. Brother Huntley has helped guide me

through some low seasons and high celebrations. When Brother Huntley came to our church in 2014, he told me on the second night of our meeting, "Last night, I preached to this church; tonight, I am preaching to you." He preached, "The Real Message of Christmas—Fear Not"! It was that night that I embraced the call God had on my life to preach and later pastor the wonderful church I now serve.

We love and thank God for the Huntleys.

Bishop and Mrs. Robert E. Henson
Flint Michigan

My first acquaintance with Wayne Huntley was in the early 1970s. As the years passed, Shirley and I grew even fonder of him and Sister Patsy.

Bishop Huntley has impacted our lives immensely through his pulpit ministry. He has also been a great source of personal encouragement and inspiration through our many personal conversations over the years.

Bishop and First Lady Huntley, Shirley, and I love you!

Josh Hodum
Pastor, Cookeville, Tennessee

The very definition of passion, care, and friendship is embodied in Brother Huntley. His anointed preaching and teaching illuminate the path of righteousness, while his authenticity and warmth create deep, lasting connections with so many. Brother Huntley has personally impacted my life in ways that only eternity will fully reveal. His kindness is genuine, never superficial, and his friendship is a gift for which I continually thank God. A true servant of the Lord, Brother Huntley exemplifies what it means to live a life of purpose, faith, and love … and as everyone knows, behind every successful pastor is a powerful, praying wife.

Thank God our era has been graced with the dynamic ministry and unwavering faith of Brother Wayne and Sister Patsy Huntley.

Gerald and Susan Huntley (brother and sister-in-law)
Bishop, Truth Tabernacle
Hickory, North Carolina
(Submitted by Susan)

I first met Wayne and Patsy Huntley while I was attending Texas Bible College in Houston. They were holding a revival in a town nearby, and my roommate invited me to attend. Riding in the car with Wayne and Patsy was also when I met Wayne's brother, Gerald. Patsy endeared herself to me when she later told Gerald, "You'd better go get that girl." I have felt her support ever since!

I only have good things to say about my wonderful sister-in-law and brother-in-law. They are the BEST of ordinary people. Loyal, True, Honest, and Trustworthy are a few words that describe their lives.

Because of their relationship with the Lord, we can count on them for their prayer and know God is listening.

Wayne told Gerald when we were in our church building program, "If you go down, I'm going with you!" We didn't, but that kind of support is immeasurable.

They give of themselves to the Kingdom of God and family and friends everywhere!

Thank you, Wayne and Patsy. You are so much loved.

Marcus Huntley (nephew)
Pastor Truth Tabernacle
Hickory, North Carolina

I am grateful for Wayne Huntley. Throughout my life, I've experienced his love, kindness, and compassion firsthand. He's taken me hunting, fishing, golfing, and more. He's been there when I needed someone to talk to when facing difficult situations. During the last few years, my family has suffered with our health, spiritual battles, and mental fatigue. Through it all, I KNOW that he's just a phone call away. If I become a tenth of the man that he is, I will consider myself a giant. I'm so thankful that God saw fit to give me the best uncle in the world.

I'm proud that I get to call you Uncle Wayne!

Love you!

Douglas and Patricia Klinedinst, Evangelist of the UPCI
National Evangelist Coordinator

Bishop Wayne Huntley has been an illuminating voice of inspiration, direction, and comfort to the body of Christ for the entirety of our ministry.

"Preach Them Out Of Hell" deeply impacted and focused our early evangelistic ministry.

I'm sure we echo the sentiments of an entire generation of ministers who are profoundly indebted to the Huntleys' labor of love and dedicated ministry.

Our beloved Sister Patsy Huntley has stood beside her husband, the man of God, demonstrating faithfulness, loyalty, and prayerful support. Perhaps unknowingly, she has left an incredibly positive impact on my wife and me. We have gleaned valuable counsel concerning ministry, family, and personal integrity, both listening and learning from this consistent and Godly woman.

My wife and I have attempted to rise in some small measure to the example these two giants of the faith have so marvelously provided.

We celebrate the ministry of Wayne and Patsy Huntley. We rejoice in the fruits of their labor made evident weekly at the Temple of Pentecost!

Dennis Landtroop (nephew)
Pastor, Carthage, Texas

While growing up in East Texas with my three siblings, there were seven words that were always sure to create excitement and bring a special joy to us. Those seven words were, "Aunt Patsy and Uncle Wayne are coming"! It meant we were in store for some great singing and preaching, food, fun, fishing, and a lot of laughter. It also sometimes included a book that Uncle Wayne would loan me to read. Those times and those books were very impactful in my life.

Those seven words became seven years when Uncle Wayne invited me to Raleigh, North Carolina, to help him plant a church that would become the TOP. I am not sure I helped very much, but it surely helped me. Those seven years were formative, informative, and transformative in my life.

Any good that my life produces is owed in large to Uncle Wayne, Aunt Patsy, and those seven years.

Christine Landtroop (niece)
Pastor's wife, Carthage, Texas

Almost four decades ago, when I married Dennis, I joined a family, and in the family was a man and woman of God that I had admired for a long time— Uncle Wayne and Aunt Patsy Huntley! Immediately, I became one of their own, and as I got closer to them, I learned three very important things, even more than I already knew:

1. God and His church are the framework that you build everything else around in your life.
2. Maximize the Moment.
3. Magnify the Positive!

God knew I needed them in my life and on my journey! The book you hold in your hands is the story of their lives, and what a glorious and devoted story it is; I know, I've had a front-row seat for the last little while!

DeWayne and Barbara Landtroop (nephew)
Pastor, Echoes of Calvary, UPC
Laurinburg, North Carolina

Wayne and Patsy Huntley are two of the most influential people I have ever met.

This impactful journey began in 1968. I was thirteen, and my parents had traveled to the UPCI General Conference. They had asked a young man from our church attending Texas Bible College to come home and bring students with him to preach the weekend services at our Gainesville, Texas, church.

I was sitting on the living room couch when the TBC boys entered through a door to my extreme right. Wayne Huntley was the last to enter the room, and yet his warm Apostolic glow immediately touched me.

As soon as he walked in, I knew he was somebody special. I could not help but notice his burden and passion as he approached prayer, worship, and altar services. Without a doubt, I knew he was a man on a mission.

As a thirteen-year-old boy, I wanted to order my life according to the "footprints" he was leaving; it was as though they were put there just for me!

Little did I know that the next time I would meet Wayne Huntley, he would be with my aunt, Patsy Sue Landtroop, and within a few months, I would gladly embrace him as "Uncle Wayne."

Uncle Wayne and Aunt Patsy often came to Gainesville to preach revivals. Their anointed ministry was so effective. Before Uncle Wayne would preach, Aunt Patsy would open her accordion and sing, "When the Lord gets ready, you gotta move," all the while walking up and down the aisles. This profoundly moved me. To this day, I still glean from memories of seeing tears dripping from her face while in passionate prayer for the lost and the Kingdom of God. I witnessed this as a young teenage boy, and it still echoes in my ears.

Aunt Patsy, who is just a few years older than I am, yet exhibits a wealth of wisdom, love, and amazing character, has commanded my allegiance to her, not only as my incredible pastor's wife but also as a mother figure.

I have noticed many others who have been blessed with the "footprints" that Uncle Wayne and Aunt Patsy have purposefully placed in their lives—a true Apostolic ministry! One of the greatest blessings I have ever received was the invitation to become a product of their ministry by planting a church in Fuquay-Varina, North Carolina.

For twenty-six years, I had the honor and privilege of working with them both. During that time, I never experienced a moment when their integrity was questionable. My love and respect for them have only grown stronger with time.

One of their many Apostolic characteristics was their amazing selfless spirit. They purposely lived below their means so they always had something to give others and the work of God.

Their anointed ministry and sometimes correction always found a way to equip me, empower me, and enrich the lives of my family and me. Through the years, their ministry has captured my heart, saturated my spirit, charged me, and enabled me to continue to <u>step forward even when I felt I could not</u>!!!

Aryck and Belinda Lassiter
Aria, Aleeya, Abriya, and Armani
Jen-Marie (Mother)
Peason United Pentecostal Church
Peason, Louisiana

Wayne Huntley is one of my heroes of the faith and spiritual father. I pay special tribute to you, a genuine spiritual trendsetter of the United Pentecostal Church International.

Coming into the church in Raleigh in the early '90s from a broken home, the Lord and a godly mother led me to you! My life would never be the same.

Not wanting to become a preacher fresh off the soccer field, the Lord saw fit to save a wretch like me and has blessed my family and me beyond measure. I found so much solace and peace in the many memories and messages you have ministered throughout my life; I am forever grateful for you.

My most significant compliment as a minister came as a direct reflection of your influence and confidence in my life and ministry. Someone told me, "The Gospel is in good hands."

So, thank you very much for your endorsement and incredible deposit of distinction in my life and that of my family. We are forever grateful for the example you have set.

I am forever grateful for the special bond and memories I cherish and reflect upon daily in the old, intimate hymns of Pentecost that you sang. These hymns promoted history and heritage and provided a foundation on which I can build my family for God. I will be forever indebted to the life and legacy of my "Second Momma."

My prayer every day is to make you proud and then do the same with my family!

Gordon and Afton Mallory
Evangelists and Missionaries to the Philippines

A number of years ago, Brother Mallory was riding around Raleigh with Brother Huntley in his little pickup. Brother Huntley casually mentioned that he was due to go to the Philippines to preach at their general conference but had decided not to go. Alarmed, Brother Mallory reached over, took his arm, and said, "My friend, if you don't go to the Philippines at this time, you'll be making the biggest mistake of your life! You have a special word from the Lord for that conference!"

Brother Huntley looked shocked at the urgency in Brother Mallory's voice and immediately said, "Okay, if you feel that strongly about it, I'll go." And go, he did! He did not know that the Philippine Church was at a crossroads and that major divisions had arisen in the fellowship. He preached, "Don't Kill the Baby." He spoke like an Old Testament prophet, telling them that they were killing revival in the Philippines by allowing spirits of unforgiveness and disunity to prevail. When he finished, brethren were on their faces, repenting with many tears flowing like fountains, then arising to fall on each other's necks with great healing in their relationships. He saved the work at that moment, and revival was reignited, resulting in the great harvest that followed. They now say there are over a million constituents.

We were ministering for some time in North Carolina, staying in the White House by the Raleigh church, when the Huntleys, Ballesteros, and the TOP family wanted to bless us with a very special 50th Wedding Anniversary celebration. The wonderful church folks went into action. For ten days and late nights, we saw cars parked at the JIM (gym) as they decorated, transforming it into a stunning wedding venue, complete with a sit-down banquet meal, elaborate wedding cake, and tasty desserts (so far beyond our 1965 wedding). We marched in to stand before Brother Huntley, Brother Ballestero, and our son to renew our vows and be blessed by all the love and giving. We were so humbled that they would do this for us.

Sitting in the bleachers in a General Conference Foreign Missions service, I (Sister Mallory) felt like passing my watch down the row to the usher in a sacrificial offering. Brother Huntley saw and wouldn't let that pass. Afterward, he went all the way to our headquarters, where they showed him several watches that had been given. Via text photos to Brother Mallory, he identified the one I had donated and repurchased it for me for $1,000. I was SO overwhelmed! His kindness to a missionary wife with his big giving heart no doubt increased the value probably ten-fold for that small offering—sincere thanks for such boundless goodness.

Nick Mahaney
Evangelist of UPCI

In March 2007, my father, Charles Mahaney, passed away. I was just starting in the ministry. I felt alone, with no voice or guidance in my life. Brother Huntley not only stepped in and filled that role but has also become the biggest influence in my ministry. The Huntleys have opened doors for me, prayed for me, corrected me, and guided me. Everything in my ministry has Wayne Huntley's fingerprints on it. The thankfulness and gratitude my wife and I have for Brother and Sister Huntley go beyond the words that I have to express. What an impact they have had in the Kingdom of God.

Vesta Mangun
Pentecostals of Alexandria
Alexandria, Louisiana

It is with hearts full of love and deep appreciation for the exemplary lives of Wayne and Patsy Huntley, who have shared their ministry as evangelists, pastors, teachers, and special speakers in conferences, camp meetings, and seminars throughout our fellowship! And as a beloved leader serving in an official capacity in their own home state, North Carolina.

His many sermons, like "The Treasure is in the Field," will long be remembered. For the past fifty-plus years, Patsy has stood alongside him, often hidden in the crowd, but in reality, it was the spiritual force that has blessed their family, their home, and their church family through her godly example.

God blessed them with a beautiful and talented daughter, Christy, and her husband, Bryan, and five outstanding grandchildren: Huntley, Christyana, Christian, Caison, and Gentson. Pastor Bryan Ballestero and his wife, Christy, are now the Lead Pastors in Apostolic succession in Raleigh, North Carolina.

The Huntley legacy will be long remembered, not only by family, friends, and the United Pentecostal Church International, but by generations to come as long as the Lord tarries.

Joel and Kristen McCoy
The Apostolic Church, Pastor
Porter, Texas

Where to begin? A hero in my eyes since I can remember. I believe Brother Wayne Huntley was every young preacher's inspiration. Years ago, while on the evangelistic field, we spoke briefly in Alexandria, Louisiana, when Brother Huntley was kind enough to hold our twin boys for a picture. I, of course, had to be next to him to help hold the babies! Little did I know that the path of life would bring us together years later when I became a pastor in Porter, Texas. He preached our

installation services because of his relationship with the previous pastor, Bishop Jerry Green, and we met again. A new friendship was born, but it felt like we had known each other for years. It wasn't long before we got to meet the Landtroop side of the family, and we fell in love with Sister Patsy, too. What an honor to share pulpits and hunting stands with this great man. What a privilege my wife and I have been gifted to spend precious time with them both. Our hearts are forever tied to the Huntleys. Their influence has been invaluable in our lives, and we will always hold their friendship as a treasured gift from God.

Bryan and Ashley Landtroop Morris
(nephew and niece)
Introduction by Bryan for Wayne Huntley before preaching.

This morning, I have a privileged task that some may consider difficult: introducing our speaker. However, there is so much to say that time will not allow.

It is difficult, perhaps, to assist the audience in identifying and understanding the prestige of Pentecost in our presence. I could spend a tremendous amount of time reviewing his world-renowned status. The number of camps, conferences, and revivals he has preached are incalculable. His relationship with God is immeasurable. The number of souls in altar calls blessed by the anointed preached Word of God are innumerable.

However, this morning, I identify his ministry as one that is not here to impress with prestige or resume. Yet, an effective ministry that is filled with burden, compassion, and great love.

This morning, you will hear at the same time both:
Authority and humility…
Concern and compassion …
Direction and discretion …
I would not be surprised if you witness both laughter and tears.

Years ago, when I was a student in college. I had a work study at the university computer lab. I didn't study much in the library. I opted rather to listen to preaching. I discovered a website that was dedicated to Apostolic preachers, and I began to listen to them one by one. Every day, I was wowed and amazed. I selected a library of sermons by a certain Wayne Huntley, and as I listened, a transformation occurred that moved me from a student of the university to a student of preaching. Instantly, I was among the audience in these conferences and revivals. The atmosphere was so real that I could feel the heat that can be identified with a red-hot Apostolic service. I could hear the worship and the congregation preaching with the preacher. I could taste the goodness of the Lord! I spent hours listening to and re-listening to recorded sermons from Wayne Huntley. I had never heard of him before, but I was caught up with the Heavenly flow and anointing of his preaching.

Shortly thereafter, I met Ashley Landtroop. In the beginning stages of our interest, she must have felt the need to campaign for courtship as she stated, "Oh, by the way, Wayne Huntley is my uncle." The insight of her wisdom inspired the depths of my mind to instantly reply, "I do." A few years later, her words echoed the "I do" in Uncle Wayne's church with Aunt Patsy directing the wedding.

I am quite confident that Bro. and Sis. Huntley's most proud accomplishments are that they are the parents of Christy.
They cherish their five grandchildren and great-grandchild.
To them, he is "Grandbuddy."
To North Carolina, he is district superintendent.
To myself and many preachers, he is pastor,
To Raleigh's Temple of Pentecost, he is bishop.

Today, his ministry is going to bless you. Would you welcome with me to this pulpit, Bishop Wayne Huntley.

Barron Price
Morton, Mississippi

Brother Huntley, I want to thank you for the tremendous impact you have had on my life and ministry. I think it was either 1972 or 1973 that you and Brother Mark Foster came to P. B. I. in Tupelo to promote the North Carolina District. It was then that the Lord placed a call within my heart to go to North Carolina. I'll never forget the joy I felt when the North Carolina District Board approved us to go to Shelby. At the time, I felt God was calling me to be a blessing to North Carolina, but I now understand that He wanted North Carolina to be a blessing to the Price family so we could be a better service to His Kingdom! I gave Shelby and the North Carolina District the best that I had for those six years, but the North Carolina District gave my family so much more.

In 1992, America fielded the Dream Team in the Olympics, but as a church planter, I felt I had already experienced the Apostolic Dream Team by observing the North Carolina leadership for two years.

I regret the unfortunate turn of events that caused you such undeserved pressure. Still, you became even more of a hero in my eyes as I witnessed your positive leadership and Christ-like actions as vicious attacks and accusations were constantly being circulated. You led us forward in positive strides without demeaning those guilty of stirring strife or defending your integrity. You simply demonstrated that integrity! I have nothing but admiration and deep respect for the Huntley family.

Probably the most significant highlight of our tenure in North Carolina was seeing Brother Huntley's dream of having a Junior Youth Camp for North Carolina fulfilled, and working that week with the Ballesteros. The success of that camp gave me the initial sense of "mission accomplished" for my purpose for that season. You also had such a positive impact on my son Jeremy's life. Without those six years in North Carolina, I don't believe he would be the asset to the Kingdom that he is today.

Thank You!

Kent and Joan Rhoads
Pastor, Oil City, Louisiana

Brother and Sister Huntley have been icons in the Pentecostal movement for as long as we can remember. We watched them from a distance with admiration, never really believing that we would get to meet them, much less spend time with them on a personal level. God saw fit for their influence to become personal to us several years ago, and for that, we are truly thankful. We've learned that whether from a distance or up close and personal, they are genuine Apostolic Pentecostals who love God and love people. We would like to thank them both for their investment in the Kingdom of God and, more specifically, their investment in us personally.

With much admiration and love.

Donnie Sheerin
Pastor, First Church
Kennett, Missouri

Wayne Huntley is my favorite preacher. He is the most prolific, passionate preacher I have had the distinct privilege of hearing and knowing. I've always loved his preaching, and there is none finer than my friend, Rev. Wayne Huntley.

I can remember as a young man when I served Missouri's youth, I would put his name down to preach at our Youth Convention and youth camps. When I started serving the Sunday School ministry in Missouri and, ultimately, the UPCI Children's Ministry, I would put his name down to preach our meetings, Train Up, and General Conference. I'd even suggest to my wife, who serves the Ladies Ministry in Missouri, that Brother Huntley would do great preaching at your conference. I've always felt that, whatever the conference, Brother Huntley would be the best preacher for it.

There is no other preacher who, with his preaching, has impacted and influenced my life and ministry more than Brother Wayne Huntley.

As I would hear him preach at General Conference or Because of the Times, I would be so inspired to become a better person and preacher. To me, Brother Wayne Huntley was <u>Superman</u>! Then, I would have the high honor of speaking for him at his amazing church, fishing with him at the lake on the farm, harvesting a turkey, the Non-Typical Hail Mary, or having him share stories and scriptures with me. Then I realized what I now know: <u>Clark Kent</u> is a bigger and better man than <u>SUPERMAN</u>!

Wayne Huntley is the real deal! He's simply stated, the best! He excels in all that he does and gives examples to younger preachers of what they can and should be.

I was so personally honored and blessed when "Superman/Clark Kent, The Wayne Huntley" recently came to First Church in Kennett, Missouri, where my wife Chae and I have been privileged to pastor for twenty years. His presence and preaching celebrated us so beautifully, and for that, I'm deeply grateful and appreciative. He exampled once again what a wonderful blessing he is to so many of us and the Kingdom of God.

Scott Smith
Columbia, South Carolina
Scott and Carolyn, Hannah, Marion, Anna, and Emma Smith

We first met Wayne, Patsy, and Christy at a Labor Day Rally in Durham, where they invited us to preach at the church on Loop Road (First United Pentecostal Church). This was a long way from the TOP, but the top is actually a way of thinking and living, and the Huntleys are tops. They took us under their wings and have been our dear friends for over forty years! Wayne is the sole reason I received Home Missions support for eighteen months, which gave birth to four churches in South Carolina.

Wayne and Patsy came and ministered to us at the funeral of our daughter, Judith. We are thankful, and we shall never forget. We've cried together, and we've laughed until we cried. Thank you for all the memories and for sharing your victories with us! From the little fireplace on King Arthur Trail to now, from Loop Road to Lake Wheeler, from Charlotte to Texas Bible College, and from Waco to the world, thank you, Jesus, for giving to us all, The Huntleys. Thank you for adding value, purpose, vision, and destiny to our lives!

Thetus Tenney
Wife of the late (great) Tom Fred Tenney

My dear Patsy and Wayne,

That greeting is in no way disrespectful, but it is a lot more familial—and that is how I feel.

With joy, I have watched both of you grow, mature, and step into leadership, changing your contribution but never changing your core.

I remember the day my husband, T. F. Tenney, announced you, Wayne, as the first recipient of the SFC scholarship to Texas Bible College. (Sheaves For Christ, the name the National Youth Department of the UPCI used to be called.) To him, you were always special, the masthead for that worthy program.

In 1981, I stood with you on the platform of the UPCI General Conference, introducing you to our fellowship as a church planter. I was impressed then with your unassuming honesty and your "just you" attitude, and you never changed.

Success in your life and work brought many changes, but not to the core of who you are. You were, you are, and always will be kind, loyal, warm, smiling, and loving, Patsy and Wayne. You are way down the road from that day in 1981, but you add a bright spot to our future. Thank you for being you and loving me.

Jimmy Toney
Pastor, Gainesville, Florida

I was a student at Texas Bible College when I was first introduced to the ministry of Bishop Wayne Huntley. He was preaching at a Texas camp, and immediately, his spirit, faith, and passion were infectious in this young preacher. I would be embarrassed to tell you how many times I have listened and re-listened to sermons over the years. Never in my wildest dreams did I think I would get the privilege to meet him, much less have a relationship with his family, but God does all things well, and I am just one of many who are indebted to Brother and Sister Huntley.

Tom Trimble
Pastor, Restoration Church
St. Charles, Missouri

While Brother Huntley is perhaps best known for his preaching worldwide (the Apostle of Alliteration!), and he and his wife, Patsy, are known for planting and establishing a premier church in North Carolina, they have made the most impact on my family and me through their compassion, time, and guidance. Several instances come to mind.

When he was the camp evangelist and I was working with the youth at a district camp meeting, I had the audacity to call his room and ask if they wanted to go to a restaurant and eat. My son Ryan was with me, and I added, "I don't have a car. Could you pick us up?" They did! Then we went and found some Blue Bell ice cream at a store and, if my memory is correct, ate it in the parking lot.

Another time, Ryan and Brother Huntley were ministering at Texaco Camp and had a layover together at DFW. My son asked if Brother Huntley would eat with him at Pappasito's, and Bishop poured into my son again.

At a very low time in my life, Brother Huntley met with me for over three hours, encouraging me to go on and make it through the challenges life had sent us.

Once, in Seattle, Washington, we were together for a youth convention. Brother Huntley and I were in the lobby elevator when a minister joined us. Decades before, this other preacher had sold out and capitulated to the trappings and temptations of the surrounding culture. At that moment, I saw the contrast: One was a caricature of ministry, while Brother Huntley was the character of ministry.

Thank you both for being examples to follow. I live by his sayings today: "Keep your dreams in front of you," "I refuse to act my age," and "Don't cry because it's over; smile because it happened."

Thank you both for your ministry through the years. Thank you for praying and taking the time to help so many other ministers. Thank you for being champions and for possessing a faith worth following.

Matthew Tuttle
Pastor, Eastgate United Pentecostal Church
Vidor, Texas

Besides my father, no ministry or minister has had a more significant impact on my life than Brother Wayne Huntley.

As a Bible school student, I would drive from Indianapolis, Indiana, to Alexandria, Louisiana, annually to hear Brother Huntley preach. Each message would challenge and convict me, but it always left me encouraged and confident that there is nothing God can't do. "Hath Israel No Sons?" is a sermon that permanently marked my life. The effects of Brother Huntley's messages were magnified when I met the messenger. He's a friend and chief encouraging officer, a leader of his home, church, and organization. Brother Huntley's preaching inspires me to be a better preacher; his life inspires me to be a better Christian.

My first personal interaction with Brother Huntley was on the mission field as an AIM worker, four years into a one-year term. Michelle had given birth to our fourth daughter. We didn't know she would be born with Down Syndrome and two holes in her heart. The darkness, doubt, and fear were tangible. I returned from the hospital the following day to find our home broken into and all our valuables stolen; this was our lowest day. After cleaning up, I noticed a "Temple of Pentecost" card in the mailbox. In the middle of our mess, Brother Huntley's handwritten note, "I believe in you, and I'm praying for you," brought a lifting and light to our heaviest and darkest day.

No doubt, he is the greatest preacher of my generation, a Christian, and a friend to all. I'm thankful God allowed me to be a part of the generation influenced by Brother Wayne Huntley.

Sergio and Rhonda Vitanza
Pastors Primera Iglesia
Wendell, North Carolina (and several other cities)

The revival that has taken place in the Spanish community of North Carolina is a direct result of the vision and dream of our pastors, Wayne and Patsy Huntley. God's favor, along with their constant encouragement and support, has enabled us to see this dream become a reality.

When Sergio moved to Raleigh and asked for a job description, Brother Huntley simply told him, "Everything Spanish." That level of confidence and trust has continued throughout the years until this day!

We are excited for their story, which includes our story, to be put into print and shared with the world!

Con mucho amor, Sergio and Rhonda Vitanza and family.

Toby and June Wall
Temple of Pentecost

Dear Bishop and Sister Huntley,

We are so thankful for you! When we landed at the TOP, we had been drifting like a ship at sea, with no safe harbor in sight, and feeling like our ship was about to go down. Once God brought us to you, we immediately felt safe. We felt wanted. We felt like we were home at last. Your love and care brought us so much comfort. You literally saved us from drowning in sorrow and despair. You put us back to work in the Kingdom, and twenty years later, we are so happy to be serving here and continually moving forward. I am so grateful our ship is still afloat!

Raymond and Beverley Woodward
Pastor, Fredericton, New Brunswick

Our friendship with the Huntleys began in the summer of 1999 when Brother Huntley and I ministered together at the Atlantic District Camp Meeting. Beverley and I were blessed to chauffeur Brother Huntley all week, enjoying many conversations with one of our heroes. (Sister Huntley wasn't able to be there due to the birth of their second grandchild.) I had never preached much beyond Atlantic Canada, but that was the week Brother Huntley invited us to minister in Raleigh, North Carolina. They warmly welcomed us to their great church the following February, and in the months that followed, I began to get phone calls that all began the same way: "Wayne Huntley said that I needed to have you minister at our church." His affirmation and kindness changed the future for this younger minister (and for hundreds of others just like me).

Over the last two decades, I've been honored to share preaching duties with my friend at many conferences and camp meetings, but it all started with his intentional investment. Like us, Sister Huntley is an "Anne of Green Gables" fan, and they had intended to visit Prince Edward Island on that trip to Canada way back in 1999. So, twenty years later, we visited the island together, spending wonderful days doing all things "Anne" and meaningful evenings listening to lots of old favorite songs and reminiscing about God's faithfulness to us all. Our lives have been abundantly enriched by our friendship with Wayne and Patsy Huntley, and we are forever grateful.

Wayne and Patsy Huntley Through the Years

Actual tree in our front yard, beautifully carved by Lisa Selvera.

The backside of our gate at the Non-Typical Family Farm

333

Twenty-fifth Anniversary

Fortieth Anniversary

337

Fiftieth Anniversary

339

Hide your eyes!

Wayne Huntley Ministering

341

Because of the Times–2019

Wayne preaching at Because Of The Times: Brother James Kilgore, Brother T. W. Barnes, and Brother T. F. Tenny

UPCI General Conference 2019

The Whole Gospel To the Whole World By the Whole Church

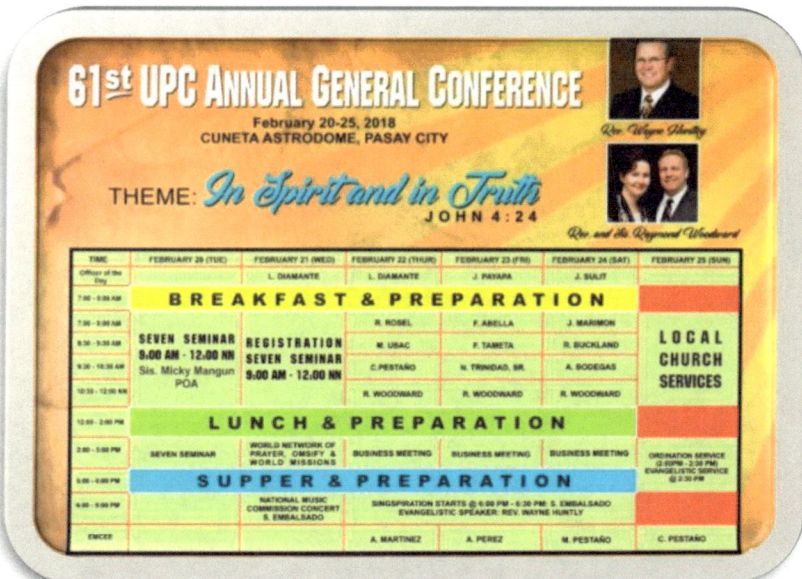

2018 General Conference of the Philippines

February 1981

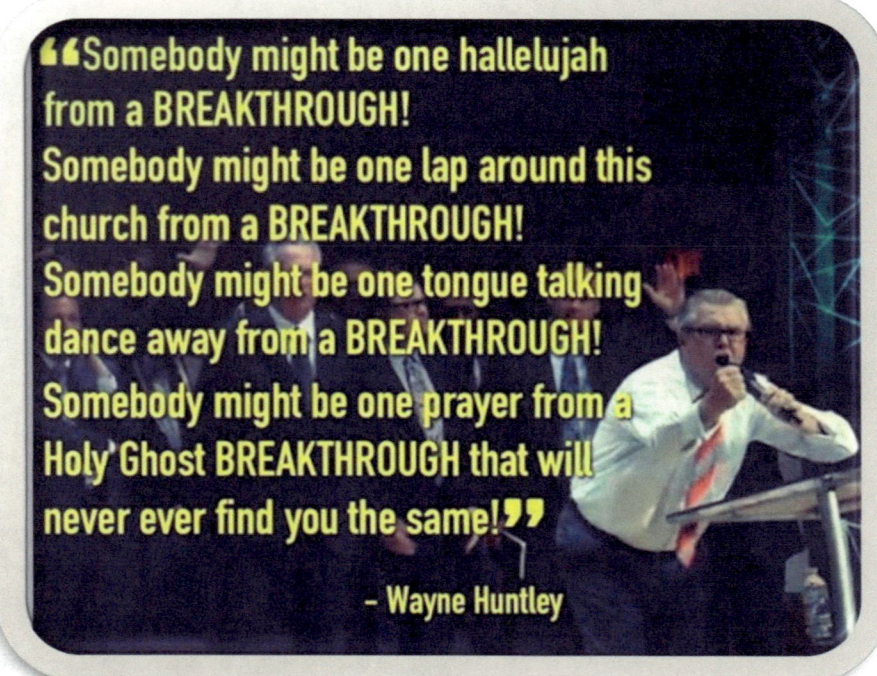

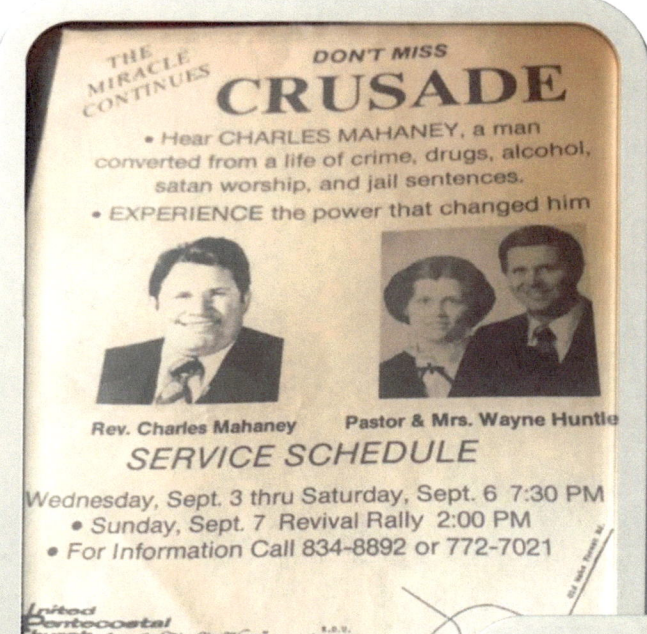

Sixty-first General Conference, United Pentecostal Church Philippines, 2018

The Huntley Family

352

Caison was five years old when he received the Holy Ghost at the Carolina Crusade Chapel Hill, North Carolina, in October 2016.

354

Christy made Wizard of Oz costumes for the Fall Festival.

Christian and Caison voluntarily escorted me off the platform when I spoke on Mother's Day.

Huntley Starr

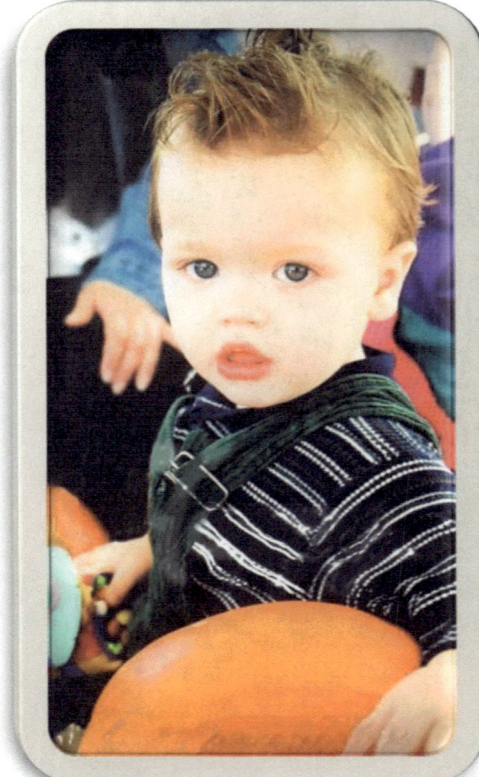

Gramommy teaching Huntley to play Hand and Foot

Huntley and Abigail Ballestero

Christyana Content

Christy and Ana wearing the dress I created

Christyana and other children praying in the altar at the UPCI General Conference.

Christyana and Jordan Blake

Clara Content Blake

Christyana and Christian

Christian Bryan

Receiving the Holy Ghost at age 5

Caison and Gentson praying for Christian

Christian and his car

Caison Judah

In 2025, Caison received the title of "Bible Quizzer of the Year" in North Carolina's Intermediate Division.

Gentson Hebron Carl

373

Gentson and Izzy

374

Wayne and Patsy in the Texas Hill Country

Made in the USA
Columbia, SC
19 September 2025